Will Israel Survive?

Will Israel Survive?

Mitchell G. Bard

First published in 2007 by
PALGRAVE MACMILLAN™
175 Fifth Avenue, New York, N.Y. 10010 and
Houndmills, Basingstoke, Hampshire, England RG21 6XS.
Companies and representatives throughout the world.

PALGRAVE MACMILLAN is the global academic imprint of the Palgrave
Macmillan division of St. Martin's Press, LLC and of Palgrave Macmillan Ltd.
Macmillan® is a registered trademark in the United States, United Kingdom and
other countries. Palgrave is a registered trademark in the European Union and other
countries.

ISBN-13: 978–1–4039–8198–1
ISBN-10: 1–4039–8198–1

Library of Congress Cataloging-in-Publication Data

Bard, Mitchell Geoffrey, 1959–
   Will Israel survive? / Mitchell G. Bard.
      p. cm.
   ISBN 978-1-4039-8198-1
   1. Israel—Foreign relations. 2. Israel—Population. 3. Israel—Economic conditions.
I. Title.
   DS119.6.B326 2006
   956.9405'4--dc22   2006038630

A catalogue record of the book is available from the British Library.

Design by Scribe, Inc.

First edition: July 2007

10 9 8 7 6 5 4 3 2 1

Printed in the United States of America.

I'd like to dedicate this book to Marcela for her patience and love, and my children Ariel and Daniel who will hopefully contribute to Israel's survival by their good deeds and commitment to the Jewish people. This book is also dedicated to the citizens of Israel who persevere despite the odds and who will ensure, along with their supporters in the Diaspora, that Israel thrives until real peace is achieved.

Contents

Preface

BECAUSE ISRAEL HAS NEVER KNOWN A DAY OF PEACE, FIGHTING EIGHT military campaigns and a daily war against terror that as recently as July 2006 escalated into a war, it is not surprising that no one talks about Israel's future. Israel's present is seen as so fraught with danger that most discussions focus on a day, a week, or perhaps a month in advance. Whenever someone proposes longer-term plans, such as the road map for peace, they're usually dismissed as naïve at best, and fools at worst, because these plans have consistently failed.

Most books about Israel, therefore, focus on reviewing the past and describing the present predicament. No one wants to admit that no solution may exist to the conflict between Israel and its neighbors, and many people see themselves as having the secret to peace. This is not a book about my prescription for peace. Sure, I have some ideas about what is likely to happen that will be discussed later, but a basic fallacy this book is meant to expose is that the absence of peace is in any way related to the lack of proposals.

The ideas presented here are based on my study of Israel for more than 20 years and can be backed up with data and references I've used over that time. My goal is to illustrate the complexity of the issues and explain why Israel's survival is open to question.

I'm grateful to the many teachers and colleagues who have helped educate me over the years. I want to especially thank David Krusch, Jennifer Feinberg, Yariv Nornberg, Ariel Scheib and Joanna Sloame for their help, my agent Lynne Rabinoff for her support, and my editor Airié Stuart for her helpful suggestions and guidance.

Hopefully, it will be possible to write a sequel to this book in the near future titled, *The Thriving State of Israel: Truly a Light unto the Nations.*

Chapter 1

Israel's Past Is Prologue

FROM ALMOST THE BEGINNING OF HUMAN HISTORY, THE JEWISH PEOPLE HAVE faced threats to their survival and overcome them. The ancient Israelites built a state that repeatedly faced enemies and ultimately succumbed to their superior power. Even then, however, some Jews remained entrenched in their homeland, and those who were exiled dreamed of returning. When at last the Jewish people regained their independence and established the state of Israel, they were blamed for turmoil in a region that had been the subject of competing interests for centuries. The desire to bring stability to the Middle East, particularly in light of the interests of modern nations in oil and trade, has led the world to focus a disproportionate amount of attention on a tiny nation whose people have asked for little more than the chance to build a home and live in peace with their neighbors. That peace has proved unachievable because the causes of the threats to Israel's future are complex and cannot be ameliorated by greater attention, inspiration, or inventiveness.

This is why the title of this book has a question mark. You might have expected the title to be, "Israel *Will* Survive." Israel might be the only country in the world whose right to exist is debated and whose future is questioned. Can you imagine anyone asking whether the United States will survive or whether it should exist? Or anyone saying "no" if asked?

Even Israelis question their future. In a September 2006 poll, for example, Israelis were asked, "To what extent are you certain the state of Israel will exist in the long run?" Nearly one-fourth of the Israelis answered they were not certain. Three-fourths of Israelis said they were in a struggle for survival and 56 percent said the country is less secure than it was a decade ago. The following month another poll found that 54 percent of Israelis feared for the existence of the state.

Despite doubts about the future, the history of the Jewish people is a story of survival. After all, what were the odds against an agrarian people, enslaved for generations, escaping their tormentors, marching out of the desert, conquering the inhabitants of a remote land that they believed was promised to them by God, and forming a nation? The Israelites, the forebears of the Jewish people, did just that.

From the time that the Israelites set up their state, they had to fight for their lives and livelihood. Like today, the battle was not just with external enemies; it was often among themselves. A Jewish monarchy evolved after it became evident that the people needed a strong central leader and the tribes could no longer govern the masses. Internal conflicts led to a split in the powerful kingdom of the Jews. This weakened their hold on the land and led eventually to their defeat and exile for more than two thousand years.

For religious and secular Jews who understand the lessons of history, the internal strife that led to the dissolution of the Jewish state is a constant reminder of what can happen to Israel if the people do not remain strong and united. From the more religious point of view, it is also prophetic of what will happen if Jews turn away from their faith.

Much later the Jewish people would discover that their promised land may be a place of milk and honey but, unfortunately, those commodities are considerably less valuable than the oil beneath the unholy ground of their enemies. In the early days of independence, however, the more serious problem was that the Jews found themselves at one of the central meeting points for the armies of empires that competed over their land and its surroundings. The Jewish people held off their enemies and maintained an independent nation for nearly 400 years before succumbing to the mighty Roman empire. This small piece of territory, formerly called the Land of Israel, continues to be fought over today.

If not for the combination of internal strife and the imperial designs of its neighbors, Israel would today be one of the oldest nations in the world, celebrating more than 3,000 years of independence rather than a mere 59.

Even after most Jews were dispersed, communities remained in Jerusalem, Safed, Hebron, and Tiberias. Many Jews were massacred by the crusaders during the twelfth century, but the community rebounded in the next two centuries as large numbers of rabbis and Jewish pilgrims immigrated to Jerusalem and the Galilee. By the early nineteenth century—years before the birth of the modern Zionist movement—more than 10,000 Jews lived throughout what is today Israel. While most Jews remained in the diaspora, they never gave up the dream of a return to Israel.

Despite the catastrophic loss of independence that lasted for centuries, it is the Jews who emerged as the victors over the long haul. It took more than 2,000 years for the Jews to regain power in their homeland, but Israel is now a prosperous nation of more than seven million citizens, while the mighty Assyrians, Babylonians, and other ancient powers that once dominated the region have been relegated to Marx's dustbin of history.

And it is not just ancient empires that the Jews have outlasted. In 1917, the Russian revolution led to the creation of a Soviet empire. That same year, the Balfour Declaration issued by Great Britain called for the establishment of a Jewish homeland in Palestine. Now, 90 years later, the Soviet Union has disintegrated, but the state of Israel has survived. "The revolution that purported to redeem mankind failed miserably," Maoz Azaryahu noted, "whereas Zionism has succeeded in reformulating Jewish existence in geographical, national and cultural terms."[1]

During the long centuries of exile that preceded the reestablishment of Israel, the Jewish people learned from their mistreatment by Christians and Muslims, and ultimately from the Holocaust, the painful lesson of what can happen if they do not have a homeland of their own. Support for Israel became almost a religion for Jews (and many non-Jews) committed to the Jewish state's survival. As Shlomo Avineri observed, "to be Jewish today means, in one way or another, feeling some link with Israel."[2] On the other hand, one reason for questioning Israel's future is the sense, reflected in polls of young American Jews, that this connection may be fraying.

Israel's survival also does not seem so certain when one realizes how many people would like to see the Jewish state disappear. Many view Israel as the greatest irritant to the Arab world, responsible for instability, terrorism, and rampant anti-Americanism. Without Israel, the critics suggest, the Arab world would have better relations with the United States and the region would be placid. History has shown, however, that U.S.-Arab relations have only gotten closer as American ties with Israel have grown stronger. Today, the

United States has good relations with every Arab state except perhaps Syria and Libya (and a slow thaw is even taking place with Muammar Qaddafi's regime). Moreover, the entire region is marked by inter-Arab and inter-Muslim conflicts unrelated to Israel. Border disputes exist, for example, between Saudi Arabia and Yemen, Iraq and Iran, and Iraq and Kuwait. Syria considers Lebanon a southern province it would like to control. Shiite and Sunni Muslims are in conflict throughout the region and are killing each other daily in Iraq while competing for power with Kurds. Christians, Muslims, and Druze fight for control over Lebanon. Hamas and Fatah fight for control over the Palestinian Authority. Iran and Iraq fought a bloody ten-year war unrelated to Israel. Iraq invaded Kuwait. If Israel disappeared tomorrow, the Middle East would still be in turmoil.

The hatred exhibited toward the United States usually has nothing whatsoever to do with Israel. The attacks on 9/11, for example, were conducted because of radical Muslims' hatred of Western values and the U.S. presence in Arab countries (in particular Saudi Arabia), and to further the Islamists' ultimate goal of the establishment of an Islamic empire. Similarly, the last two wars that the United States has fought in the Middle East with Iraq had nothing to do with Israel.

Impatience with the instability of the region and the conviction that America has the power to do something about it have led to persistent calls for U.S. engagement. But what can the United States do about the conflicts mentioned above? The answer is little or nothing. Consequently, the focus is on the one dispute in which the United States does exert some influence, namely, the conflict between Israel and its neighbors. A major Democratic Party theme of the 2004 presidential election, for example, was that President George W. Bush's failure to be more actively involved in peacemaking was largely responsible for the ongoing Palestinian-Israeli violence. That the violence began on President Bill Clinton's watch and was partly an outgrowth of the failure of his engagement was ignored (more about that later).

The idea of U.S. intervention is not a partisan one; rather, it is a cardinal tenet of the State Department. American officials have long believed that they can solve the Arab-Israeli conflict through diplomacy. Since the United States has influence on only one party to the conflict, Israel, any American plan necessarily focuses on pressuring Jerusalem to make concessions that the diplomats hope will satisfy the Arabs.

The United States has been pursuing diplomatic efforts in the Middle East for nearly six decades and the one thing they have in common is failure. Even President Bush, who said he wanted to avoid the pitfalls and mistakes of his predecessor, was dragged into Middle East diplomacy. He enunciated a plan in 2002 that gave way to the road map for peace (backed also by the European Union, Russia, and the United Nations) and, ultimately, neither plan brought the parties any closer to ending the conflict. This outcome was consistent with the past, as not a single U.S. peace plan has been successful, yet diplomats and other wishful thinkers continue to hold out hope that some comprehensive plan can be devised to bring about peace. You can't blame the diplomats for trying because it is their job to pursue negotiated solutions to problems, but you can fault them for their naïveté given their purported expertise on the region.

This naïveté is not unique to the United States. Others, including many Israelis, believe in the existence of a magic formula that will end the conflict. The implication is that we just need the Einstein of diplomacy to figure out the secret, but this is an illusion. The absence of peace has nothing to do with the inadequacy of previous plans.

I am not suggesting that it is a mistake to seek peace or to work toward ending the conflict; however, this approach is too simplistic. The job of diplomats is to devise political solutions to political problems, but the Arab-Israeli conflict is not a purely political dispute. If it were, a settlement could be reached to which all the parties could agree. President George H. W. Bush's secretary of state, James Baker, offered the best example of the naïve view that the difference between Arabs and Jews was no different than a disagreement between, say, the United Auto Workers and General Motors. Baker's great accomplishment was in convening a conference in Madrid where the Palestinians and several Arab states, including for the first time the Saudis, sat at the same table with Israel. Unlike a president handling a labor dispute, however, he couldn't force them to agree and little came out of the meeting.

The conflict between Israeli Jews and their Arab and Muslim neighbors has lasted now for more than a century because it is nothing like a management-labor negotiation. It is not even like most international conflicts, which are based largely on political and geographical disagreements. The Arab-Israeli conflict does indeed involve such elements, but it is also rooted in psychology, history, and religion. The inability to appreciate all these components is the reason why American peace initiatives have consistently ended in failure and why Israel's survival cannot depend on them.

On one level, the entire conflict is really about geography. Two people, Jews and Palestinians, claim one piece of land as their own. Since neither the Jews nor the Arabs were prepared to allow the other to rule over them, the only logical solution to the antinomy anyone has ever come up with is to divide the land. The British suggested this first in 1937 when Lord Peel offered a plan to split Palestine. A decade later, the United Nations arrived at the same conclusion in proposing and adopting the partition resolution to create Jewish and Arab states in Palestine. In neither instance, or any negotiations since, have the Palestinians been prepared to accept a state in only part of what they claim to be their homeland. The Zionists reluctantly accepted the partition ideas because they were prepared to settle for half a loaf to insure they had any loaf at all. At root, the persistence of the geographic dispute boils down to the Palestinians' refusal from 1937 to the present to accept the idea of a Jewish state living beside a Palestinian state in Palestine/*Eretz Yisrael* (the land of Israel, as Jews prefer to call the pre-state area).

Beyond this basic point, however, geography is also a factor because it shapes the deployment of military forces, the availability of water, and the drawing of boundaries. Israel's view on these issues can be understood only if you appreciate the relative size of Israel vis-à-vis its enemies and the landscape of the area.

Because Israel attracts so much media attention, it is perceived to be much larger than it is. People who have not visited Israel often have a difficult time comprehending just how small and vulnerable the country is. Israel is actually the size of New Jersey, but that doesn't really capture the relationship between size and security. For example, before 1967, at its narrowest point Israel was just nine miles wide. President George W. Bush says driveways in Crawford, Texas, are longer than that.

To give another sense of the geography, on one of my trips to Israel, I toured a community called Gush Etzion. It is in the West Bank, so the rest of the world considers it a settlement (actually, it is a bloc of 18 communities), but it is less than a 15-minute drive, six miles south of Jerusalem. We stood on a hilltop and the guide said to look to the west. The tower we could see not far in the distance, he said, was the Crowne Plaza Hotel in the center of

Jerusalem. He then told us to look to the left of the hotel, farther in the distance. It was a bit hazy but, he said, that was Tel Aviv. We were literally looking across the width of the country. It would be as if you came to visit me in Washington, D.C., and I took you to the top of the Washington Monument and said, "Hey look, you can see San Francisco."

In 2005 I took a helicopter tour that lifted off from an airport along the beach of Tel Aviv. We flew all of seven minutes before we reached the 1967 border. It is said that President Bush's policy toward Israel was strongly affected by a similar helicopter tour of the area that Ariel Sharon gave him when Bush was still governor of Texas. Once you see the geography firsthand, it's easier to understand what Israelis mean when they talk about the need for secure and defensible borders.

Forget the nine miles across the midsection of Israel. If you go to Jerusalem, Jews and Arabs are separated by only a *few feet*. The Temple Mount, on which sits the Dome of the Rock and the al-Aqsa Mosque, is literally on top of the Western Wall, the holiest site in Judaism. Around the corner is the church of the Holy Sepulchre. How do you draw lines between Jews and Arabs, Christians, and Muslims?

Israel's greatest weakness may be its size. It will never be geographically or demographically comparable to its neighbors. More worrisome, the military advantage it once had because of its size—short supply lines—has been largely erased by its enemies' acquisition of long-range missiles that can blanket the country. More ominously, its advantage is also threatened by the potential for an enemy with nuclear weapons to devastate the country with three bombs or fewer. In the missile age, it is questionable whether secure and defensible borders are still achievable.

Topography also matters. Travel up to the Golan Heights, a region Israel captured in 1967, which rises from 400 to 1,700 feet in the northeast corner of Israel, and overlook the Hula Valley, Israel's richest agricultural area. Prior to the Six-Day War, the Syrians controlled the region and used that vantage point to shell Israeli farmers below. Anyone who has been there immediately understands why Israel is reluctant to withdraw from this territory. North Carolina's long-time senator Jesse Helms, never regarded as a great friend of Israel, went to the Golan for the first time and said that he wished all of the other senators could see the landscape so they would understand why Israel can't give up that strategic high ground.

Geography is not relevant only to the dispute with the Palestinians. A peace agreement between Israel and the Palestinians that settled their territorial issues would not end the threats against Israel. The mere presence of a Jewish state in the area considered by many Muslims to be Islamic land is sufficient provocation to maintain a state of belligerence, as is the perceived subservience of Muslims in Israel to Jews. Thus, for example, a resolution of the Palestinian issue would have no impact on Iran's rejection of Israel's right to exist. Israel doesn't "occupy" an inch of Saudi or Kuwaiti or Libyan land, yet these nations consider themselves enemies of Israel.

These geographic realities have a key impact on the psychology of the conflict as well. Though rarely discussed, relations between the parties are shaped by raw human emotions such as fear, shame, humiliation, honor, and revenge. For example, in June 1967, Israel defeated the combined military might of the Arab world in just six days. For the Arab world, this was not just a political or military defeat; it was also humiliating. How could this puny state of Jews, inferiors according to Islam, defeat the warriors of Allah? The Arabs were overwhelmed by a sense of shame and dishonor.

In 1973, Egypt and Syria attacked Israel. They undoubtedly hoped to destroy the Jewish state, but they knew this would be difficult, if not impossible, because of Israel's military strength and its support from the United States. What was more important, however, was to restore the Arabs' honor. The war accomplished this objective. Though Israel won the war, the Arabs, especially the Egyptians, saw it as a victory because they had surprised the Israelis and nearly defeated them. (Many people forget that Sadat was assassinated during a 1981 "victory parade" commemorating the success of the 1973 war.)

Some people claim the war could have been avoided altogether had Israel responded positively to peace overtures Egyptian President Anwar Sadat made in 1971. But Sadat was not talking like a man interested in peace when he threatened to go to war if a political solution was not achieved, and when he demanded Israel's complete withdrawal from the Sinai and a resolution of the Palestinian refugee problem while at the same time declaring he would never establish diplomatic relations with Israel. Moreover, those who want to blame Israel for the war that followed underestimate the psychological damage of the 1967 war. Sadat could not have made peace in 1971 because it would have been from a point of weakness and dishonor. In an interview, Sadat told the *New York Times* about his childhood and how people would fight for 50 years over a meter of land: "our land . . . means our honor here . . . and one dies for this honor." After 1973, having erased the stain of humiliation, it was possible for him to seriously discuss normalizing relations with Israel.

The psychological impact of the two wars on Israel was almost a mirror image of the effect on the Arabs. In 1967 Israelis came out of the war beating their chests and telling everyone how they were the toughest kids on the block. The country was in a state of euphoria and believed it had miraculously overcome the threat of annihilation. Israelis also believed they had proven the Arabs couldn't defeat them and assumed the Arab states would therefore feel compelled to make peace. It didn't happen. Six years later, Jewish Israelis were shocked on their holiest holiday, Yom Kippur, by an attack on their northern and southern borders by the armies of Syria and Egypt. Though they prevailed on the battlefield, they had come so close to defeat that the psyche of the entire nation was shaken (in fact, Prime Minister Golda Meir had contemplated suicide). From that point on, Israel assumed a fortress mentality and, even as the military grew stronger—it is sometimes misleadingly referred to as the fourth most powerful in the world—Israelis always have had in the back of their minds a little voice warning them that Israel could be destroyed. This subconscious fear shapes all Israeli negotiations.

This feeling is compounded by the even more deep-rooted trauma of the Holocaust. Two-thirds of European Jewry was murdered by the Nazis and the creation of Israel was prompted in part by that catastrophe. All decisions related to Israel's ultimate security are shaped by the fear of annihilation. Menachem Begin, a Polish-born Jew, for example, decided to order a preemptive strike to prevent Iraq from acquiring a nuclear capability that, he believed, Saddam Hussein could use to destroy Israel. Discussions of territorial compromise have also been influenced by this anxiety, as evidenced by Abba Eban's objection to demands that Israel withdraw to the 1967 borders; he said these were the "Auschwitz borders," by which he meant Israel's existence would be endangered if it were to agree to such an insecure boundary.

In the most recent conflict during the summer of 2006, as in 1973, psychology again was evident in the claims of Hizbollah. Despite being defeated militarily in every battle, and despite the devastation of the surrounding countryside, the group's prestige was enhanced in much of the

Arab world because it inflicted severe pain (economic and physical) on the Israelis and seemed to have fought them to a draw. Hizbollah's willingness and ability to stand up to Israel was a source of pride for the Arabs and Muslims that contrasted sharply with what the "Arab street" viewed as the gutless behavior of Arab leaders who have done nothing to confront Israel in more than three decades.

One last example of the psychology of the Arab-Israeli conflict is perhaps more obvious: revenge. What does the terrorist group Hamas say after Israel assassinates one of its leaders? Does it announce the need to immediately sit down and negotiate? No; it declares its intention to exact revenge—a pure, nonpolitical, emotional reaction. The desire for revenge is very strong; Arabs can carry it with them for generations. Revenge is one way Arabs erase shame. Harold Glidden, a former member of the State Department Bureau of Intelligence and Research, observed that the Arabs feel it necessary to take vengeance "to restore to the Palestinian Arabs what was wrongfully taken" and "eliminate the shame that had been visited on them and on the other Arabs by their defeats by Israel."[3] Hussein Agha and Robert Malley also noted that Hamas reflected the Palestinians' "psychological condition" and came to power to "exorcize the disgrace" and to provide "revenge."[4]

Glidden explained why Israelis were wrong to assume that their victory in 1967 would compel the Arabs to make peace, an argument that applies as well to why militarily defeating Hamas or Hizbollah or any other terrorist group would be equally ineffective today in stimulating an interest in coexistence. Rather than prompting them to pursue peace, the adverse military balance "produces an emotional need for revenge, and this need is deepened rather than attenuated by each successive defeat." Like the Egyptians, the Palestinians feel shame must be eliminated. "This cannot be done by making peace," Glidden said, "before vengeance has been taken."

While a strong Israel helps deter Arab aggression, it also causes the Arabs to seek increased military power to compete with their enemy. "The Arabs fear a strong Israel," Glidden wrote, "because they cannot conceive that any strong state (whether Israeli or Arab) would not use its power and influence to dominate and control the others. . . . This felt danger from Israel is what lies behind the long-reiterated fears of Israeli expansion and Israel's alleged desire to take over the Arab territory 'from the Nile to the Euphrates.'" It doesn't matter that Israelis see themselves as peace loving and find such claims absurd, as well as demonstrably false, given their withdrawals from Sinai, the Gaza Strip, and parts of the West Bank, which total approximately 94 percent of the territory Israel captured in 1967. As Israeli-Arab newspaper editor Bassam Jabber explained, Israel has to persuade the people in neighboring countries that it has no intention of conquering the whole region or plundering its resources.[5]

Westerners place peace high on their priority lists. But for Arabs, Glidden said, "the emotional need for vengeance to eliminate the ego-destroying feeling of shame" takes precedence. As an example, Glidden cited the Shiite chief Mujtahid of Iraq who said in August 1938, long before the creation of Israel, that a jihad for Palestine was everyone's duty, and that if the Arabs lost they would suffer "humiliation, death and eternal shame."

Jews do not have the same need for revenge, but Israel is not above pursuing enemies who are believed to merit punishment. In most cases Israel has sought to arrest terrorists, but it has also engaged in targeted killings and, most famously, sent Mossad hit teams after the perpetrators of the massacre of Israeli athletes at the 1972 Munich Olympics.

History also matters. Jews have lived in the land of Israel without interruption for at least 2,000 years. By comparison, the Arabs can claim an association of, at best, a little more than 1,000 years. The only independent state in the Land of Israel was a Jewish monarchy that lasted more than 400 years. What historical right do Palestinians have to independence given that they have never had a state in all of recorded history?

Even the term "Palestine" has nothing to do with the people who today call themselves Palestinians. The territory is believed to have been named for the Philistines, an Aegean people who, in the twelfth century B.C.E., settled along the Mediterranean coastal plain of what is now Israel and the Gaza Strip. In the second century C.E., after crushing the last Jewish revolt, the Romans first applied the name Palaestina to Judea (the southern portion of what is now called the West Bank) in an attempt to minimize Jewish identification with the Land of Israel. The Arabic word *Filastin* is derived from this Latin name.

Ironically, one local Palestinian Arab leader, Auni Bey Abdul-Hadi, told the British Peel Commission in 1937, "There is no such country as Palestine! 'Palestine' is a term the Zionists invented! There is no Palestine in the Bible. Our country was for centuries part of Syria." The distinguished Arab-American historian, Philip Hitti, testifying against partition before the Anglo-American Committee in 1946, said "There is no such thing as 'Palestine' in history." Representatives of the Arab Higher Committee to the United Nations also submitted a statement to the General Assembly in May 1947 that said Palestine was part of Syria. A few years later, Ahmed Shuqeiri, later the chairman of the PLO, told the Security Council: "It is common knowledge that Palestine is nothing but southern Syria."

Given this history, one could argue the Jews were there first and have title to the land, and while Arabs have long been present, there's no basis for the Palestinian demand to have a state. These historical facts play into the Israeli view of the merits of the Palestinian case, as do more recent developments, notably the evolution of a Palestinian national consciousness and a desire for self-determination. The recognition of these historical changes has gradually led the majority of Israelis, including former political hardliners such as Ariel Sharon, to accept the reality of Palestinian nationalism and the virtual inevitability of the establishment of the first Palestinian state.

Another example of how history influences policy is the unilateral Israeli withdrawal from Lebanon in 2000. Many Israelis argued the evacuation set a bad precedent because it was universally regarded in the Arab world as a retreat forced by the steadfast resistance of Hizbollah. The Palestinians took this as a model and thought they too could use terrorist tactics against Israel to force it to give up territory. After a five-year war marked by horrific suicide bombings and other terrorist attacks that took more than 1,000 Israeli lives, Israel unilaterally withdrew from the Gaza Strip. While I would argue Israel's withdrawal was not a direct result of the war, but was a wise strategic decision that saved lives and ameliorated the demographic problem (discussed in chapter 4), the Palestinians saw the disengagement as another example of how resistance could yield positive results.

In the case of both withdrawals, Israel thought that by ending its provocative occupation it would gain security. Israel did what the peace activists had campaigned for—namely trading land for peace. In reality, however, the trade yielded not peace but terror. After Israel left Lebanon, Hizbollah built up its arsenal and continued to launch rockets into Israel, culminating in the attack on July 12, 2006, in which three soldiers were killed and two taken hostage—a provocation that led Israel to again cross into Lebanon. A UN peacekeeping force deployed in Lebanon after Israel withdrew in 2000 was supposed to prevent such attacks but did not. This was a repetition of the failure of the UN peacekeepers whose precipitous removal had contributed to the 1967 war and reinforced Israel's historical mistrust of the United Nations. Similarly, following the disengagement from Gaza, the Palestinians continued attempts to infiltrate terrorists into Israel and to fire rockets at civilian targets on an almost daily basis. When Hamas kidnapped an Israeli soldier days before the Hizbollah attack, it too precipitated an Israeli military response.

This recent history led Prime Minister Ehud Olmert to suspend the principal initiative on which he campaigned for office, namely, the unilateral withdrawal from a significant portion of the West Bank. The Israeli people have now had two case studies of what they get in exchange for ending occupation and are not about to make the same mistake a third time.

The historical roots of the conflict are also evident in discussions about Jerusalem. It is sometimes suggested that the city be internationalized, as envisioned in the original UN partition plan. After all, the argument goes, this is a holy city to three major religions, so why should it be under the sole control of Israel? The Palestinians also claim that the city should belong to them and it should be under their control.

The Israeli response is to look to history. The partition resolution did not see internationalizing Jerusalem as a permanent solution; nevertheless, for the first two years after the 1948 war the United Nations reiterated its position on the city but abandoned the idea of internationalization as Jordan tightened its hold on Jerusalem. It was only after Israel retook the city in 1967 that the world body regained interest in the city's fate. In the 19-year interim, while the UN stood silent, Jordan had occupied the city, desecrated synagogues and other holy places, and refused to allow Jews access to the Western Wall.

Israelis also see little merit to the Arab claims to Jerusalem since it was never the capital of any Arab state, and for most of Islamic history, it was considered insignificant, a neglected backwater town. The Palestinians certainly never had any special claim to the city. This history, along with the 3,000-year Jewish connection to the city King David built, helps explain the Israeli insistence that Jerusalem remain the undivided capital of Israel.

In suggesting a variety of factors that contribute to the conflict between Israel and its neighbors, I do not mean to imply that politics has no role to play. Clearly, politics is very important as the conflict is shaped by competing nationalisms. Jewish nationalism—Zionism—holds that the Jews are a nation like any other, entitled to self-determination in their homeland, which is Israel.

Contrary to the smears of anti-Semites and the United Nations, Zionism has nothing whatsoever to do with racism. Anyone can be a Zionist. You can be black, brown, or yellow. You can be from the United States, India, Thailand, or Mars. In fact, if it were possible to quantify Zionism, I would argue that the most rabid Zionists are the black Jews from Ethiopia who for centuries looked forward to returning to their homeland, unaware that white Jews existed. And Israel's heroic rescue of these Jews constitutes a dramatic rebuttal to the racism calumny. As William Safire put it, "For the first time in history, thousands of black people are being brought to a country not in chains but in dignity, not as slaves but as citizens."[6]

On returning to their homeland, however, the Jews found other people living in the same area. Over time, Palestinian Arabs also developed a nationalistic view that they too were entitled to self-determination in Palestine. Palestinian Arab nationalism is largely a post–World War I phenomenon that did not become a significant political movement until after the 1967 Six-Day War and Israel's capture of the West Bank; nevertheless, today it is undeniable.

During much of the 1950s and 1960s, pan-Arabism also clashed with Zionism as Egyptian President Gamal Abdel Nasser sought to unify the Arab world. That worldview has been supplanted now by pan-Islamism, which brings me to the final and, perhaps most important factor in the current conflict—religion.

The Jewish people can base their claim to the Land of Israel on several grounds: uninterrupted Jewish settlement from the time of Joshua onward; the Balfour Declaration of 1917; the League of Nations Mandate, which incorporated the Balfour Declaration; the United Nations partition resolution of 1947; Israel's admission to the UN in 1949 and the recognition of Israel by most other states. Fundamentally, however, the reason that the Jewish homeland had to be in such an inconvenient place, surrounded by hostile neighbors and lacking the one valuable resource that made those neighbors relevant to the rest of the world, is the belief that this is the land promised to Jews by God Almighty. It is Jerusalem where Jews hope to perfect the world and bring about a peace that will usher in a messianic age. And the Muslims take Judaic theology seriously. That is why they closed the Golden Gate to the Old City, where it is said the Messiah would enter Jerusalem. They also built a cemetery in front of the gate as a barrier because the Messiah is supposed to belong to the priestly caste that is prohibited from entering a cemetery.

The religious connection to Israel was crucial to the early Zionist movement. After all, if the goal was to find a haven from anti-Semitism, why did it have to be in the area that had come to be called Palestine? In 1903, after pogroms in Russia, Theodor Herzl himself had proposed creating a homeland in Uganda. That idea was rejected by the Zionist movement and Herzl maintained that he saw Uganda as only a temporary refuge from anti-Semitism until a homeland could be created in Israel. The fact is that Zionism has profound religious roots. Many prayers speak of Jerusalem, Zion, and the Land of Israel. The injunction not to forget Jerusalem, the site of the temple, is a major tenet of Judaism. The Hebrew language, the Torah, the laws in the Talmud, the Jewish calendar and its holidays all originated in Israel and revolve around its seasons. Religion, culture, and history make clear that it is only in the Land of Israel that the Jewish commonwealth could be built.

It is not only Jews, however, who have a religious attachment to the land. This is the same area where Jesus Christ was born and Christianity emerged. The papal desire to cleanse the region of infidels led to two centuries of bloody crusades (1095–1291), marking the last time Christians were dominant anywhere in the Middle East. Today, Israel remains a focal point of Christianity and the one place in all the Middle East where Christians can live and practice their faith freely. Some Christians also support a Jewish state because they believe the return of all Jews to Israel and their subsequent destruction in an apocalyptic battle will bring about the resurrection of their messiah.

Muslims also have a theological connection to the Land of Israel, although theirs is perhaps more tenuous. They believe that Mohammad took his night flight to heaven from the Temple Mount, and, other than Jerusalem, no other area of Israel holds much significance to Muslims. Even Jerusalem is of marginal importance. It is not mentioned in the Koran and was never a capital or major political center in the Islamic empire. Still, the presence of Jews in this land, and more important, their control over an Islamic holy place is anathema to them.

The Islamic religion has a more fundamental problem with the existence of a Jewish state, however, that derives from the Muslim view that the world is divided into two realms, the House of Islam and the House of War, the Dar al-Islam and the Dar al-harb. The Dar al-Islam is all those lands in which an Islamic government rules. Non-Muslims may live there on Muslim sufferance and, strictly speaking, a perpetual state of *jihad*, or holy war, is imposed by the law. The outside world, which has not yet been subjugated, is called the House of War. It is then a religious obligation for Muslims to subjugate the infidels and it is unacceptable for non-Muslims to rule over Muslims or for non-Muslims to control Muslim territory. This is absolutely basic to understanding the intractability of the Israel-Islamic conflict. It is inconceivable that Hamas or Islamic Jihad or Hizbollah or any other fundamentalist group can accept the existence of a Jewish state in the body of the Islamic world. Israel is a cancer (a reference they often use) that must be excised, and there is nothing that anyone can do to change their minds. If Israel were to withdraw tomorrow from all of the West Bank, all of East Jerusalem, and give every inch of the Golan Heights to Syria, there still would be no peace, because the Islamists will not be satisfied with a return to the 1967 borders; they demand that the border be the Mediterranean Sea.

The Muslim antipathy to nonbelievers is not restricted, incidentally, to Jews. Small sects, such as the Baha'i, are ruthlessly persecuted. Most Christians have been driven out of the few Muslim countries where they lived and the radical attitude toward them is expressed in the popular saying, "First the Saturday people, then the Sunday people."

When the conflict between Jews and Arabs and Muslims is viewed in its full geographical, psychological, historical, political, and theological complexity, there is no mystery why it has persisted for more than a century. The questions we still have to answer are whether it is possible to find an end to the conflict despite its complexity and whether Israel can survive even if this is impossible.

Chapter 2

The End of the
Arab-Israeli Conflict

THE ARAB STATES NEVER WANTED TO SEE A JEWISH STATE CREATED IN the Middle East and for a long time tried to destroy it. The general perception remains that a conflict exists between Israel and the Arab states and that Israel's security remains an issue. In fact, the Arab world has fractured and is no longer united against Israel, as individual states pursue their own interests, which they fear would be jeopardized by fighting Israel. Moreover, states that once relied on the Soviet Union for arms and political support lost their principal non-Arab ally with the collapse of the Berlin Wall, and their armies are no match for the Israelis. The decisions of Egypt and Jordan to sign peace treaties proved that conflict between Arabs and Israel is not inevitable. The Palestinian issue remains an obstacle to a more comprehensive peace, but the Arab states are not prepared to go to war on their behalf and limit their commitment to rhetoric and modest financial support. This is indicative of the shift that has occurred as the conflict with Israel has transformed from a war over land and ideology to one based on religion.

On November 27, 1947, the United Nations General Assembly expressed the international community's consensus that the best option for resolving the conflicting claims of Jews and Arabs in Palestine was to divide the country and create a Jewish state and an Arab state. Had the Palestinians accepted that decision, they would be celebrating along with Israel their 59th birthday instead of nearly six decades of statelessness.

Following the partition vote, the Arabs made no secret of their intentions, announcing their plan to use force to prevent the implementation of the resolution. These threats were immediately followed by outbreaks of violence in Palestine and throughout the Arab world where Zionism quickly became a capital crime and Jews who had lived in relative peace and security, in some cases for centuries, suddenly found themselves in grave danger.

The international community set an unfortunate precedent at that time—one it has followed ever since—by failing to provide the means to implement the UN's decision. Though the partition resolution called for the creation of a commission to carry out the UN's wishes, it was never supported. As a result, violence escalated in the months preceding the withdrawal of the British, who had governed the area following World War I. When the British left, Israel declared its independence. Within hours of the announcement on May 14, 1948, five Arab armies invaded the newborn state and the secretary-general of the Arab League announced: "This will be a war of extermination and a momentous massacre which will be spoken of like the Mongolian massacres and the Crusades."

After defeating the Arab armies in the war that followed, Israel hoped the Arabs would be prepared to accept the Jewish state and live in peace, but that was not the case. The most any of the Arab states would agree to was an armistice agreement; none entertained the notion of a peace treaty. For the next 30 years, Israel fought a series of wars that were portrayed as battles for survival, but only one really posed a threat to the existence of the Jewish state. In 1973, when Egypt and Syria launched a surprise attack on Yom Kippur, the holiest day of the Jewish calendar, they came so close to defeating Israel that Prime Minister Golda Meir considered deploying nuclear weapons as a last resort. Thanks in large measure to a massive resupply effort by the United States and the bravery of the Israel Defense Forces, the soldiers reversed the situation on the battlefield. Though no one realized it at the time, and few understand it even today, the turning point in the Arab-Israeli conflict was 1973. Israel was surprised and nearly defeated, yet it staved off destruction and proved that for the foreseeable future no combination of Arab armies could conquer it. Equally important, the United States intervened at a critical moment, albeit only with supplies, and demonstrated that it would not permit Israel to be overwhelmed.

Since 1973 Israel has not fought a war with an Arab state. Think about that. Despite the common perception of the region in a constant state of turmoil with the Arab-Israeli conflict as the principal source of instability, it has been more than 30 years since Israeli and Arab armies met on the battlefield. Israel did fight with the Palestinian Liberation Organization (PLO) in Lebanon and

Syrian forces were very briefly engaged, but the Lebanese army didn't really fight in either 1982 or 2006 and Israel's other military campaigns have been with the irregular forces of the Palestinian terrorist groups and Hizbollah.

Though formally maintaining a state of belligerency, Iraq, Saudi Arabia, Libya, and Syria have avoided attacking Israel. Although Syria has used Hizbollah and Palestinian terrorists as proxies to attack Israel, Syria has not launched an attack from Syrian soil since 1973. Syria avoided a fight even after Israel invaded Lebanon in 2006 and had its troops sitting on the Syrian doorstep.

The 1973 war was a watershed for a variety of reasons. One was that it put an end to the Arab fantasy of destroying Israel, in part because the United States had clearly chosen a side for the first time and made it clear it would not allow Israel to be defeated. As noted in chapter 1, a critical psychological breakthrough was also achieved whereby Egyptian honor was restored. President Anwar Sadat made a strategic decision to shift alliances from the Soviet Union to the United States and make peace with Israel. Once he had made this commitment, he was willing to sacrifice the interests of the wider Arab world and specifically those of the Palestinians to advance Egypt's own parochial interests.

Sadat's determination to go it alone was especially evident in his reaction to the initiatives of President Jimmy Carter. Despite the revisionist histories and apologetics of Carter's former advisors and admirers, a major catalyst for Sadat's decision to go to Jerusalem in 1977 and declare his willingness to make peace was that he thought Carter's policies were so bad, he was afraid they would interfere with his goal of regaining the Sinai and ending the conflict with Israel. Once Egyptians felt the humiliation of 1967 had been erased, Sadat was able to defy the rest of the Arab world and make a deal with Israel for several reasons. A courageous and visionary leader, he wielded absolute control over his nation and did not need to win support for his policies from the army or the public before making decisions. Egypt saw itself as the leader of the Arab world because of its long history, its military power, and its sheer size and population. The heritage of the Egyptian people also gave them confidence that they were special and did not require the permission of others to act in their interests. Despite being ostracized by other Arab states in the years immediately following the signing of the treaty, the Egyptians held fast and eventually were accepted back into the Arab fold, though they have never again wielded the same degree of influence they enjoyed in the 1950s, 1960s, and early 1970s.

The peace treaty has never been popular in Egypt, and throughout the nearly three decades since it was signed, the government has never made any effort to improve relations with Israel. For several years, Egypt recalled its ambassador from Tel Aviv because it disapproved of Israeli policy toward the Palestinians. President Hosni Mubarak, who succeeded Sadat after he was assassinated, has visited Israel only once—for Prime Minister Yitzhak Rabin's funeral—in the 25 years he's been in power. Furthermore, anti-Semitic articles, television shows, and cartoons are regularly published in the government-controlled press. But still, Egypt has kept this cold peace despite repeated calls from other Arabs to renege and to fight the Israelis during the Lebanon war and at different times during the conflict with the Palestinians.

As long as Egypt remains committed to peace with Israel, it is unlikely that any coalition of Arab forces could ever challenge Israel and threaten its survival without weapons of mass destruction. The one important caveat is that this could change almost overnight. While most analysts focus their concerns on Iran and terrorism, the most serious potential danger to Israel and regional stability comes from Egypt. As noted above, the Egyptian people have never been encouraged to embrace the idea of coexistence with Israel. To the contrary, they have consistently been fed propaganda that reinforces their stereotypes of Jews and their misperceptions of Israelis.

Israel has benefited from the fact that Egypt is not a democracy. If it were up to the popular will, it is doubtful that the peace treaty would have survived this long, though that does not necessarily mean that Egyptians desire war. It does indicate, however, that future relations with Israel are almost entirely dependent on the disposition of the Egyptian dictator. The people of Egypt did not want, demand, or make peace with Israel; it was Anwar Sadat who decided to end the conflict and who was sufficiently powerful to impose his will on the country. He paid for that decision with his life. When his vice president replaced him, there was no assurance that Mubarak would fulfill the treaty commitments. To his credit, despite the pressures he has faced over the last quarter-century, he has never wavered. While he has scrupulously observed the treaty, however, he no doubt learned a lesson from his mentor's assassination. He has never made any effort to strengthen the agreement or to go beyond the letter of the treaty. Diplomatic contacts have become more routine, trade has grown significantly, and there has been a modest amount of tourism (though almost entirely in one direction, from Israel to Egypt). The relationship still lacks, however, the warmth Israelis envisioned.

Since the future of the treaty depends on the individual leading Egypt, Mubarak's successor is vitally important to Israel. The Egyptian leader is now 79 and his days in office are numbered. He has made no secret of his desire to have his son replace him, though this idea has generated a great deal of criticism among Egyptians who resent the idea of a pharaonic-type family dynasty. If Gamal Mubarak does become president, it is not clear what his position will be toward Israel, though the expectation is that he will continue his father's policies.

The succession in Egypt typifies the difficulty the United States faces in the region. The Bush Administration has made the advance of democracy the centerpiece of its Middle East strategy, yet it has been unwilling to challenge the autocratic rule of President Mubarak. Egypt is not viewed as a threat to U.S. interests so it is not a priority to push for democracy there. Consequently, only muted protests have been issued by the United States when reformers have been arrested. The clear message sent to Egypt and the rest of the Middle East, though, is that the United States prefers the dictator it knows and believes is sympathetic to an unknown, possibly democratic alternative who is more likely to be a rabidly anti-American militant Islamist.

Israel has similar fears. While it is certainly disappointed with the quality of its relationship with Egypt, which is always referred to as a "cold peace," it is still peace. Considering what happened in the relatively free election held in 2006 in the Palestinian Authority, which brought Hamas to power and eliminated hope for peace negotiations, it is not surprising that Israel and its supporters would be unenthusiastic about elections elsewhere in the Muslim world. The worst-case scenario would be for a radical Muslim takeover of Egypt and the creation of an Islamic theocracy. It is not such a farfetched idea. Egypt was the birthplace of one of the Muslim world's most radical movements, the Muslim Brotherhood, whose offshoots include Hamas. This would put a radical regime right on Israel's borders, one with a large, well-trained army equipped with some of America's most sophisticated weapons. Consider the current balance of power: Egypt has 450,000 soldiers and another 254,000 in reserve compared to Israel's standing force of 186,500 and 445,000 reserves. Egypt has approximately 3,000 tanks and 500 aircraft while Israel has 4,000 and 800. Alarmingly, even today, Egyptian war games are directed toward Israel.

It has been a serious concern for some time that the United States has continued to sell military equipment to a regime that faces no external threats. The Clinton Administration, for example, offered Egypt Patriot antimissile batteries. Who did Egypt think was going to shoot missiles at them? Its neighbors were no match for the might of the Egyptian military and showed no signs aggression. The threat Egypt does face is internal, primarily from Islamic fundamentalists who have murdered tourists and government officials. What use are Patriots or new F-16s and M1-A1 tanks against Muslim clerics? The usual "if we don't sell them arms someone else will" argument doesn't apply here either. Undoubtedly other nations would like to sell the Egyptians arms, but what would Egypt use to pay for them? Egypt is an American welfare client. The purchase was financed out of the $1.2 billion in military aid we provide. The U.S. taxpayer is buying arms the Egyptians don't need. There is an economic argument to be made in favor of such sales. It is a way to go around the limitations of the defense budget to pump money into the U.S. defense industry. Companies can then produce more weapons and, in theory, lower the overall cost of the ones the U.S. military buys, keep production lines open, and create jobs.

You might ask why we don't just buy the weapons for our own forces and accomplish the same result? Simple: diplomatic cowardice. The Egyptians want new toys and if the United States doesn't give them what they want, they'll throw a tantrum. Clinton's defense secretary, William Cohen, justified the sale of weapons to the Egyptians by saying they would be insulted and consider it a breech of our friendship if the United States did not make the sale. Cohen's comment reflected the longstanding foreign policy doctrine that the United States applies to the Arab countries—what I call the policy of indulgence. Give our friends what they want to keep them happy. Heck, it worked for years with the Saudis, why not apply it across the board?

The money would be far better spent on butter than guns. The Egyptian population continues to explode while imports of food skyrocket and unemployment grows worse. In a country where half the population and two-thirds of the women are illiterate, wouldn't it be better to buy books than missiles? The misery created by domestic problems is exploited by the radical fundamentalists and creates political instability. For this reason, non-military assistance would be more effective in strengthening the government and resisting radical fundamentalists.

✡

What is the disposition of the other Arab states? The other countries of immediate concern to Israel are those on its other borders—Jordan, Lebanon, and Syria.

Jordan was always the most reluctant participant in the conflict with Israel. Zionist leaders first began negotiating with the monarchy in the 1940s and kept up a steady dialogue with the Hashemites who have ruled the country since it was carved out of Palestine by Winston Churchill in 1921. In 1967, King Hussein was drawn into the fighting with Israel, and lost the territory, including Jerusalem, that his grandfather had conquered in 1948. Having learned his lesson, he sat out the 1973 war. He held out hope that he would regain the West Bank in negotiations with Israel, but he came to the realization that the Palestinians would never accept his authority and his fellow Arab leaders would not support the expansion of his country (as they had never accepted his occupation from 1949 to 1967). He renounced his claim in 1974 when the Arab League declared the PLO to be the "sole legitimate representative of the Palestinian people." From that point on, Jordan had no territorial dispute with Israel, and King Hussein was held back from reaching a formal agreement only by the fear of suffering Sadat's fate in normalizing relations before the Palestinian issue was resolved.

Following the Oslo Accords in 1993 (in which Israeli and Palestinian negotiators laid out a path to peace), however, Hussein saw an opening and, though a final settlement was not reached between Israel and the Palestinians, he gambled that he could get away with a separate peace. The gamble paid off as he achieved peace with his most powerful neighbor, avoided the ostracism of the Arab world that Egypt suffered and, most important, physically survived. In addition, he regained the approval of his patrons in America who had been angered by his ill-considered support of Iraq following its 1991 invasion of Kuwait. By reinforcing the U.S. view that Jordan could play a moderating influence in the region, he also earned additional financial and military support. Despite entreaties from the Palestinians and other Arab states, Jordan has adhered to the treaty it signed with Israel in 1994. Like Egypt, Jordan has not gone much beyond the letter of the treaty to promote a spirit of peace, but Israel is more than satisfied with the removal of another border state from the coalition of rejectionists.

As in Egypt, it is conceivable that the situation could radically change in Jordan, and Israel has reason to be vigilant toward its eastern neighbor. The majority of the Jordanian population is Palestinian and the territory is part of historic Palestine. While Israel and its supporters naturally are focused on the threat Palestinians in the West Bank pose to them, the Jordanians have always been equally concerned about the possibility that the Palestinians will focus their ire in Jordan's direction.

In addition to a potential Palestinian coup, an even greater danger may be the prospect of a fundamentalist revolution similar to Iran's. As in much of the region, a strong radical undercurrent is present in Jordan and the monarchy has been very careful to keep a tight rein on the fundamentalists. In April 2006 Jordan arrested several members of Hamas who were suspected of planning a terrorist attack against senior members of the government on orders from Hamas leaders in Damascus. This followed an earlier threat uncovered when Jordanian officials learned that Hamas had smuggled weapons, including bombs and rockets, into the kingdom. That discovery led Jordan to cancel a planned visit by Palestinian Foreign Minister Mahmoud Zahar of Hamas.

Tensions between Hamas and Jordan are nothing new. In 1998 the government warned leaders of the Islamic resistance movement in Jordan to refrain from making statements inciting violence or obstructing the Palestinian-Israeli Wye River agreement that had just been signed. This admonition came after a Hamas bomb attack on an Israeli school bus in the Gaza Strip and a statement by the Hamas politburo chief in Amman, Khalid Mashal, condemning the Wye agreement and vowing to continue the war against Israel.

In 1999 five commercial offices in Amman registered under the names of Hamas leaders were closed, several of its members were detained, and arrest warrants were issued. In September 1999 Khalid Mashal, Ibrahim Ghousheh, Mousa Abu Marzook, Sami Khater, and Izzat Rasheq were arrested after returning from a trip to Tehran. Marzook, who held a Yemeni passport, was deported. Mashal, Ghousheh, Khater, and Rasheq, all Jordanian citizens, were given the choice of being tried for membership in an illegal organization or leaving Jordan. Ultimately, the four men were deported to Qatar. Jordanian officials had grown increasingly worried about the close ties that Hamas was developing with the radical Muslim Brotherhood and with Iran and Syria. Computer files confiscated from the Hamas offices contained sensitive information about the kingdom and Jordanian figures. Records revealed the locations of arms and explosives caches around the kingdom and indicated that around $70 million had been transferred to Hamas from abroad over the previous five years. Subsequently, Hamas became an "illegal and non-Jordanian" organization whose presence was no longer tolerated.

The Palestinians and especially Hamas are a threat to King Abdullah (who is married to a Palestinian). It is in the interest of Abdullah's monarchic rule that Palestinian nationalism is suppressed and that no additional Palestinians are allowed into Jordan. Throughout the second intifada from

September 2000 to 2006 (an uprising that might more accurately be called the Palestinian war), Jordan turned away at its borders Palestinians trying to flee the violence, and even those just wishing to pass through on their way to Mecca for the Muslim pilgrimage, for fear they might try to stay. Jordan also shares with Israel the desire to prevent a strong Palestinian state from emerging in the West Bank and therefore, together with the Israelis, can maintain a vise around the Palestinians to prevent them from developing a threatening military capability. Should Jordan itself shift course as a result of the end of the monarchy or ascendance of Islamists, it does not have the military capability to endanger Israel's survival, but it could become a terrorist base or potential partner in a radical coalition that would make Israelis more uncomfortable.

On Israel's northern border, Lebanon has been its most troublesome neighbor for the last three decades. The threat, however, does not come from the Lebanese government or even from the majority of Lebanese people. It has been almost entirely a result of alien forces that established separate states within Lebanon. First came the PLO, which established a base in Lebanon following the expulsion of its leaders from Jordan in 1970. The PLO had succeeded in establishing a state within a state in Jordan, but when it became clear the Palestinians were intent on overthrowing the monarchy, King Hussein waged war against them and drove them out of the country, in the process killing more Palestinians in one month (Black September) than Israel has killed in 60 years.

Following Black September, the PLO recreated and expanded its terrorist infrastructure in Lebanon. Unlike Jordan, however, Lebanon had no strong central government. Worse, the country is comprised of religious factions that had achieved an uneasy balance of power over the decades. That balance was upset by the Palestinians and helped set off a civil war, which then gave the Syrians the pretext to send in troops to quell the violence. But after the war ended, they refused to leave. Believing that Lebanon was really part of southern Syria, the government of Hafez Assad was determined to gradually swallow the country.

By the late 1970s, the PLO had begun using Lebanon as a base for attacks against Israel, which ultimately provoked an Israeli response. Though the PLO was forced out of Lebanon in the resulting war, the decision to create a buffer zone to protect its northern border led to an 18-year occupation by Israeli forces in southern Lebanon.

Israel never had any territorial claims to Lebanon and the Lebanese had no real grievance with the Israelis other than the general Arab dissatisfaction with its creation. Israelis also believed they had a better chance to reach an accommodation with Lebanon because, unlike the other Arab states, it has a significant Christian population. The Lebanese Christians have no religious objection to the existence of a Jewish state, and many see Israel as an ally in the fight against radical Muslim hegemony. The Christian president of Lebanon, Amin Gemayel, actually signed a peace agreement with Israel in 1983, but by that time Syria was the real authority in Lebanon and forced him to abrogate the treaty. Since then, the Christian population has steadily declined and lost influence to the growing Muslim majority.

As long as Syria remained the occupying power in Lebanon, it was impossible for the Lebanese to pursue an independent policy toward Israel. Peace was held hostage to the demands of the Syrians. In the meantime, another threat to Israel emerged as Iran began to look for ways to expand its influence through Shiite populations in the Arab world. In most Arab countries, the majority of the Muslim population is Sunni; however, the Lebanese Muslims are predominantly Shia. Toward the end of 1982, Iran sent emissaries to assist in the establishment of a revolutionary Islamic movement in Lebanon. The radical Shia group that emerged was Hizbollah (or Party of God). Led by religious clerics, the organization aspires to create an Iranian-style theocracy in Lebanon and, ultimately, to establish Islamic governments across the Arab world. In recent years Hizbollah has become part of the Lebanese political process, but it also uses terror as a means to achieve its goals.

As its organizational infrastructure developed, Hizbollah, with Iranian and Syrian assistance, began to establish an extensive military network in the Baalbek area. Its militias subsequently spread into the Shia neighborhoods in southern and western Beirut as well as into southern Lebanon. From bases along the border, Hizbollah has repeatedly carried out terrorist actions against Israelis and launched rockets into northern Israel. Israelis have not even been safe outside their homeland. On March 17, 1992, Hizbollah bombed the Israeli Embassy in Buenos Aires, killing 29 and injuring more than 250 people. Two years later, on July 18, 1994, the AMIA Jewish community center in Buenos Aires was bombed; 87 people were killed and more than 100 injured. Eight days later, the Israeli Embassy in London was car bombed by two Palestinians linked to Hizbollah.

After Hizbollah launched an unprovoked attack on an Israeli patrol on July 12, 2006, in which three soldiers were killed and two taken hostage,

Israel launched a major operation to disarm the terrorists and push them far enough from the border that they could not threaten its citizens with rockets. A mixture of indecisiveness, poor planning, international pressure, and Hizbollah fortitude prevented Israel from destroying Hizbollah as a fighting force. During the course of the month-long fighting, 159 Israelis were killed and more than 2,000 wounded; two million lived under threat of rocket attacks; 500,000 Israelis were displaced from their homes; 15 percent of the entire Israeli population was forced to live in bomb shelters; Israel's tourist industry, which had finally started to recover from the Palestinian war, was devastated; fires sparked by Katyusha rockets destroyed more than 16,000 acres of forests and grazing fields, and the total cost of the war was estimated in excess of $5 billion.

It is still too early to assess the final outcome. Much will depend on whether Lebanon fully implements the UN resolution calling for the deployment of its troops along the border with Israel and the disarming of Hizbollah. It remains to be seen whether the UN force will do what it failed to do for the previous six years, namely prevent Hizbollah from threatening Israel. And it is not yet evident if the Lebanese people will turn on Hizbollah for the destruction it brought on the country or if the group's leader, Hassan Nasrallah, will emerge even more popular and lead a radical takeover of the country.

Clearly, Israel did not win the decisive victory it expected, but I believe Israel still came out ahead. Even Nasrallah was forced to admit he made a mistake and miscalculated the Israeli response to the provocation he ordered. While some critics have suggested Israel's ability to deter war suffered, the fact that it responded with such ferocity to the attacks from Lebanon more likely strengthened its deterrent posture by showing the extent it is willing to go in response to a serious provocation. Perhaps the most important achievement of the war was that Hizbollah no longer holds territory along the border with Israel. The Lebanese army and an international force now stand between the group and Israel, minimizing Hizbollah's ability to threaten Israel. While some Lebanese were impressed by Hizbollah's actions, others felt Hizbollah's recklessness devastated the country. If the latter view becomes the dominant one, Hizbollah will lose popularity, thereby slowing the radical Islamization of Lebanon. While anger toward Israel over the destruction will be slow to dissipate, the conditions now are better than ever before to achieve a future agreement between Lebanon and Israel. If, however,

Nasrallah's popularity instead grows, it is conceivable that Lebanon will become an Islamic republic tied to Iran and will act as a terrorist base to threaten Israel and export radicalism throughout the region.

The principal impediment to peace with Lebanon has been Israel's other northern neighbor, Syria. After Syrian forces entered Lebanon in 1976, Syria essentially controlled the country until international pressure forced the evacuation of the occupation troops in 2005. Even now, its allies and intelligence agents hold great power. Until Syria reaches an agreement with Israel, the Syrians will do everything in their power to prevent the Lebanese from negotiating a separate deal.

Although the Syrians have shown little interest in peace (as I discuss in greater detail in chapter 8) they have also been reluctant to fight Israel. They have been happy to host the headquarters of various terrorist factions in Damascus (despite promises to the Bush Administration to shut down the offices) and to provide weapons and other logistical support to terrorists in the Palestinian Authority and Lebanon. Hizbollah has been viewed as a proxy used by Syria to keep pressure on Israel while avoiding any direct provocation that might cause Israel to attack Syria. Syria has kept its own border quiet except for trying to engage Israeli forces in the 1982 Lebanon war, during which the Israelis destroyed or damaged 18 of the 19 Syrian missile batteries and, in one day, shot down 29 Syrian MiG fighters without the loss of a single plane. Syria and Israel carefully avoided confrontations for the remainder of that war, and in 2006 Israel was careful not to give the Syrians a pretext for a fight. They did send warplanes over Assad's palace in Damascus as a warning that he was not beyond Israel's reach. In addition, during the clash with Hizbollah, although the Israelis could have intercepted arms deliveries bound for the terrorists in Syria, they instead purposely waited until shipments crossed the border into Lebanon.

Syria's ability to wage war was seriously damaged by the fall of the Soviet Union, which had been its patron for decades. Its arsenal is now comprised largely of Soviet-era weapons and it has no superpower to provide diplomatic support for its actions. Because of its support for terror, its interference in Iraq and its general intransigence, Syria has become increasingly isolated internationally. Even within the Arab world, Syria has little support because of its interference in Lebanon and its alliance with Iran.

Since the war with Hizbollah, however, Syrians officials sounded increasingly belligerent as when Assad ominously suggested on Syrian TV in August

2006 that there are alternatives to peace. Israel also detected suggestions of operations across the Golan Heights frontier that raised fears that the young, inexperienced Syrian president might make the same miscalculation Nasrallah admitted. For some time, Israeli military planners have warned of a possible lightning strike by Syria, aimed at seizing the Golan Heights. Syria hopes the international community would then intervene to prevent Israel from fighting to get the territory back. Though the largely barren Golan Heights is less important to Syria than the more prosperous southern province otherwise known as Lebanon, it is still possible that Assad will feel the need to take pre-cipitous action to erase the humiliation of his troops' expulsion from Lebanon and of Hizbollah's standing up to Israel while he did nothing. It seems more likely, however, that Assad, fearing the might of the Israel Defense Forces, will continue to keep the border quiet.

✡

Beyond its immediate borders, Israel faces little direct danger from the Arab states. Saudi Arabia has a tiny population and though it has spent billions on state-of-the-art weapons, its military is no threat to Israel. The Saudis contribute to the war against Israel primarily by using their position as the leading oil producer to pressure the United States and other governments to undermine Israel. They give lip service to the Palestinian cause and con-tribute what for them is a trifling amount of aid, but otherwise are not involved. Since Israel holds no Saudi territory, the question is why the Saudis are at war with Israel. The public reason is the Palestinian cause, but no one believes the Saudis care much for the Palestinians. The real reason is that the Saudis are perhaps the most openly anti-Semitic people on earth, who under-write terrorists fighting Israel, schools that deny Israel's existence, and supporters of the extremist Wahhabi sect of Islam. To give just a few examples of the Saudis' bigotry, in 1937 King Ibn Saud said, "Our hatred for the Jews dates from God's condemnation of them for their persecution and rejection of Isa (Jesus) and their subsequent rejection of His chosen Prophet." He added "that for a Muslim to kill a Jew, or for him to be killed by a Jew ensures him an immediate entry into Heaven and into the August presence of God Almighty."[1] King Faisal said in a 1972 interview that Jews murdered children to take their blood and mix it with the bread they eat on Passover.[2] In 1984 the Saudi delegate to the UN Human Rights Commission conference on religious tolerance said, "The Talmud says that if a Jew does not drink every year the blood of a non-Jewish man, he will be damned for eternity."[3] In 2002, Dr. Umayma Ahmad Al-Jalahma of King Faisal University, said Jews use human blood to prepare pastries for Purim.[4] More recently, the official website of the Saudi Supreme Commission for Tourism stated in 2004 that the policy of the Saudi Arabian government is to deny visas to "Jewish People." The Saudis might want to act on their feelings toward Israel, but despite spending billions for sophisticated weapons from the United States and elsewhere, the Saudi army does not pose a serious threat to Israel.

The danger posed by Saudi Arabia is primarily indirect, which makes it more insidious. As the principal funders of radical Islamic education around the world, the Saudis are the ones who help create schools and educational materials that produce the radical Muslims who join the ranks of Hizbollah, Hamas, and al-Qaeda. At one Saudi financed school, for example, Israel was blackened out on a map and replaced with "Palestine," and an eleventh-grade textbook relates that one sign of the Day of Judgment will be that Muslims will fight and kill Jews, who will hide behind trees that say, "Oh Muslim, Oh servant of God, here is a Jew hiding behind me. Come here and kill him." This school was not in Riyadh or Islamabad, it was in the state of Virginia. If this is what can be taught in a U.S. school, one can only imagine what students learn in the Saudi-funded madrasas. Given this sort of education, it is no mystery why 15 of the 19 hijackers on 9/11 came from Saudi Arabia.

Saudi support for terrorism and al-Qaeda, in particular, is not restricted to extremists in the kingdom. A classified American intelligence report published by the *New York Times* in 2002 revealed that an October 2001 survey of educated Saudis between the ages of 25 and 41 found that 95 percent of the respondents supported Osama bin Laden's cause. According to a UN report quoted in *Gulf News* (December 28, 2002), "al-Qaeda was able to receive between $300 and $500 million over the last 10 years from wealthy businessmen and bankers whose fortunes represent about 20 percent of the Saudi GNP, through a web of charities and companies acting as fronts."

The Saudis also have been heavily involved in supporting Palestinian terror. They were the largest financial backer of Hamas during the 1990s, and in 2002 the Saudis held a terror telethon, which raised more than $100 million for families of Palestinian "martyrs," including the families of suicide bombers. In September 2005 Israeli authorities arrested an Israeli-Arab Hamas activist who confessed to receiving instructions for the group's field operatives and hundreds of thousands of dollars from its headquarters in Saudi Arabia.

Despite their disposition, the Saudis have periodically gone on a peace offensive. In 2002 King Abdullah, then the crown prince, proposed a plan to distract attention from the Saudi terrorists' role in 9/11. The initiative—which offered Israel "normal relations" in exchange for a withdrawal to the 1967 borders and a resolution of the Palestinian refugee issue—was resurrected after the 2006 war in Lebanon. The fact that the Saudis would push a peace plan rather than joining Iran or Hizbollah in calling for a holy war against Israel is further indication of the lack of desire of Arab states to fight with Israel.

This is even more true of the smaller gulf states, several of which are prepared to have normal relations with Israel. States such as Qatar and Oman established trade ties that would have become more robust if not for the pressure placed on them by the Arab League. These countries are far more interested in commerce than ideology or religious fundamentalism. The same holds true for North African countries such as Morocco and Tunisia (all of these countries broke off formal relations after the outbreak of Palestinian violence in 2000). The major exception has been Libya, which has been a part of the rejectionist camp since Muammar Qaddafi came to power in 1969. Even the Libyans, however, have been no danger to Israel. Though they gave some support to the war effort in 1973 and have fought rhetorically since, the Libyans were neutralized as a threat after the United States attempted to assassinate Qaddafi in 1986 and the Soviet Union collapsed. Moreover, following the Iraq war, Qaddafi gave up his nonconventional weapons and managed to get his country off the U.S. list of countries sponsoring terror.

The Arab country that had been most threatening to Israel, at least rhetorically, was Iraq under Saddam Hussein. Iraq saw itself as the leader of the rejectionists and always contributed to the Arab war effort. In the 1991 Gulf War, Iraq fired 39 Scud missiles at Israel, killing 74 people (two died in direct hits, four from suffocation in gas masks and the rest from heart attacks) and frightening the entire population with the prospect of Iraq using chemical weapons. Even after losing that war, Saddam continued his threats against Israel, supported Palestinian terrorists, and was believed to be rebuilding his nonconventional capability to the point where he might again threaten Israel. The U.S. war and removal of Saddam from power has eliminated Iraq as a threat to Israel; its new leadership has shown no desire to continue

Saddam's belligerence toward Israel. Some people have held out hope that a democratic Iraq could have warm relations with Israel given the millennia-old ties between Jews and that historic area. That dream was at least temporarily put to rest by the outspoken criticism of Israel's campaign against Hizbollah. Whether Iraq turns into a greater danger will depend on what happens during and after the U.S. occupation of the country. Should Iraq become a new base for terrorists or a radical Islamic stronghold, it could once again become a threat to Israel.

While it is possible for the situation to change and for worst-case scenarios to play out, for practical purposes the Arab-Israeli conflict has come to an end at the governmental level. Today, Israel's principal enemy is militant Islam, and the Arab states have all but accepted Israel as an inconvenient reality in their midst. The informal end of the conflict at the state level occurred in late 2001 when Israeli prime minister Ariel Sharon declared that PLO chairman Yasser Arafat was irrelevant and isolated him in his headquarters in Ramallah. Television pictures showed Arafat sitting in a small candlelit room with a gun beside him as he made desperate calls to Arab leaders begging them to come and save the Palestinians from the Israelis. To his dismay, no one answered his pleas.

Five years later, the picture is even clearer. Israel has again mounted a major operation against Palestinian terrorists and no Arab state has lifted a finger or protested. Even in the face of what Palestinians have claimed is a humanitarian crisis, Arab states have only reluctantly contributed a pittance in financial aid. Meanwhile, people throughout the Arab world and journalists in the government-controlled press of Arab states openly talk about being tired of the Palestinians and their unwillingness and inability to put their house in order and reach an agreement with Israel. The Palestinians have learned—or should have by now—that their Arab brethren really don't care about them and see them primarily as pawns in the wider propaganda war with Israel. As long as the Palestinians remain stateless, the Arab states can complain about Israel's policies and try to wring concessions out of the rest of the world, particularly the Europeans, if their parochial demands are not met. The Arab states are willing only to send relatively paltry sums of money to help the Palestinians, make pious declarations of support, and engage in anti-Israel rhetoric in international forums, none of which has gotten the Palestinians any closer to achieving independence.

Similarly, the Arab states were silent as Israel attacked Hizbollah in Lebanon. No Arab state was prepared to go to war to defend Lebanon, and

Arab leaders made no secret of their belief that the Muslim radicals brought the disaster on themselves.

The fact that the Arab states are unwilling to defend their fellow Arabs doesn't mean that they have come to love Israel. Most, if not all, of the Arab states still would prefer that Israel did not exist, but they have neither the military power nor or the financial wherewithal to pursue the war any longer. Although to date only Egypt and Jordan have signed formal peace agreements with Israel, the gulf states and some North African nations have been willing to engage in trade and limited diplomacy with Israel. The main obstacle to closer ties is the continuing peer pressure of the Arab League to maintain the facade of a united anti-Israel front while the Palestinian issue remains unsettled.

The good news for Israel is that the danger of facing the conventional armies of its neighbors has been greatly reduced. Though still unlikely in the short term, the possibility at least exists now of reaching informal, if not formal understandings with much of the Arab world.

The bad news is that the war is now with religious fanatics with whom no political compromise is possible. Despite the wishful thinking of the diplomatic class, the conflict with Hamas and Hizbollah cannot be resolved because they are driven by a religious rather than a political agenda. They believe Allah has given them marching orders to reconstitute the Islamic empire and, ideally, expand it throughout the world. For them, Israel is a cancer in the Islamic body that must be excised.

Israel cannot achieve the type of peace its citizens long for if radical Muslims have a foothold near its borders. So long as the Islamists are denied nonconventional weapons, however, they can only terrorize Israel, not threaten its existence. The war Israel continues to mount against Hizbollah and Hamas is motivated by their determination to remove this danger. The Arab states silently cheer Israel on because they understand that the region would be better served by quiet than by instability and, more important, that the Islamic radicals want to undermine their regimes and create Iranian-style theocracies throughout the region.

The Palestinian conflict today is not really about land, it's about religion. Israel has proved willing to trade land for peace, but experience has shown the Israelis that no territorial compromise is sufficient to satisfy the Palestinian leadership (see chapter 8). The current Palestinian agenda is dominated by Hamas, which is unambiguous about its commitment to Israel's destruction because of the view that Jews cannot rule over Muslims or Islamic territory. The tilt toward Islamism in the Palestinian Authority illustrates the potential for changes in the region to dramatically alter the strategic picture. For example, Islamists could conceivably come to power in Egypt and Jordan and those countries might then form a coalition with Syria and Iran aimed at destroying Israel. At the moment it is farfetched, but these are the types of scenarios that Israeli war planners must at least consider.

What is striking is that the region has not become more radicalized. Following the revolution in Iran in 1979, the fear was that fundamentalism would sweep across the Middle East, endangering oil supplies to the West and the future of Israel. Not one country around Israel, however, followed in the footsteps of Iran. It is also important to reiterate that Israel is not at war with all of Islam, only the radicals. This is evident from the peace treaties with two Muslim states and from its diplomatic relations with other majority Muslim governments in Turkey and Mauritania and its economic interests or trade offices in Morocco, Tunisia, Oman, and Qatar. In September 2005 Israel had a major breakthrough in meetings with Pakistani officials. Publicity about the contacts led to pressure on Pakistan to say it wouldn't recognize Israel until the Palestinians had a state. Nevertheless, this was a major development, spurred in large part by Israel's close and rapidly improving relationship with India. That same month, the Tunisian president sent a personal letter to Sharon praising his "courageous" withdrawal from Gaza.

The times have changed dramatically from the days when Arab officials always walked out of the room when an Israeli spoke. Abba Eban, Israel's UN ambassador, used to tell a story about walking into a restaurant where Iraq's UN ambassador was eating. When the Iraqi saw Eban, he got up and left. Eban said he liked having the power to keep him from enjoying a meal. Today, Israeli and Arab ambassadors eat in the same restaurants and may even share a table.

No one should confuse the Arab states' unwillingness to engage in a war with Israel as a permanent acceptance of Israel's presence in the Middle East. If the balance of power in the region shifts and a coalition of Arab governments can form with the capability to destroy Israel, especially if they acquire weapons of mass destruction, it is possible the conflict will be renewed. It is more likely, however, that most Arab states will do the minimum required to satisfy their populations that they don't accept Israel—namely, spout pious slogans about the Palestinian cause, sponsor anti-Israel resolutions at the UN and other international forums, support terrorists, and engage in anti-Semitic rhetoric. It isn't pretty, and it isn't peace, but Israel can survive.

Chapter 3

The Return of the
Muslim Empire

The former Israeli prime minister Benjamin Netanyahu likes to say that Israel lives in the Middle East not the Middle West. While Americans prefer to believe in universalism, the notion that people everywhere are basically the same, the truth is that differences exist. This does not necessarily mean one group of people is better than another, just that they may have different values and beliefs. Netanyahu's point, however, is that the people of the Middle East have important distinctions that make Israel's neighborhood very different from America's. While Israel's friends would like to see it have the type of relations with its neighbors that the United States has with Canada and Mexico, the reality is that this is unlikely. The main reason is the prevalence of radical Islam and its adherents, whom I will call, for lack of a better term, Islamists. The Islamists believe they have received divine instruction that the land now called Israel is Islamic land that must be restored to the Muslims and, furthermore, that the Jews are an impediment to their ultimate redemption. This is not their opinion, it is the will of God and therefore beyond dispute. A holy war is underway that can have only one conclusion in the minds of the Islamists, leaving Israel with no choice but to prepare for a future of hostility. Still, dealing with Israel and the Jews is only the first step in the Islamist mission of remaking the entire world in their image.

Americans, especially, are reluctant to suggest that religion plays a role in the Middle East conflict because of the fear that they will be labeled bigots.

Just as Jews are viewed as trying to silence their detractors by screaming "anti-Semitism," the Muslims try to intimidate their critics with accusations of Islamophobia. In the United States, that is the worst that is likely to happen to anyone who has the courage to denigrate the behavior or beliefs of Muslims. Elsewhere, critics face physical danger. When Salman Rushdie published the novel *The Satanic Verses* (1989), which some Islamists thought was heretical, an edict was issued calling for his death. Similarly, there was widespread rioting and other threats of violence following the publication by a Danish newspaper of cartoons of Muhammad. When Pope Benedict gave a speech in the fall of 2006 in which he quoted from a medieval text that referred to Muslims using violence to spread their faith, the Muslim world erupted in fury—some people chose to demonstrate that theirs is the religion of peace by killing a nun, burning churches, and threatening to murder the Pope.

By contrast, anti-Semitic caricatures of Jews are common, especially in the Arab press, which regularly depicts Jews as Nazis, murderers, bloodthirsty barbarians, and worse. In response to the cartoons of Muhammad, the Iranian government thought it would be a clever idea to hold a contest soliciting cartoons denying the Holocaust. Even in that vile case, Jews did not riot because they were offended. They did not threaten to assassinate Iran's president. As one observer put it during the Danish controversy, offending Muslims may get you sentenced to death, while offending Jews will only get you talked to death.

The fear of offending Muslims has been evident in the behavior of U.S. officials who bend over backward to praise the Islamic faith and distinguish between radicals who pervert the "authentic" Islam by subscribing to terrorism and those who do not. President George W. Bush, who sees the world divided between good guys and bad guys, described the evil Muslims as "Islamofascists," but this also provoked anger. Even as Shiite and Sunni Muslims attack each other's mosques and slaughter each other in Iraq, political correctness demands that Islam be referred to as a religion of peace.

In America, hatemongers are even given humanitarian awards. In 2006, for example, the Los Angeles County Human Relations Commission (LACHRC) voted to give a "human relations award" to Maher Hathout of the Islamic Center of Southern California and Muslim Public Affairs Council. Among other things, Hathout has said that Arab governments that meet with Israelis would be "flushed down in the cesspools of history of treason," labeled Israel an "apartheid state," and said that Arabs have to "throw a bomb in a market or send somebody to suicide" because they don't have the "ability to target real targets in Israel."[1]

Another example of the successful propaganda and intimidation campaign was the case of an imam in Cleveland who called himself the Ambassador of Islam. After a number of favorable articles appeared in the press about what a wonderful, tolerant fellow he was, someone produced a tape of him at an Islamic Jihad fund-raising event where he said the Muslims should direct "a rifle at the first and last enemy of the Islamic nation, and that is the sons of monkeys and pigs, the Jews." This is a phrase that struck me as odd the first time I heard it, but it is a staple in the rantings of Muslim anti-Semites. For example, in a weekly sermon in April 2002, Sheikh Muhammad Sayyid Tantawi, the highest-ranking cleric in the Sunni Muslim world, called the Jews "the enemies of Allah, descendants of apes and pigs." Saudi Sheikh Abd Al-Rahman Al-Sudayyis, imam and preacher at the Al-Haraam mosque, the most important mosque in Mecca, beseeched Allah to annihilate the Jews. He also urged the Arabs to give up peace initiatives with them because they are "the scum of the human race, the rats of the world, the violators of pacts and agreements, the murderers of the prophets, and the offspring of apes and pigs." In one speech, Hizbollah chief Hassan Nasrallah referred to the "historical catastrophe of the establishment of the state of the grandsons of apes and pigs—the Zionist Jews—on the land of Palestine and Jerusalem."[2] On November 8, 2005, government-owned Syrian TV broadcast an interview with the deputy minister of religious endowments in which he stated that Syria serves as "the last line of defense" against "Zionist plots which aim to put on the throne of the Middle East the descendants of . . . those whom the Koran called the descendants of apes and pigs."[3]

This imagery is not new. According to Bat Ye'or's book, *The Dhimmi*, in the ninth century, the Qadi, Ahmed B. Talib, required Jews to wear patches on their shoulder that bore the image of an ape (Christians had badges with pictures of a pig) and to nail onto their doors the sign of a monkey. Jews over the centuries have been called many disparaging names associated with their looks or wealth, but why the comparison to animals? Islamists find their inspiration in texts that say that Jews were transformed into animals for violating the word of God. The divine punishment of Jews is mentioned in three Koranic verses: "They are those whom Allah has cast aside and on whom His wrath has fallen and of whom He has made some as apes and swine. . . ." (5:60); "You have surely known the end of those from amongst you who transgressed in the matter of the Sabbath, in consequence of which we condemned them: Be ye like apes, despised" (2:65); and "when, instead of amending, they became more persistent in the pursuit of that which they were forbidden, we condemned them: Be ye as apes, despised" (7:166).

While Islamists do not hesitate to make it clear they are at war with the West, the West does not want to be perceived as fighting the Muslim world. This is not just a post-9/11 phenomenon. Nearly a decade earlier, in 1992, Edward Djerejian, assistant secretary of state for Near Eastern affairs and a former U.S. ambassador to Syria and Israel, delivered the first official statement on U.S. policy toward Islamism in a speech titled "The United States, Islam and the Middle East in a Changing World." He said, "If there is one thought I can leave with you tonight, it is that the United States government does not view Islam as the next 'ism' confronting the West or threatening world peace."

Djerejian was wrong. Nevertheless, let me begin by stating the obvious: not all Muslims are terrorists, not all Muslims are intolerant or in any way hostile. I say this knowing the apologists for Islamism will ignore this qualification and focus only on the critical analysis, which they will try to discredit by shouting "Islamophobia" without addressing the substantive facts.

That said, the public relations campaign to portray Islam as the religion of peace and love ignores the history of Islam and the reality of the radical Islamist agenda. As Efraim Karsh, a leading historian and head of Mediterranean studies at King's College London, and others have written, Islam is a religion of imperialism, but this has escaped the scrutiny and opprobrium of the leftist, third world, nonaligned groups and individuals who myopically view the United States as imperialist and colonialist with Israel as its tool.

A short review of Middle East history can easily put the lie to the fantasy of benevolent Islam peacefully coexisting with the rest of the world until twentieth-century Western imperialists enslaved the Muslims and provoked them to the type of violence we saw on 9/11. First, however, it is important to understand that long before Muslims came into conflict with the West, they were fighting among themselves for power and to determine the true path of Islam. A split occurred between the Muslims whose power was based on their relationship to the prophet and those who were later converts or didn't have close ties to Muhammad.

The majority of Muslims today are Sunni who follow the first four caliphs, who they believe followed the practices of Muhammad and his companions. The Shiites reject the first three caliphs and accept the fourth, Ali, Muhammad's son-in-law, because they believe he was closer to the prophet. Other theological and practical distinctions exist, but this is the core of their differences and at various times throughout the last fourteen centuries, these two groups have sought to delegitimize each other and have often fought for supremacy (as in Iraq today).

A uniting principle, however, is the Muslim view of the world as divided into the House of Islam and the House of War, the Dar al-Islam and the Dar al-harb. The Dar al-Islam is all those lands in which a Muslim government rules by Islamic law. The Dar al-harb is made up of *harbis,* infidels who have not accepted the supremacy of the Muslim state and the primacy of the Muslims. It is the duty, moreover, of Muslims to pursue a jihad until the whole world is either converted or subjugated. Jihad literally means "struggle," and this struggle against nonbelievers need not be violent, but Islamists—such as the members of Hizbollah, Islamic Jihad, and Hamas—interpret it literally as a holy war.

The Muslim attitude toward Jews is reflected in various verses throughout the Koran, the holy book of the Islamic faith. "They [the Children of Israel] were consigned to humiliation and wretchedness. They brought the wrath of God upon themselves, and this because they used to deny God's signs and kill His Prophets unjustly and because they disobeyed and were transgressors" (Sura 2:61). According to the Koran, the Jews try to introduce corruption (5:64), have always been disobedient (5:78), and are enemies of Allah, the Prophet, and the angels (2:97–98).

Still, as "People of the Book," Jews and Christians are protected under Islamic law. The traditional concept of the *dhimma* (writ of protection) was extended by Muslim conquerors to Christians and Jews in exchange for their subordination to the Muslims. Peoples subjected to Muslim rule usually had a choice between death and conversion, but Jews and Christians, who adhered to the Scriptures, were allowed as *dhimmis* (protected persons) to practice their faith. This protection did little, however, to insure that Jews and Christians were treated well by the Muslims. On the contrary, an integral aspect of the *dhimma* was that, as infidels, the *dhimmis* had to openly acknowledge the superiority of the true believers—the Muslims.

In the early years of the Islamic conquest, the *jizya* (tribute), paid as a yearly poll tax, symbolized the subordination of the *dhimmis*. Later, the inferior status of Jews and Christians was reinforced through a series of regulations that governed their behavior. The *dhimmis,* on pain of death, were forbidden to mock or criticize the Koran, Islam, or Muhammad, to proselytize among Muslims, or to touch a Muslim woman (though a Muslim man could take a non-Muslim as a wife). *Dhimmis* were excluded from public office and armed service, and were forbidden to bear arms. They were not allowed to ride horses or camels, to build synagogues or churches taller than mosques, to construct houses higher than those of Muslims, or to drink wine in public. They were not allowed to pray or mourn in loud voices as that might offend the Muslims. The *dhimmis* had to show public deference toward Muslims, always yielding the center of the road to them. A *dhimmi* had little legal recourse when harmed by a Muslim. Since his oath was unacceptable to an Islamic court, he could not give evidence. To defend himself, he would have to purchase Muslim witnesses at great expense. *Dhimmis* were also forced to wear distinctive clothing. In the ninth century, for example, Baghdad's Caliph al-Mutawakkil designated a yellow badge for Jews, setting a precedent that would be followed centuries later in Nazi Germany.

At various times, Jews in Muslim lands were able to live in relative peace and thrive culturally and economically. The prosperity of some Jews, such as the physician and philosopher Maimonides, gave rise to the idea that Jews enjoyed a "golden age" in tenth-century Spain whereas, as Princeton University historian Bernard Lewis has written, "The Golden Age of equal rights was a myth, and belief in it was a result, more than a cause, of Jewish sympathy for Islam."[4] The position of the Jews was never secure, and changes in the political or social climate would often lead to persecution, violence and death. Jews were generally viewed with contempt by their Muslim neighbors; peaceful coexistence between the two groups involved the subordination and degradation of the Jews.

When Jews were perceived as having achieved too comfortable a position in Islamic society, anti-Semitism would surface, often with devastating results. On December 30, 1066, Joseph HaNagid, the Jewish vizier of Granada, Spain, was crucified by an Arab mob that proceeded to raze the Jewish quarter of the city and slaughter its 5,000 inhabitants. The riot was incited by Muslim preachers who had angrily objected to what they saw as inordinate Jewish political power.

The treatment of the Jews was relatively benign compared to the Muslim behavior toward other people who were in the path of their armies. The propagators of the "peaceful Islam" myth would have you believe that Muslims simply went from town to town carrying a Koran and inviting people to read it, who were then so struck by enlightenment, they immediately converted to this new faith. Perhaps some converts were attracted this way, but most had a very different encounter with the early Muslims.

In 632 Muhammad's followers marched out of the deserts of Arabia and began to create one of the world's great empires, stretching across parts of Asia, the Middle East, North Africa, and into Spain. For roughly 1,300 years the Muslims dominated that region of the world. The Muslim empire slowly fragmented into competing kingdoms that were still unified by the Arabic language and the adherence of the majority of the people to Islam.

The first major external threat to this empire came in the eleventh century when Pope Urban II called for a crusade to regain Palestine from the infidels. In 1099 crusaders captured Jerusalem and celebrated by herding all the Jews into a synagogue and burning them alive. Jews supported Muslims for most of the empire's existence because other rulers—especially Christians—treated them even worse. During the two centuries that the crusaders controlled Palestine, Jews were persecuted but their communities remained entrenched throughout the country. Given their mistreatment at the hands of the Christians in the Middle East and especially in Europe, it is not surprising that the Jews sided with the Muslims who, in 1187, recaptured Jerusalem after Saladin, a young Kurdish officer from Mesopotamia (now Iraq) invaded Palestine and expelled the crusaders. The Muslims maintained control over most of their empire until it began to crack in the thirteenth century when the Mongols invaded from eastern Asia and seized the lands of present-day Iran and Iraq.

The Mongols were stopped by an army of slaves known as Mamelukes, who had been mobilized by Egypt to defend the empire. The Mamelukes then turned on their masters, and seized power in Egypt, Syria, and much of Arabia. One more foreign army took a crack at building an empire in the Middle East—this time it was the Turks. They defeated the Mamelukes and in 1516 and 1517 absorbed Egypt, Syria, and the western empire into what became known as the Ottoman empire after the dynasty founded by Osman I. Though the Turks were Muslims, they had a more tolerant attitude toward Jews, and the Jewish community began to flourish again in Palestine.

Palestine wasn't an important province for the Turks; they paid little attention to it and let the country in general and Jerusalem in particular deteriorate.

While the Jews were by no means thrilled about being *dhimmis* in the Ottoman empire, the seeds of rebellion were growing elsewhere as a new idea began to take hold throughout many parts of the world early in the nineteenth century—nationalism. The French Revolution had inspired people to seek their independence, and by the close of the century some Turks in the heart of the empire were growing increasingly dissatisfied with the autocratic control of the Ottoman rulers. These Young Turks, as they were called, were led by the charismatic Mustafa Kemal Ataturk. Their goal was to institute a variety of reforms including the separation of mosque and state, a separation enshrined in the modern republic's constitution. The Ottoman empire had been steadily declining and World War I led to its final breakup and the weakening of Muslim control over the region. Britain and France divided up the region and created new political entities, usually with their allies installed as the heads of the governments. The newly independent Arab nations that emerged in the succeeding decades vacillated as pawns in the cold war between the United States and the Soviet Union, and between variants of socialism, nationalism, theocracy, democracy, and autocracy. All of these nations had one consistent feature: Islam was the state religion. The Saudis remained the most fervent adherents to their own strict brand of Islam, Wahhabism (which holds that Muslims have lost their way and must return to a pure form of Islam, as defined by the Saudi clerics), but still allied themselves with the United States rather than the godless communists. Jordan, an artificial creation of the British, and for a time Iraq, Lebanon, and Iran, which were all ruled by nonreligious leaders, also were allied with the West.

Egypt emerged as the most important state in the region because of its size, history, and leadership; the Muslim Brotherhood, a radical Islamist political movement, originated there in opposition to governments viewed as corrupt, too pro-Western and insufficiently committed to the faith. A threat to the regime, the Brotherhood was ruthlessly suppressed, but offshoots of the organization sprang up elsewhere in the region, in Saudi Arabia, Jordan, and Syria. After the Syrian branch tried to assassinate President Hafez Assad in June 1980, for example, membership in the Brotherhood was declared a capital offense, and Assad sent his army to raze their stronghold in the city of Hama and killed an estimated 20,000 people in 1982.

The turning point for the Islamists was the Iranian revolution in 1979. Under the Pahlavi dynasty established in 1925, the country was secularized and allied with the West. This greatly benefited the Jews, who were emancipated and played an important role in the Iranian economy and cultural life. On the eve of the Islamic Revolution in 1979, 80,000 Jews lived in Iran. In the wake of the upheaval, tens of thousands of Iran's Jews, especially the wealthy, fled, leaving behind vast amounts of property. When the Ayatollah Khomeini's followers succeeded in forcing the shah to flee the country, Khomeini returned from exile, instituted *Shariah* (Islamic law), and began to purge the country of Western influences. Khomeini also sought to export the revolution and provoke the replacement of the Arab governments in the region with Islamic republics. Iran subsequently became the patron—spiritual and financial—for most of the region's Islamists. The Iranian model of revolution, its institution of Islamic law and its anti-Western philosophy characterize the rhetoric of many extremist groups. The weapons, training, and literature that are the backbone of Islamist violence are bankrolled by Tehran.

Iran has been linked to numerous anti-West and anti-Israel terrorist attacks that range from hostage taking and airplane hijackings to carrying out assassinations and bombings. Some of these incidents include the seizing of more than 30 Western hostages in Lebanon between 1984 and 1992, the bombings of the U.S. Embassy and the French-U.S. Marine barracks in Beirut in 1983, the 1992 terrorist attack on the Israeli Embassy in Buenos Aires, and the bombing of the Argentine Jewish communal building in 1994.

Iran has grown increasingly involved in the Palestinian Authority and is trying to build alliances to promote violence against Israel. In October 2005 a senior Palestinian intelligence official revealed that Iran promised a reward of $10,000 to Islamic Jihad if it launched rockets from the West Bank toward Tel Aviv. The money was transferred from Iran to Syria, where Ibrahim Shehadeh, Islamic Jihad's head of overseas operations, forwarded it to the West Bank. Deadly weapons were also smuggled into the hands of Iranian-sponsored groups such as Hizbollah and used against Israeli civilians in commando-style raids. During the 2006 war, the world learned that Iran had given Hizbollah long-range missiles that could reach Tel Aviv, as well as anti-ship missiles, one of which disabled a new ship in Israel's Navy.

Part of the ignorance of Western analysts and the wishful thinking of the general population is the belief that the Iranian mullahs and other Islamists have grievances that can be addressed. For example, Osama bin Laden is routinely described as interested in removing U.S. forces from the Middle East and overthrowing the Saudi monarchy, but those are just stages toward his real goal. Bin Laden and his fellow Islamists wish to begin by Islamicizing individual Arab nations, then the region—which requires the destruction of the cancer in the Islamic heart, that is, Israel—recreating the empire by expanding Islamic rule and regaining control of Spain, and spreading the faith globally to become the dominant power in the world.

If Israel withdrew from 100 percent of the Gaza Strip, 100 percent of the West Bank, 100 percent of the Golan Heights, and 100 percent of Jerusalem, Hamas and Islamic Jihad would not stop murdering Israeli women and children. Rather, they would intensify their terrorist campaign in the belief that they had forced Israel to withdraw that far, so eventually they could force the Jews into the sea. The unwillingness to accept a Jewish state in their midst also is a common thread among Islamists and some Muslims perceived as being moderate. Yasser Arafat, for example, was often portrayed as a secular leader but he was not. The Islamists from the more extreme movements may have seen him as an apostate, but Arafat was a Muslim who was no more willing to accept Jewish sovereignty over Muslim land than the leaders of Hamas or Islamic Jihad. That is one reason why he would never end the conflict with Israel.

For years, Palestinians would say that their goal was a "secular democratic" state in Palestine. What was interesting is that this was a slogan used exclusively for Western consumption. While the prospect of a truly democratic Arab state is farfetched given the region's history, the notion of a secular one is almost beyond imagination. Not surprisingly, the discussions of Palestinian statehood in Arabic always made clear that the Palestinian state would be rooted in Islam and, though the Palestinians have never succeeded in writing a final constitution, every draft has declared Islam to be the official religion of any future state.

Islamists believe they are on the march. Hamas used its terror campaign, it believes, to force Israel's withdrawal from the Gaza Strip. Iran's support for terrorists throughout the region, its defiance of the international community's efforts to curtail its nuclear program, and its ability to suppress internal dissent show that Iran is a power to be reckoned with on the regional and world stage. Hizbollah's ability to survive a conflict with Israel shows how an insurgency can fight and "win" against infidel forces constrained by Western values. The Judeo-Christian emphasis on self-preservation is no match for the self-sacrificing spirit of Islamists who seek martyrdom; they are led by strong, charismatic leaders who command and receive total obedience.

The goals of overcoming Western decadence, corruption, and backwardness, recreating the Muslim empire and destroying Israel have widespread public appeal in the Muslim world. The ideology of Islamism has not spread at the state level in part because the notion of recreating the Muslim empire implies the destruction of existing nation-states whose current regimes are unwilling to sacrifice their power to embrace Islamism.

As I said at the outset of this discussion, in no way do I mean to suggest that all or even a majority of Muslims are Islamists. Approximately 15 percent of the citizens of Israel are Muslims, and a great variety of views exist among Muslims and among Muslim states. Israel, for example, has long had a relationship with Morocco and, during the Oslo period, started to have interactions with some of the Gulf states. More recently, Israel had its first substantive meetings with Pakistan. If Islamists were the dominant force in the Muslim world, Israel would be in far more serious danger; however, if only 10 percent or even 1 percent of the world's 1.5 billion Muslims adhere to the genocidal views of bin Laden, Nasrallah, and others, that is a significant enough number to pose an ongoing threat to Israel and the West.

The war waged by fundamentalists is primarily directed at the West, but it first must be won in the Arab world. A main reason that most of the Arab League refused to support Hizbollah's war on Israel is that Hizbollah is a radical Shiite group created, funded, and armed by Iran. Its Arab critics were from regimes dominated by Sunni Muslims who understood that the radical Shiites in Lebanon were a threat not merely to Israel but to their own countries. The other Arab leaders, unlike most analysts outside the region, recognized that Hizbollah's principal goal was to take over Lebanon, institute a Shiite theocracy, and spread Iran's influence deeper into the heart of the Arab world. They also knew that Iran would see this as the start of a domino effect that, the Iranian Mullahs hoped, would eventually allow the Shiites to undermine, if not overthrow, the Sunni-dominated governments. Youssef Ibrahim, an Egyptian-born American who served as a senior Middle East regional correspondent for the *New York Times*, noted that while the West rightly fears the Islamists, the Arab states worry about "an ascendant Shiite 'arc of menace' rising out of Iran and peddled in the Sunni world by Syria."[5]

The differing visions of Islam that contributed to the earlier fracturing of the Muslim empire are ongoing impediments to its restoration. The revolutionary zeal of bin Laden and others to remake the region in their image of Islam requires erasing borders and dismantling nations, which is naturally opposed by those in power and counter to the nationalistic trends of strengthening the individual states at the expense of the *ummah*, the collective Islamic community.

It is also important to note that Islam isn't simply at war with the Jews. Christians are also nonbelievers. Muslim students are taught, for example, that the Day of Judgment won't come until Jesus Christ returns to Earth, breaks the cross, and converts everyone to Islam. One reason for the focus of Muslim wrath on Israel is that the Jewish state is the last refuge in the region for Christians and other non-Muslim populations. For all their professions of tolerance, the Muslim states have decimated non-Muslim populations and either persecute the remaining nonbelievers or ignore them because their numbers are so small. Christians were once a majority in Lebanon; today the community is a shrinking minority. A small Coptic Christian community remains in Egypt where it faces a variety of restrictions, and the Baha'i live under constant persecution in Iran. A handful of Jews remain in Egypt, Lebanon, Yemen, and Iraq; the rest fled or were expelled in the 1940s and 1950s, and a majority immigrated to Israel. The Muslims have succeeded in remaking the rest of the region as an exclusive enclave. The religious war in the Middle East is now primarily (but not exclusively) between the Shiite radicals and the Sunnis who rule most Arab states. The conflict is most obvious in Iraq where Muslims blow each other up on a daily basis with little comment or interest by the outside world, or for that matter, by their fellow believers.

The success the Islamists have had in terrorizing the international community has created the impression that they are winning World War III. Given the reluctance of the rest of the world to fight back, it is not surprising that the radicals appear ascendant. On the other hand, this post-9/11 defeatism is reminiscent of the years immediately following the Iranian revolution in 1979. At that time, a major U.S. ally had been overthrown, America had been humiliated by the hostage affair, and some feared that Iran was the first domino to fall in the march of Islam to restore the caliphate. Despite the dire predictions of the time, however, not one more domino fell in the area. One of the principal targets of the Shiites, the Saud dynasty, has remained intact, and the gulf states remained under their existing monarchs. The Assads in Syria, the Hashemites in Jordan, and Mubarak in Egypt faced fundamentalist subversion and ruthlessly suppressed it. Even the apparent Islamist advances in the Palestinian Authority and Lebanon have proven illusory. In the case of the former, Hamas won the 2006 election because of widespread Palestinian frustration with the corruption of Fatah and the better organization of the Islamic party, not because of any dramatic shift in Palestinian society toward Islamism. Since coming to power, the group's representatives have been unable to perform basic acts of governance, such as insuring security, providing jobs, and paying employees. Moreover, the irredentism of the Hamas leadership alienated the international community and provoked an international boycott that has left the economy in shambles. The Palestinian Authority has all but disintegrated into chaos and internecine fighting.

Even the claim that Hamas drove the Israelis out of Gaza is widely recognized by Palestinians as nothing more than propaganda. Israel left on its own terms because Prime Minister Ariel Sharon recognized that holding on to the territory worsened the Palestinian-Jewish demographic imbalance between the Mediterranean Sea and the Jordan River, kept 8,000 Israeli settlers as targets of suicide bombers, and put thousands of soldiers at risk to protect Jews who were adding nothing to the nation's security. The Palestinian people were not fooled by the rhetoric of the terrorists, as is evident by this comment from Mohammed Ahmed Moussa, a grocer in Jabaliya, who said, "Let's be frank. If Israel didn't want to leave Gaza, no one could have forced them out. Those who claim the rockets and attacks made them leave are kidding themselves."[6]

In Lebanon, Hizbollah had replicated the PLO's feat of creating a state within a state. Like Hamas, Hizbollah declared victory following Israel's withdrawal, but even Hizbollah's charismatic leader Hassan Nasrallah was forced to admit afterward that he had miscalculated how Israel would respond to his group's act of war. Contrary to media reports suggesting widespread support among its followers in the south, most of Hizbollah's supporters fled the battlefield. The Shiite mufti of Tyre said Hizbollah didn't ask the community about the war and the Shiites didn't authorize war or ask to be dragged into one. Non-Shiites feel even more strongly. It will take some months before the full impact of the war is known; in the short run, one outcome has been to slow, if not completely halt, Hizbollah's efforts to establish an Iranian-style theocracy.

This was also a setback for Iran, which saw its principal proxy castigated by the international community. More telling was the fact that much of the Arab world dissociated itself from Nasrallah and rejected his call to join a holy war against Israel. The Arab media was openly critical of Hizbollah. For example, in August 2006 the Saudi paper *Al Watan* labeled their kidnapping of an Israeli soldier "irresponsible" and Kuwait's *Assi Assa* newspaper called Nasrallah an "adventurer" who was "unaware of his actions" and "does not understand what he has done to Lebanon."[7]

✡

For many people, 9/11 marked the start of an international war between the West and the Islamists. This was perhaps the formal beginning, but the war actually began earlier, possibly with the Iranian revolution and the taking of American hostages, or certainly with the first bombing of the World Trade Center. It did not take long to find out who were America's allies and who were aligned with the terrorists. On 9/11, the Israelis mourned with the American people while the Palestinians held a parade.

One of the difficulties in fighting this war is the reluctance to acknowledge that it *is* a war because it is rooted in religion. No political leader wants to be portrayed as waging a war on a faith that has more than a billion followers. A second problem is that the Islamists fight by their own rules, ones that the Western world does not recognize, in which civilians are used as shields and prisoners may be tortured and brutally murdered. A third challenge is that the enemy is not obvious and has few known bases of operation. The individual terrorists are typically not wild-eyed fanatics whose appearance would trigger alarms. Contrary to conventional wisdom, they are also rarely poor or persecuted people seeking vengeance. Some may indeed wish to avenge some real or imagined injury, but most of the Islamists want to spread Islam and to fight those they believe are impeding its influence. The Islamists often congregate in specific mosques where particular clergy inspire them to use terror as a means to accomplish their objectives, but most are in loose-knit groups that have little or no contact with each other and are under no central authority.

We did know that one of the principal bases for Islamists involved in 9/11 was Afghanistan. I wrote in September 2001, however, that for this to be a serious war on terrorism, we could not limit our counterterrorism operations to Afghanistan. If the 9/11 attack really was worse than Pearl Harbor, as many said at the time, I argued that we should mount a World War II–style campaign targeting Iran, Syria, Lebanon, and the Palestinians, but held open the possibility of using nonmilitary measures against them. I also acknowledged such a campaign wasn't likely to happen in part because the U.S. State Department would do everything in its power to prevent it for fear of upsetting our Arab friends. Instead, I predicted, the United States would attack Iraq, even if Saddam had nothing to do with 9/11, because we had other reasons to try to take him out—not the least of which was the need for Dick Cheney, Paul Wolfowitz, Donald Rumsfeld, and the other Bush Sr. administration returnees to make up for their failure to complete the job in 1991. The results of the war that did bring about Saddam's demise are now the subject of debate and may not be fully apparent for some months or years; one thing that is clear now is the need to continue to fight the Islamists.

In the relativistic political world of the West, it is too difficult to imagine that genocidal threats are more than rhetoric, but Jews learned from bitter experience that when a homicidal maniac threatens murder and has the means to do it, you should take him seriously. The West has not yet learned this lesson.

Having written several books on the Holocaust, I have often been struck by the fact that Hitler made no effort to disguise his intentions. Although during the war the Germans went to great lengths to conceal the final solution, in the years prior to the war Hitler publicly stated that he would exterminate the Jews—yet his remarks were dismissed as rhetoric. Now the Iranian president threatens to wipe Israel off the map, the leader of Hizbollah says he wants to kill every last Jew, and Hamas calls for Israel's obliteration, and their statements are met with the same lack of concern. Islamists also inspire comparisons to Hitler by their frequent denial of the Holocaust, typified by Iranian President Mahmoud Ahmadinejad's remark that the Holocaust was "a legend" invented by the Jews and that he did not accept that "Hitler killed millions of innocent Jews in furnaces and sent them to concentration camps."[8]

Islamists pose a threat to the whole world but Israel is on the front line. Neither Israel, the United States, nor the entire Western world can fight a religious war with Islam. The Islamists are spread throughout the world and it would take a true world war in which every nation agreed to participate to eradicate the danger. Given that the European Union cannot even bring itself to put Hizbollah on its list of terrorist groups and take the steps the United States has implemented to cut off funding to the organization, it is unrealistic to expect a concerted global effort to fight Islamism.

The real battle must be fought among Muslims. Islam must have a reformation. As Muslims rightly note, Christianity was once a religion that was as much associated with war and intolerance as peace. It was the Christians who maintained for centuries that Jews killed Christ, instituted the Inquisition, and mounted the Crusades. A reformation did take place and Christians changed some of their beliefs about Jews. One may still find fault with elements of Christianity, but it no longer poses a military threat to the lives of nonbelievers. The church arrived at these changes through its own processes, albeit with some outside influence. Similarly, non-Muslims cannot force change on the Islamic world. During the controversy over Mel Gibson's film *The Passion of the Christ*, there were Jews who were so concerned about the film's content and its potential harmful effects, they were determined to explain the truth about the Gospels to Christians. It was absurd. Christians had to debate the issues among themselves. Similarly, no matter how knowledgeable anyone may be about the Koran and Muslim traditions, it is not for others to interpret Islam.

It will also be up to what Youssef Ibrahim, Contributing Editor for the *New York Sun*, calls the silent Arab majority to speak out. These are Muslims who believe that

> 7th century Islam is not fit for the 21st century challenges: Women do not have to look like walking black tents. Men do not have to wear beards and robes, act like lunatics and run around blowing themselves up in order to enjoy 72 virgins in paradise. And that secular laws, not Islamic Shariah, should rule our day-to-day lives. And yes, we the silent Arab majority, do not believe that writers, secular or otherwise, should be killed or banned for expressing their views. Or that the rest of our creative elite—from moviemakers to playwrights, actors, painters, sculptors and fashion models—should be vetted by Neanderthal

Muslim imams who have never read a book in their dim, miserable lives. Nor do we believe that little men with head wraps and disheveled beards can run amok in Lebanon, Saudi Arabia, Iran and Iraq making decisions on our behalf, dragging us to war whenever they please, confiscating our rights to be adults, and flogging us for not praying five times a day or even for not believing in God.[9]

The problem at the moment is that the trend in the Muslim world appears to be in the direction of radicalization rather than reformation. Just as non-Muslims are cowed into silence by Muslim threats of violence, the fear of speaking out within the Islamic world is even more pronounced. It is rare to find Muslim leaders with the courage to condemn even the most heinous terrorist attacks, let alone the broader Islamist agenda.

September 11 was a turning point. It put Muslims on the defensive. Public opinion polls had previously indicated that they were unpopular and misunderstood, but those feelings had been based on perceptions that the Arabs were blackmailing us with high oil prices, that they were savages who saw violence as the way to resolve their grievances, and that they were primitives riding camels in the deserts while forcing their women to hide behind veils. After 9/11, these negative stereotypes were reinforced and magnified by the perception that Americans were not only targets, but were considered by Muslims enemies who should and could be killed on a large scale. Though often put in crude terms that offend the sensibilities of the universalists, the fundamentalist Christians see the threat clearly. The Pope articulated in an indirect way the religious war that he recognizes is underway when he quoted from the medieval Byzantine emperor Manuel II Paleologus who said, "Show me just what Muhammad brought that was new, and there you will find things only evil and inhuman, such as his command to spread by the sword the faith he preached."

The Muslims' faith in ultimate victory is based in part on their belief that time is on their side. In many ways their historical perspective is much wiser than that of most other peoples. After all, when Americans talk about the "good old days," they might be referring to the 1950s or 1960s. When Muslims reflect on their glorious past, they refer to the 950s or the 1250s or the 1450s. And who can blame them for such nostalgia? The Muslims had an empire that lasted for more than a thousand years, stretching from Asia to Spain. During that period, Muslims were the dominant force in their half of the world in almost every aspect of civilization from science to literature to architecture.

Given the perspective of centuries, the current situation in which Israel is viewed as the region's dominant power (and the U.S. is the global super-power) is considered a temporary phenomenon. Thus, for example, you hear Arabs say such things as, "The Crusaders conquered Palestine and it took 200 years to drive them out, but we did. Now the Zionists have conquered Palestine, and it may take us 200 years, but we'll drive them out as well." From the Muslim perspective, they've only been working toward this goal for 100 years and they've still got another 100 to go. Or, as the political adviser to Palestinian Prime Minister Ismail Haniyeh of Hamas puts it bluntly in the title of his new book—The End of the Jewish State: Just a Matter of Time.

Chapter 4

The Demographic Bomb

BESIDES FAITH, ON WHAT DO MUSLIMS BASE THEIR OPTIMISM THAT TIME IS on their side? There are two main reasons—the demographic bomb and the atomic bomb. This and the following chapter explain the reasons for the Islamists' optimism. Discussions of Israel's security dilemma focus on the dangers posed by conventional armies in Syria and Egypt, terrorists based in the Palestinian Authority and elsewhere, and potential attacks using weapons of mass destruction, especially nuclear weapons, from Iran. These are, of course, serious concerns; however, the gravest long-term threat to Israel's future may be internal—namely, the erosion of the state's Jewish democratic character by a shift in the demographic balance as the anti-Zionist Arab minority grows.

Today, Israel has a population of more than seven million, and even after absorbing approximately one million immigrants from the former Soviet Union in the last decade, the Jewish population is still only 5.3 million. Approximately 4.7 million Palestinians live in Israel, the West Bank and Gaza Strip. If the circle is expanded to include the rest of the region, the Arab and Muslim population is roughly 300 million. No matter how many babies the Zionists produce, they are not going to catch up. The Muslim birth rate in the region is about double that of the Jews in Israel. Muslims often talk of the woman's womb as a weapon in their battle to destroy Israel: "The woman who rocks the baby's cradle with one hand, rocks the nation with the other." As a result, some Muslims believe they can swamp the Jews by numbers alone.

Since 1967 Israel has faced a demographic dilemma. If it were to annex the disputed territories, it would have to incorporate a large Palestinian Arab population. Even if the Palestinians never became a majority and only constituted a sizable minority, they would undoubtedly use Israel's democratic process to erode the Jewish character of the state. For example, they might elect candidates to the Knesset that would vote to eliminate the role of the chief rabbinate in matters of personal status or to change the state's symbols or holidays. Some Israelis have suggested the way to prevent the Palestinians from turning the Jewish state into another Arab nation would be to deny them the right to vote. In that case, Israel would cease to be a democracy. Since no Israeli prime minister has been able to square the circle and figure out how to annex the territories and maintain Israel's Jewish democratic character, even the supposedly right-wing leaders who are advocates of "Greater Israel" eschewed annexation. In fact, one of those hardliners, Ariel Sharon, decided to take the exact opposite step and withdraw from the Gaza Strip, thereby significantly improving the demographic ratio of Jews to Arabs.

Sharon recognized the harsh reality that the population between the Mediterranean Sea and Jordan River is today approximately 10.3 million: 4.7 million are Palestinians, meaning that if Israel annexed the West Bank and Gaza Strip, the Jewish population today of that "Greater Israel" would be a bare majority—52 percent. According to Israel's leading demographer, Sergio DellaPergola of Hebrew University, the proportion of Jews is likely to fall to 47 percent by 2020, and to 37 percent by 2050.

Now that Israel has freed itself of the Gaza albatross, the demographic balance has improved. Approximately 2.3 million Palestinians live in the West Bank and another 1.3 million Arabs are Israeli citizens. The total population of Israel and the West Bank is 9.3 million, meaning Israel's 5.3 million Jews comprise 57 percent of the total, a comfortable majority unless you consider the potential of the 40 percent Arab minority to influence the character of Israel's democracy. Furthermore, in the absence of massive immigration, given the higher Arab birth rate, the Jewish majority is bound to shrink.

Reading demographic projections of the Middle East is a little bit like counting angels on the head of a pin; the estimates are always imprecise because of the impossibility of anticipating changes in variables such as fertility rates and immigration. Earlier predictions, for example, were based on what was an exceptionally high Arab birth rate, but the most recent figures show that the Arab population, especially in Israel, has experienced a declining birth rate. Those trying to minimize the demographic issue trumpet this as evidence that it is not as bad as doomsayers suggest and that the trends of the past do not necessarily reflect the future. These optimists do not always acknowledge that the birth rate of Israeli Jewish women is holding steady at 2.7 children per woman and remains well below the 4.7 per Arab woman. In addition, the average age when Jewish women have their first child is 27.5 years compared to 23.2 for Muslims.

One study suggested the assumption that Arabs in the West Bank and Gaza pose a demographic threat to Israel has been exaggerated because the actual population in the territories is significantly lower than what is reported by Palestinian Authority (PA) officials. According to a study by a team of independent researchers, the 2004 Palestinian Arab population was closer to 2.4 million than to the 3.8 million cited by the PA. The independent study arrived at its figures largely by deconstructing PA statistics, but DellaPergola has challenged the result, saying his estimate of 3.4 million Palestinians is based on Israeli data. (The CIA estimates the population for the West Bank and Gaza at 3.6 million.) Even if the new study is more accurate, it only has a minimal impact on the demographic reality. According to Israeli census figures, the population of Israel today is approximately 7 million. If we add the 2.4 million Arabs that the new study says live in the territories, the total population from the Jordan River to the sea would be 9.4 million, including about 3 million Israeli Arabs. The Jewish population is roughly 5.3 million or 56 percent, slightly better than DellaPergola's estimate of 52 percent.

These overall statistics also distort the debate over the disengagement from Gaza where the demographic picture was crystal clear. According to the new study, the Arab population there is more than one million. The Jewish population was 8,500, which means the percentage of Jews was a fraction of 1 percent of the total population in Gaza.

The independent study focused solely on discrediting the PA statistics and did not address the crucial issue of future trends, which DellaPergola shows are clearly in the Arabs' favor. Although the new report argues that the growth rates in Israel and the territories have been lower than previously forecast (they use data for the last four years only), even these figures show that the growth rate for the Arabs remains higher than that of the Jews, so the proportion of Jews should continue to decline. Not surprisingly, the authors of the study also conclude that Israel faces a demographic threat, though they say it is exaggerated and there is time to evaluate policy options.

The Israeli Central Bureau of Statistics, however, suggests the situation may be even worse. The bureau said that the proportion of Jews *within the current borders* of Israel is expected to decline from the present figure of 78 percent to 70 percent in 2025 because of the higher birth rate among Israeli Arabs. According to one of Israel's preeminent demographers, Arnon Sofer of Haifa University, prior to the disengagement from Gaza the majority of the population between the Jordan River and the Mediterranean Sea was Palestinian. Having rid itself of responsibility for Gaza, the proportion of the population in areas held by Israel dropped to 40 percent. Nevertheless, Sofer says that natural growth projections indicate that Arabs, including Israeli Arabs, will once again become the majority in the areas controlled by Israel by 2020.

Recognition of this demographic threat was a prime motivation for Ariel Sharon's dramatic shift from settlement builder to disengagement advocate. To forestall a second evacuation, many friends of Israel are trotting out old arguments regarding the imperative of defensible borders and going as far back as 1967 to cite a U.S. Joint Chiefs of Staff memo that outlined Israel's need to retain some territory captured during the Six-Day War. Those same advocates are quick to point out, rightly, that UN Resolution 242 did not call for Israel to withdraw from *all* the captured territories, so they should also be aware that the Joint Chiefs were equally careful in specifying that Israel retain *some* but not all of the West Bank. Moreover, while the geography may not have changed in the last 40 years, the demography has changed dramatically, and that too has strategic implications.

Most Israelis do not believe Israel should keep the entire West Bank and believe that peace requires at least some territorial compromise. Ariel Sharon, the father of the bulk of the settlements, asserted that there will be such compromises. His successor, Ehud Olmert, ran for prime minister on a platform promising a unilateral "realignment" in the West Bank in which the vast majority of settlements, mostly small and relatively isolated, would be evacuated and the population transferred either within the 1967 borders or to settlements annexed to Israel. There is a general consensus in Israel that the future boundaries of Israel will incorporate five settlement blocks. These blocks include roughly 70 percent of the Jews living in the West Bank, the other 30 percent, roughly 60,000 Jews, are expected to move either to those blocks or within the 1967 borders.

Even after establishing borders and consolidating its Jewish majority, Israel still faces demographic challenges presented by the Israeli Arab birth rate, which is double that of the Jews' declining rate, and declining immigration. On the eve of Rosh Hashanah 2006, the proportion of the Israeli population that is Jewish was 76.2 percent, down from 77.8 percent five years ago. While the Arab population will not become a majority in the foreseeable future, it is likely to become a sizable minority that can wield far greater influence on politics and society than it does today. Israelis know that the Jewish birth rate is not going to improve dramatically, and most Israelis probably are happy about that since the women who are producing large families are principally ultra-Orthodox Jews whom the secular majority consider a threat to their way of life (a subject I will return to in chapter 8).

✡

Israeli policies are exacerbating the demographic situation, particularly in Jerusalem, where the security wall (and here it is almost entirely a wall rather than a fence) is being built with little apparent regard for population projections. In its effort to incorporate as much of the land as possible in and around Jerusalem, the barrier has also enclosed thousands of Palestinian Arabs inside the city. In fact, unbelievable as it may seem, Israel has now brought a Palestinian refugee camp within the borders it has drawn for Jerusalem.

One extreme measure that Israel took to minimize the demographic imbalance was to issue a directive in 2002, which later became a law, freezing the naturalization process of all Palestinians from the West Bank and Gaza Strip residing in Israel as the spouses of Israeli (usually Arab) citizens. The law meant that these couples either had to divorce, stay married and live separately, or move to the territories. Although no one knows how many couples this law applies to and few instances could be cited where security concerns were raised about one of the partners, the government argued the law was needed to protect the nation's security. The law was challenged in court, and the Israeli Supreme Court ruled by a 6-5 margin in 2006 that the law should be extended while it was revised. The court's majority also acknowledged that the state had the right to protect itself by insuring a Jewish population majority.

The law illustrated how the demographic reality has become a major strategic concern of Israeli officials and has led even many of the most hawkish Israelis to conclude that Israel must withdraw from additional territory to remain a democratic Jewish state. This is the majority view, though a minority holds out hope that the status quo can be maintained until a sufficient number of Jews immigrate to Israel to erase the Arab advantage. A very small minority advocates the radical view that an exchange of populations should be on the agenda that would require the transfer of Palestinians to Jordan or elsewhere. I will discuss the alternatives in greater detail in the chapter on peacemaking, but for now I will focus more narrowly on the notion that the demographic challenge can be overcome by the mass immigration of Jews to Israel.

Many people argue that it is impossible to predict the future and that most past population projections have proven inaccurate. Earlier doomsday predictions were upset by large influxes of immigrants, and many Israelis believe this will still be their demographic salvation. After the influx of Jews from the former Soviet Union in the 1990s, this view was temporarily vindicated; however, there remain only about 10 million Jews in the entire world outside Israel, and a large number would have to decide to move to Israel to offset the demographic trend. This is especially unlikely given that roughly 75 percent of the Jews outside Israel live in the United States from which very few emigrate. In 2006, immigration to Israel dropped to 21,000, an 18-year low.

Nevertheless, the one hope for staving off the demographic threat is immigration. Not surprisingly, Prime Minister Sharon announced shortly after the disengagement in 2005 that Israel's goal was to absorb one million new immigrants by 2020. Israel achieved a similar goal over the last 15 years, when more than one million Jews from the former Soviet Union immigrated to Israel and temporarily mitigated the demographic impact of the Arab population. Now, it appears the pool of Jews in that region has run dry, and those Jews who are leaving prefer other destinations. After averaging almost 80,000 immigrants per year in the 1990s, the numbers have dropped dramatically since 2000 and fewer than 10,000 came in 2005. So many Russian Jews moved to Germany—two out of every three Jews from the former Soviet Union who were eligible—that the Israeli government pressured the

Germans to change their immigration policy to make it more difficult for Russian Jews to choose Europe over Israel.

Another interesting aspect of Israel's demographic thirst is its willingness to accept many immigrants who are not Jewish. Estimates suggest that as many as one-fourth of the immigrants from the former Soviet Union are not Jewish but are still eligible according to the law of repatriation. Many also slipped in because the immigration authorities did not scrutinize their applications too carefully.

The willingness to look the other way is even more apparent in the case of people in Ethiopia claiming to be Jews. Today, approximately 100,000 Ethiopian Jews live in Israel. For almost three decades, one of the major obstacles to Ethiopian Jews being brought to Israel was the belief by the Orthodox establishment that they were not Jews. The reasons are complex but include the fact that the Ethiopian community was separated from the rest of the Jewish world for centuries and had very different practices, notably the unawareness of the Oral Law, that is, the laws interpreted by rabbis. It was, therefore, not too surprising that rabbis making the determination of their Jewishness had their doubts. Ultimately, in 1973, the Sephardic Chief Rabbi recognized them as Jews and cleared the way for the community to be brought to Israel.

After Israel believed it had brought all of the Jews home, large numbers of Ethiopians began to come out of the hinterlands of Ethiopia to claim Jewish heritage. Most of these Jews, or more likely their relatives, had converted at some point to Christianity. The Israeli government was resistant to the idea of bringing these former Jews who wanted to return to the fold to Israel. The perception was that Ethiopians just wanted to get out of one of the world's poorest nations and saw Israel as a good place to escape to. Israeli officials believed the whole Ethiopian population of 70 million would immigrate if it could. Still the government came under increasing pressure from activists as the number of these Ethiopians, who became known as Falash Mura, began congregating in Addis Ababa. Advocates for these people began to provide humanitarian assistance as well as Jewish instruction. Horror stories about the living conditions of the Ethiopians were circulated to further pressure the Israeli government to accept them.

Finally, Israel agreed to accept the Falash Mura, albeit at a snail's pace of a few hundred a month. Why not a large airlift such as Operation Solomon, which brought what was then believed to be the last 14,000 Ethiopian Jews?

Primarily because it was opposed by the Ethiopian government, which was profoundly disturbed by the perception that their country was so bad that thousands of people were desperate to leave. The Israeli government still didn't believe these Ethiopians were Jews and complained that many reverted to Christianity once they arrived in Israel. Many Ethiopian Jews in Israel also opposed accepting the Falash Mura because they believed this group had chosen the easy way out in Ethiopia by assimilating to gain acceptance while they who had remained Jewish endured persecution.

So why would the government reverse its policy and agree to accept the Falash Mura? The answer is probably related to the demographic threat, which is now so serious that the government is prepared to accept large numbers of immigrants whose Jewishness it doubts. Stephen Spector's book *Operation Solomon* says that in 2001 Jewish Agency officials explicitly linked the Falash Mura question to the state's demographic needs. The element of desperation is also evident in the government's willingness to accept large numbers of people who will be a short-term drain on the economy and will take years to become productive. Unlike the Russians, who arrived highly educated and skilled, the Ethiopian Jews are coming from a far less sophisticated society. While the Ethiopian Jews who came in the earlier rescues have had a good deal of success integrating and contributing to Israel's economy, it took many years for them to do so, and it is now estimated to cost approximately $100,000 to absorb each new Ethiopian immigrant.

The pool of Falash Mura is potentially enormous. As Israeli officials feared, after bringing in the first group, still more emerged. It is very likely that after Israel empties the camps in Addis Ababa, which now have an estimated 3,000 people, and take in the other 15,000 Falash Mura believed to be in the city of Gondar and other areas, thousands more will claim Jewish heritage. (In fact, 8,000 more were "discovered" in early 2007.)

Demography appeared to trump economics and religion; however, the government agreed to bring only 300 Falash Mura a month. To help pay for this, the American Jewish community committed to raising $100 million. Following the war in Lebanon in the summer of 2006, the Israeli government was moving toward reneging on its commitment and said that budgetary shortfalls created by the need to rebuild northern Israel meant that only 150 Falash Mura would be allowed to immigrate each month. This provoked a firestorm of protest, primarily in the United States, which led the government to reverse the decision and agree to continue to bring in 300 people per month.

Assuming Israel does not plan to accept millions of Ethiopians as immigrants, it will be necessary to bolster the population from elsewhere. But where are there large populations of Jews left? If the entire Jewish population outside of Israel were to immigrate, the population would increase by less than 10 million, but clearly every Jew will not move to Israel. Over the last three years, an average of only 23,000 people made *aliyah* (the Hebrew word for "going up" used to indicate immigration to Israel). Further, a 2006 survey indicated that many immigrants are returning to their native countries.

Every time there is an economic calamity or outbreak of anti-Semitism, Israel expects large numbers of Jews to abandon their native lands for their Jewish homeland. For example, the collapse of the apartheid regime in South Africa was expected to stimulate the mass exodus of Jews there, but only about 16,000 of the more than 100,000-strong community made *aliyah*. In 2005 the figure was 102. The economic crisis in Argentina was also supposed to prompt a large wave of immigration, but again, only a relative handful (roughly 10,000 out of a population of 250,000) made *aliyah* during the last few years. In 2005, 397 Argentine Jews settled in Israel.

The emergence of Islamic extremism and outbreaks of anti-Semitism are expected to lead European Jews to flee to Israel, but so far it is not happening. In France, for example, Jews tell me they see no future for their community of 600,000, yet only 2,900 Jews immigrated in 2006, and the average of the prior five years was fewer than 2,000.

The only other large population from which Israel can attract immigrants is the United States. Consequently, some Israelis hold out hope that their salvation in the demographic war is that American Jewry will emigrate. This is one reason why Israeli officials repeatedly come to America and emphasize the importance of *aliyah*. The pitch that Israel is the Jewish homeland, however, has not motivated more than a couple of thousand Jews annually. Undeterred, Israel's Jewish Agency sponsored a survey that found that 500,000 American Jews said they "would consider" making *aliyah*. The survey results, ballyhooed in 2005, renewed Israeli optimism that the demographic dilemma will ultimately be ameliorated by American Jews. Unfortunately, the ludicrous data in the Jewish Agency survey is likely to feed Israeli delusions for years to come and, worse, allow at least some Israelis on the political right to believe that they do not have to make territorial or other compromises with the Arabs.

The more uncomfortable reality is that American Jews are not going to save Israel—at least not through *aliyah*. Most American Jews do profess an affinity to Israel—about 74 percent according to American Jewish Committee polls—but this has translated into an annual average immigration of fewer than 1,500 per year over the last 15 years (2,045 in 2005). The reason that American Jews' affection for Israel has not led to mass immigration can be largely explained by the nature of American Zionism and how different factions see their contributions to Israel's survival. Most American Jews love Israel; they believe that it is the Jewish homeland and that its existence is vital for the security of the Jewish people. The commitment to Israel can be expressed politically, spiritually, culturally, and religiously without leaving one's home in the United States. This is what it means to be an American Zionist.

For Israelis, it is an oxymoron to call oneself a Zionist while saying that you have no intention of moving to Israel. Moreover, Israelis like to tell American Jews that they are the ones whose survival is at stake. Benjamin Netanyahu, for example, said in October 2006, "There is no future for Jews in the Diaspora, because of assimilation and intermarriage. . . . The only future for the Jews is in Israel. The only hope for the Jewish people in the Diaspora is Israel." Jewish Agency chairman Zeev Bielsky made a similar remark on the eve of the United Jewish Community's General Assembly, the world's largest annual gathering of Jewish leaders. "One day the penny will drop for American Jews," Bielsky told the *Jerusalem Post*, "and they will realize they have no future as Jews in the U.S. due to assimilation and intermarriage. . . . We have to get them to move to Israel, and then Ariel Sharon's vision of one million *olim* (immigrants) from America will come true."[1] One of Israel's most famous authors, A. B. Yehoshua, provoked an uproar at the centennial meeting of the American Jewish Committee when he said that only Israel can ensure the survival of the Jewish people. "[Being] Israeli is my skin, not my jacket. You are changing jackets . . . you are changing countries like changing jackets. I have my skin, the territory." Later he told the *Jerusalem Post*, "It seems to me obvious that our Jewish life in Israel is more total than anywhere outside Israel."[2] Yehoshua's views were well known. He'd said similar things many times in the past. Still, his remarks roiled the crowd of some of the most active Jews who are perfectly satisfied with their interpretation of Zionism, which is based on the level of comfort Jews feel in the United States, the belief in America's strength and values, the limited impact of anti-Semitism, and the conviction that the United States is the principal defender of Jews around the world and the ultimate guarantor of Israel's survival.

Today, American Zionism comes in a variety of flavors, some that parallel the archetypal forms of Zionism and others that are products of the American experience. The following general descriptions will undoubtedly provoke howls of outrage from people who believe they are the exceptions but will nevertheless illustrate the predicament Israel faces.

A growing segment of American Jewry has hoisted the Herzlian banner of political Zionism, holding the view that the most important guarantee of Israel's survival is the U.S.-Israeli relationship. While a variety of Jewish organizations engage in promoting the relationship, the American Israel Public Affairs Committee (AIPAC) is by far the most important. Beyond the institutional clout of the formal pro-Israel lobby, Jews also exert disproportionate influence through the political process by virtue of their contributions of time, money, and energy to campaigns. Still, political Zionist influence is circumscribed. While the pro-Israel lobby may set some parameters for policymakers, its principal influence is on funding issues decided by Congress; matters of diplomacy, war, and peace are usually beyond its reach. For example, Congress unanimously voted in 1995 to move the U.S. embassy to Jerusalem by 1999 and to recognize the city as Israel's capital. Twelve years later, the embassy remains in Tel Aviv and successive administrations (the most pro-Israel in history) have refused to accept Jerusalem as Israel's capital. More recently, during the conflict with Hizbollah in Lebanon, the Israeli campaign was largely dictated by the president's position, which was initially supportive but ultimately turned on Israel and forced what some Israelis believed was a premature cease-fire. The lobbyists were helpless to do anything about it. Typically, Congress defers to the Executive branch on matters of foreign policy, so even on issues where the pro-Israel lobby "wins"—such as the imposition of restrictions on funding for the Palestinians—the legislation is effectively neutered by including waivers that allow the president to ignore the law.

Political Zionists rarely stray from the Israeli government line and can change positions 180 degrees if a new prime minister comes to power whose policy differs from his predecessor. They view Israel as the party truly interested in peace and believe the United States should support its policies. Political Zionists put the onus of peacemaking on the Palestinians and demand that they meet their obligations before Israel makes concessions. This group includes Jews who support territorial compromise and believe

peace is possible if the Palestinians accept Israel and take the necessary measures to end terror. It also includes Jews who oppose territorial compromise, or
who are willing to accept only limited withdrawal because they believe that
peace is unlikely and that the best outcome Israel can achieve is a state where
there is no conventional war and limited terror.

Though doomsayers continue to worry about Arab Americans or Muslims
gaining influence, Jews remain the dominant political force on Middle East
issues. If anything, the fear of the Arab lobby helps reinforce the view that
American Jewish political activism is essential to forestall a catastrophic shift
in U.S. Middle East policy. This is one reason why political Zionists argue,
more to themselves than aloud, that they can do more for Israel by remaining
in the United States.

A small segment of the American Jewish community, typified by Americans for Peace Now and other left-of-center political groups, support the
existence of Israel but have little good to say about it. Their main focus is criticism of Israeli policies, particularly vis-à-vis the Palestinians. These progressive
Zionists tend to be young, usually too young to have lived through the Holocaust, partition, or any of Israel's wars. They often focus on human rights and
social justice but don't have the grounding in Jewish political history to place
these issues in proper context.

Unlike political Zionists who believe Israelis acting through their
democracy should decide what's best, progressives believe Israel must be
saved by the United States; that is, as long as policymakers adopt *their* pre-
scriptions for Israel. Increasing attention, particularly at the college level, has
been given to self-identified liberal, progressive Jews who eschew establishment Jewish organizations. Many of these Jews declare fealty to liberalism
while expressing support for the Palestinian Authority, which does not
respect the liberal values they otherwise espouse, such as freedom of speech,
freedom of religion, freedom of assembly, women's rights, and gay rights.
While often casting themselves as the peace camp, progressive Zionists focus
on Israel's faults and the need for Israel to make concessions (particularly
regarding the dismantling of all settlements and withdrawal from "occupied
territories"). Little or nothing is demanded of the Palestinians whose failure to
positively respond to past Israeli concessions and whose continuing use of terrorism are rationalized. They see Palestinians as having legitimate grievances

and tend to ignore Islamists, pretending they are irrelevant as long as other Palestinians express moderate views.

Often the progressives find their natural allies in liberal causes and engage in anti-American, anti-war crusades that are hijacked by anti-Israel forces. While not going to the extreme of the anti-Zionists, their criticism is often used by Israel's detractors to show that even Jews agree about the evils of Israel's actions. They have limited clout, but they often undermine efforts by political Zionists to present a united front on major issues of peace and security. Progressive Zionists have little interest in immigrating to Israel because they see it as a flawed nation. They believe the best way to bring about change is to save Israel from itself by convincing the United States to coerce Israel to adopt the policies they endorse.

Besides the political Zionists, perhaps the fastest growing segment of the American Zionist community consists of Jews who don't want to talk directly about Israel but are interested in the society and culture. Cultural Zionists typically don't want to hear about history or politics; they are happy to listen to Israeli music or read Israeli literature. The nonpolitical, nonreligious, and largely nonintellectual connection to Israel is popular with younger Jews who will pack a hall to hear a concert by an Israeli hip-hop artist but avoid any Israel-related lecture. For these Zionists, a trip to Israel is a chance to experience the culture of Israelis firsthand, but it is more of a novelty than a way of life they wish to pursue.

A small but far more homogeneous group of mostly Orthodox Jews are committed to Israel because of their interpretation of the Torah. Religious Zionists are typically well informed and tend to be politically conservative. They are very philanthropic, but much of their support goes directly to private Orthodox institutions in Israel and Judea and Samaria rather than to state institutions or secular causes. Many of these Jews spend a significant amount of time in Israel, but will not make *aliyah* until they are retired, if at all. The handful that move earlier tend to be ulta-Orthodox and have a contradictory impact on the demographic dilemma. These Jews increase the Jewish population because they typically have larger families than secular Israelis; but since many move to Judea and Samaria and join the more extreme movements opposed to territorial compromise, they aggravate the political situation.

Few Jews from other denominations are motivated to support Israel by their faith. On the contrary, many Conservative and Reform Jews are unhappy with Israel because of the lack of support their movements receive in Israel, because of the periodically raised question as to "Who is a Jew," and because of the monopoly held by the Orthodox rabbinate over critical institutions such as marriage and divorce. While Orthodox Jews see their support as contributing to the strength and well-being of Israel, non-Orthodox Jews fear the influence of religion in politics and the exacerbation of secular-religious tensions.

A dying breed, traditional Zionists are mostly Jews who lived through Israel's formative years, contributed to its defense during crises, and show their support through establishment Jewish structures such as Jewish federations, the Jewish National Fund, and Israel Bonds. They believe Israel is the Jewish homeland and that it is most important as a haven in the event of a future catastrophe. These Zionists are typically pillars of their communities and often active politically. While many acquired their Zionism from their parents, they've been less successful in passing their passion on to their children or grandchildren. The traditional Zionists have usually traveled to Israel many times to visit, often maintain second homes there, but aren't willing to completely give up their lives in America.

For many years, a strong Zionist movement was found among Jews who were involved in organized labor and advocated socialism. With the collapse of the Soviet Union and the weakening of the American labor movement, this strand of Zionism has all but died out. Today, the organizations that call themselves Labor Zionists tend to be either political Zionists associated with the Israeli Labor Party or progressive Zionists.

Since the early days of Zionism, there have always been Jews who have gone over to the other side and sought to delegitimize Israel. Since a Jew supporting Israel is a dog-bites-man story, some Jews have discovered that a quick route to a modicum of celebrity is by acting like the man biting the dog, by attacking Israel and Zionists. This has always been and remains a tiny minority that has no interest in *aliyah*. Still, anti-Zionists have been a nefarious influence, particularly on college campuses where they are often found teaching courses about Israel and leading anti-Israel organizations. These anti-Zionists also should not be confused with classic religious anti-Zionists who opposed the creation of Israel on religious grounds because they believed the messiah should come first.

Since its origins, Zionism has never been monolithic, but one of the features of American Zionism today is the breakdown in the tradition of presenting a unified face to the gentiles. This was provoked originally by left-wing Israelis during Likud prime minister Yitzhak Shamir's term, who violated the unwritten rule against lobbying against the elected government when abroad. When Labor's Yitzhak Rabin came to power, rather than return to the old convention, right-wing Israelis came to the United States to undermine his policies.

Currently, Israelis use pluralism as a code word to encourage American Zionists to oppose the government when the opposition is in power. Practically this has meant that the left attacks governments associated with the right and vice versa. This seemingly straightforward model broke down, however, during the debate over disengagement from Gaza as the American Zionist left backed the right-wing Sharon government. Meanwhile, right-wing American Zionists have abandoned the tradition of supporting the democratically-elected government of Israel and stake out positions independent of the government.

The fragmentation of American political Zionism has undermined its raison d'etre. If American Zionists cannot strengthen Israel through their political activity, the justification for remaining in the United States disappears. This brings us to the more painful reality of American Jewish life: the admission that most American Jews are too scared to make *aliyah*. Ignore personal security for a moment, and consider both the difficulty of making a living in Israel and the living standard compared with what many of us are accustomed to in the United States.

Life in Israel isn't easy. Add to the economic challenges the sense of threat. Compared to most major American cities, the real danger in Israel is minimal but the anxiety is far greater. Forget immigration. During the five years of war with the Palestinians, many Jews were afraid to visit, canceling or postponing trips, even as evangelical Christians continued to make pilgrimages. Besides concern with terrorism, most American Jews do not have the sense of duty or responsibility to defend Israel that would allow them to overcome their fears and serve in the Israel Defense Forces, or to send their children to the army.

American Jews are still incredibly committed to Israel, as exemplified most recently by the commitment to raise $500 million to help rebuild northern Lebanon after the war with Hizbollah. Israelis derisively call this "checkbook Zionism." This is the reality, however, as American Zionists vote with their money, not their feet. Consequently, it is a fantasy to believe half a million Jews will leave their comfortable lives in the United States for the challenging life in Israel. This means the demographic problem is likely to grow worse; this in turn will be a disincentive to a negotiated peace agreement because many Arabs will believe they can achieve their objective of destroying Israel by overwhelming the Jews with the sheer weight of their population.

It is more difficult to be optimistic about how Israel can overcome the demographic threat, but it is important to keep this gloomy scenario in perspective. At the beginning of the twentieth century, the British believed Palestine couldn't absorb any more people. At that time less than a million people lived in an area that now supports more than 10 million. Later the British admitted that the Jews enlarged the absorptive capacity of the country.

After Israel's independence, one of the most remarkable aspects of the state's development was the ingathering of the exiles. The integration of people from more than 100 countries was nothing short of astounding. Consider that the Jewish population doubled in just the first three years of statehood. Less than 60 years ago, fewer than 600,000 Jews lived in Palestine; today Israel's total population is more than seven million. Long before the movie *Field of Dreams*, Herzl had his own dream: If you build a state, Jews will come. That dream became a reality, and it remains alive.

Chapter 5

The Nuclear Apocalypse

Terrorism creates strains on the nation but does not threaten Israel's existence. The demography of the region alone will not destroy Israel and will only become a serious factor years from now. Similarly, a water shortage is a long-term concern that might provoke war but will not directly harm Israel's security. A conventional war could lead to Israel's demise, but no constellation of forces exists at the moment that are likely to challenge Israel's superior military. Of all the threats to Israel's long-term survival, one danger overshadows all the rest—an enemy with nuclear weapons.

The possibility that a Middle Eastern Arab or Muslim leader might acquire a bomb has long been a concern; however, the discovery that the Islamist regime in Iran has secretly been developing a nuclear capability has made the threat far more imminent. It has forced Israeli decision makers, as well as other leaders around the world concerned with peace and stability, to face difficult choices about whether to accept new members to the nuclear club or to take whatever measures are necessary to stop them.

In a September 2006 poll, more than half of the Israelis surveyed said Iranian nuclear weapons were their biggest concern. Is it any wonder when they hear Ayatollah Ali Khamenei declare that "The only way to confront the Zionist enemy is the continuation and fortification of resistance and Jihad," and hear current Iranian president Mahmoud Ahmadinejad agree with Ayatollah Khomeini's desire to "wipe Israel off the map"? Ahmadinejad, who also denies the Holocaust, added, "God willing, with the force of God behind it, we shall soon experience a world without the United States and Zionism."[1]

President George W. Bush said on February 16, 2005, "Iran has made it clear that they don't like Israel, to put it bluntly. And the Israelis are concerned about whether or not Iran develops a nuclear weapon, as are we, as should everybody. Clearly, if I was the leader of Israel, and I listened to some of the statements by the Iranian ayatollahs that regarded the security of my country, I'd be concerned about Iran having a nuclear weapon as well. And in that Israel is our ally, and in that we've made a very strong commitment to support Israel. We will support Israel if their security is threatened." The president's support is reassuring, but Israelis know they cannot afford to rely on others for their security. The memory of the Holocaust and the trauma of the October 1973 Yom Kippur War do not allow Israeli leaders the luxury of hoping that the nuclear threat will disappear, especially given the apparent determination of the Iranians to build their own bombs.

While *aliyah* is the idealistic reaction to the "demographic bomb," the realistic response has been the atomic bomb. Israel is widely believed to have developed a nuclear bomb in the 1960s to insure it had the ultimate weapon in its arsenal and the capability to offset its quantitative disadvantage in manpower and weaponry. Possession of these weapons is one of the reasons for the shift in attitudes toward Israel that has resulted in the end to the Arab-Israeli conflict. Paradoxically, while Israel's nuclear weapons have deterred Arab armies, they have not scared terrorists. These weapons are a deterrent only if a country is prepared to use them. There is a widespread belief, reinforced by the ambiguous statements of Israeli officials (who never acknowledge having the bomb, but say they will not be the first to introduce them into the region), that Israel would only use its arsenal if it was attacked with nuclear weapons or if the country itself was on the verge of destruction. Currently, none of its enemies can threaten it with nuclear weapons, so Israel is left with a stockpile of powerful weapons that it isn't willing to use and that don't deter terrorist attacks.

Thanks to the United States, Israel has maintained a qualitative military edge over its enemies, but that margin has eroded over the years as the United States has sold increasingly sophisticated weapons to Arab states. The key to ultimate victory in the minds of many Muslims, however, is the acquisition of nuclear weapons, which will immediately erase Israel's advantage as well as its deterrent. Moreover, given Israel's small size and close proximity, a sophisticated arsenal is not required to pose a mortal threat.

With the prospect of Iran or other Islamic nations in the region acquiring a nuclear capability, the demographic threat may fade to insignificance. Moreover, the Israeli fantasy of massive immigration may do nothing but create a more inviting target for the likes of Hizbollah leader Nasrallah, who has said if all the Jews gather in Israel "it will save us the trouble of going after them worldwide."[2] Psychology factors into the decision-making process regarding nuclear capabilities. Since the collapse of their empire and the ascendancy of the West, Muslims generally have felt a degree of embarrassment because of their inability to match the technological advancements of the infidels. Increasingly, however, Muslims feel confident that they will ultimately defeat Israel because, they believe, progress is now on their side. While they acknowledge that they fell behind much of the rest of the world in the last century, oil wealth has allowed them to slowly begin to catch up to the technological advantage of the Israelis.

Though Israel has never openly admitted it has nuclear weapons, the Muslim world, along with everyone else, has long assumed Israel has the bomb. While building up stocks of nonconventional weapons to use against Israel, several states have wanted to achieve their own nuclear capability. Countries such as Libya had hoped to use their oil wealth to purchase either a bomb or the technology to build one but never succeeded. Of the Arab nations, Iraq came the closest to having nuclear weapons until its program was put out of commission in 1981, when Israel destroyed its reactor in Osirak. At the time, the Israelis were internationally condemned, even by the United States, for taking what was viewed as an aggressive and drastic preemptory measure. Ten years later, when the United States found itself at war with Iraq, the Bush Administration expressed its gratitude for what Israel had done and its relief that American forces did not have to worry about facing a nuclear Iraq. Saddam Hussein did not abandon his ambition to obtain a nuclear weapon, and it was the widespread, though ultimately mistaken, belief that he was developing a bomb that led most Americans to support President George W. Bush's decision to wage a second war on Iraq.

Though many states may harbor a desire for nuclear weapons, today the one country that is most actively pursuing a bomb is Iran. Initially, the principal reason the Iranians sought a bomb was the fear that their rivals in Iraq might get one first, thereby shifting the balance of power decisively against them. The U.S. defeat of Iraq and overthrow of Saddam Hussein, however, has eliminated the only real Arab threat to Iran's goal of becoming the region's superpower, with or without nuclear weapons. Still, the current Iranian regime is determined to develop their own bomb for several reasons. One is national pride. Having a nuclear weapon allows Iran to join an exclusive club of nations and is an indication of technological advancement. A nuclear weapon is also a symbol of military strength that would give Iran the power to potentially intimidate or even destroy its enemies. The ability to achieve a nuclear capability would be another indication that Allah is on the side of the believers. The Iranians also maintain that they need nuclear weapons to deter Israel even though they know Israel poses no threat to them. For Iranians, it is also a matter of justice that they should have as much right to nuclear weapons as the United States, Israel, or any other country. Iranians want to reverse 300 years of Western ascendancy, return the splendor to their 6,000-year-old civilization, and become the leaders of the Islamic world. Obtaining nuclear weapons is a key element of this strategy.

These are all legitimate arguments. Similar ones could be advanced for virtually any country that wished to pursue a bomb, but the international community views nuclear weapons as especially dangerous and destabilizing. The consensus is that expanding the nuclear club is detrimental to world peace. This has certainly not stopped other countries from seeking their own weapons. India and Pakistan each felt the need to obtain bombs to deter each other, and it appears that North Korea has also succeeded in building a nuclear weapon. The prospect that Iran could also go nuclear is viewed as a grave danger to Western interests and especially to Israel: It will indeed shift the balance of power in the region, and the current leaders of Iran have given the world reason to believe they might use a bomb if they have the capability.

The Iranian attitude toward Israel today represents a painful reversal in a relationship that goes back to biblical times. Israel actually had very good relations with Iran during the rule of the Shah, who provided Israel with oil and was viewed as a key ally in Israel's "periphery policy," an attempt to encircle its enemies with a ring of friends, which also included non-Arab Turkey and Ethiopia. The relationship with Iran evaporated overnight following the revolution that brought the Islamists to power in 1979. Since then, Iran has been the most belligerently anti-Israel nation in the world. The situation grew even more worrisome in 2006 with the election of Mahmoud Ahmadinejad as president. Immediately after assuming office, Ahmadinejad began making public statements that were shockingly ignorant, such as denying the Holocaust, and boldly threatening, as exemplified by his call for Israel to be wiped off the map.

Even before Ahmadinejad took power, Israel was concerned about Iran's pursuit of nuclear weapons. While it was long assumed that Iran was interested in acquiring a bomb, it was not until 2002 that it became clear that Iran was not only actively working on one, it had been covertly doing so for nearly 20 years. Perhaps as early as 1989 North Korea began helping Iran develop a nuclear program, starting with the building of dozens of underground tunnels and facilities for the construction of nuclear-capable missiles. Iran has been North Korea's principal customer for arms, missiles, and nuclear technology. The fear, particularly since the North Koreans tested a nuclear device in October 2006, is that North Korea could export to Iran plutonium, weapons design data, or even a warhead. North Korea has little in common with the Muslim world beyond an antipathy toward the West, but it is prepared to share its technology for cash, which it desperately needs to bolster its weak economy, feed its starving population and, more important from the regime's perspective, underwrite its military machine.

In the mid-1990s, Russia agreed to build a 1,000-megawatt light-water reactor in the southern Iranian port city of Bushehr. To allay U.S. fears that the fuel Russia is providing for the plant could be diverted to a weapons program, the Russians agreed to take back the spent fuel rods from the plant, but Iran has not agreed to this. The Iranians want to produce their own nuclear fuel, which they say would only be for reactors to produce energy. Iran does not need to produce its own fuel, however, because Russia promised to provide the fuel throughout the operating lifetime of the reactor. While Iran maintains it only wants to produce nuclear energy, the fact that Iran is one of the world's largest oil producers with some of the world's largest crude oil reserves raises questions as to the urgency of its need for alternative energy sources. Moreover, since Iran admitted in June 2005 that it conducted experiments to create plutonium, which is used only in weapons and not for energy production, few people believe the Iranians are sincere. The Bushehr project has provided valuable training for Iranian technicians and engineers, but the Russians have dragged their feet—some believe purposely—and the date for completing the plant has repeatedly been delayed. The reactor fuel was due to be delivered in 2006; it now appears it will not go online before at least 2007.

A third major contributor to the Iranian program has been China, which signed a ten-year nuclear cooperation agreement in 1990 that allowed Iranian nuclear engineers to obtain training in China. In addition, China has already built a nuclear research reactor in Iran that became operational in 1994. Chinese experts have also been involved in the supervision of the installation of centrifuge equipment that can be used to enrich uranium. In 2002 Iran revealed that it had purchased special gas from China that could also be used to enrich uranium for the production of nuclear weapons. The gas purchase was supposed to be reported to the International Atomic Energy Agency (IAEA), but it wasn't.

Though North Korea, Russia, and China have provided technology to Iran, the "brain" behind the Iranian nuclear program is believed to be Abdul Qadeer Khan, the father of Pakistan's nuclear program, who passed secrets and equipment to Iranian officials. Initially it was feared that once Pakistan produced an arsenal of "Islamic bombs," they would be provided to other Islamic nations. As it turned out, Pakistan was not prepared to share the weapons or even its know-how despite its religious affinity with Israel's Muslim enemies. Instead, Khan, Pakistan's principal nuclear engineer, helped Iran develop a nuclear program for more mundane, personal financial reasons. Khan became involved in helping Iran in the mid-1990s. Pakistani investigators have told the International Atomic Energy Agency (IAEA) that centrifuges built by Iran closely resemble the design of Pakistani centrifuges. Khan also helped the Iranians create a secret procurement network involving companies and middlemen around the world. In March 2005, former Iranian president Hashemi Rafsanjani admitted that Iran developed its nuclear program in secret, going to the black market for material. Meanwhile, the head of IAEA disclosed that Iran obtained through the Khan network the blueprint for casting the uranium required in making the core of a nuclear warhead.

The quickest way for Iran to complete a weapon would be to openly build a gas centrifuge plant to make weapons-grade uranium. Iran has chosen instead to continue a covert program that has been difficult to monitor. The IAEA has repeatedly criticized Iran for failing to reveal "the scope and nature" of its nuclear program. In 2002 two previously unknown nuclear facilities were discovered in Iran. The first one, located in Arak, produces heavy water that could be used to produce weapons. The other is in Natanz, where Iran has been testing centrifuges used to enrich fuel.

In February 2003, President Mohammad Khatami announced the discovery of uranium reserves near the central city of Yazd and said Iran was setting up production facilities "to make use of advanced nuclear technology for peaceful purposes." This was an alarming development because it suggested Iran was attempting to obtain the means to produce and process fuel itself, despite the agreement to receive all the uranium it would need for civilian purposes from Russia.

The Iranian government, confronted in February 2004 with new evidence obtained from the secret network of nuclear suppliers surrounding Khan, acknowledged it had a design for a far more advanced high-speed centrifuge to enrich uranium than it previously revealed to the IAEA. This type of centrifuge would allow Iran to produce nuclear fuel more quickly than the equipment that it reluctantly revealed to the agency in 2003. This revelation proved that Iran lied when it claimed to have turned over all the documents relating to their enrichment program. Complaints about the continuing revelations concerning the nuclear program met with defiance from Iranian officials. In June 2004, for example, Iranian foreign minister Kamal Kharrazi made clear Tehran's nuclear ambitions. "Iran has a high technical capability and has to be recognized by the international community as a member of the nuclear club. This is an irreversible path." Iran took further steps down that path by approving the establishment of a secret nuclear research center to train its scientists in all aspects of atomic technology and announced plans to build two nuclear power plants in addition to the Bushehr reactor. Iran also admitted that it conducted experiments to create plutonium. Iran had said that the experiments were completed in 1993 and that no plutonium had been separated since then, but an IAEA investigation found that it had processed uranium as recently as 1998.

The Iranians have also repeatedly defied the IAEA since at least 2004 and reneged on agreements with European countries that sought to avoid a confrontation. For example, Iran broke the seals on nuclear equipment monitored by UN inspectors and resumed building and testing machines that could make fissile material for nuclear weapons after it had agreed not to. Iran also began converting raw uranium into the gas needed for enrichment in violation of an agreement to suspend "all uranium enrichment activity."

Today, the main debate is not over whether Iran can develop nuclear weapons but when it will have a bomb. The experts have conflicting views and their estimates have repeatedly shifted. On May 23, 2006, Israeli chief of staff Dan Halutz said that Iran could have the weapons some time between 2008 and 2010. Earlier, Israel estimated that Iran would be nuclear-capable by 2005. About the same time that Israel revised its estimate of Iran's progress, a U.S. intelligence review roughly doubled the time Iran would need to manufacture the key ingredient for a nuclear weapon from five to ten years. Still, the analysis concluded that Iran is acquiring and mastering technologies that could be used for weapons. The head of the IAEA, Mohamed ElBaradei, suggested the Iranians were potentially closer to building a bomb than either the U.S. or Israeli intelligence analysts predicted. Even though it may take two years for Natanz to become fully operational, ElBaradei warned in December 2005 that once the facility is running, the Iranians could be "a few months" away from a nuclear weapon. Rather than slow down its program, it appeared that the international attention was stimulating Iran to accelerate it, as pronouncements from Tehran suggest further progress in the development process.

Regardless of the time frame, the possibility of Iran obtaining nuclear weapons is particularly troubling because of the way that its history, religion, and politics combine to make a potentially lethal cocktail. President Mahmoud Ahmadinejad believes the most important task of the Iranian Revolution was to prepare the way for the return of the Twelfth Imam, who disappeared in 874 and brought an end to Muhammad's lineage. This imam, the Mahdi or "divinely guided one," Shiites believe, will return in an apocalyptic battle in which the forces of righteousness will defeat the forces of evil and bring about a new era in which Islam ultimately becomes the dominant religion throughout the world. The Shiites have been waiting patiently for the Twelfth Imam for more than a thousand years, but Ahmadinejad may believe he can now hasten the return through a nuclear war. It is this apocalyptic worldview, Middle East scholar Bernard Lewis notes, that distinguishes Iran from other governments with nuclear weapons.

Lewis quotes a passage from Ayatollah Khomeini cited in an eleventh-grade Iranian schoolbook, "I am decisively announcing to the whole world that if the world-devourers [the infidel powers] wish to stand against our religion, we will stand against the whole world and will not cease until the annihilation of all of them. Either we all become free, or we will go to the greater freedom, which is martyrdom. Either we shake one another's hands in joy at the victory of Islam in the world, or all of us will turn to eternal life and martyrdom. In both cases, victory and success are ours."[3]

There are those who think that Muslims would never use nuclear weapons against Israel because innocent Muslims would be killed as well, but history disputes this reasoning. Saddam Hussein did not hesitate to use poison gas on his own people. During the war in Lebanon in 2006, Hizbollah did not worry that firing rockets into cities with large Arab populations such as Haifa and Nazareth would kill non-Jews (24 of the 52 Israeli fatalities were non-Jews). Muslims murder each other every day in post-Saddam Iraq. In Iran's ten-year war with Iraq as many as one million Muslims were killed. Ayatollah Ali Akbar Hashemi-Rafsanjani explicitly said he wasn't concerned about fallout from an attack on Israel. "If a day comes when the world of Islam is duly equipped with the arms Israel has in [its] possession," he said, "the strategy of colonialism would face a stalemate because application of an atomic bomb would not leave any thing in Israel but the same thing would just produce damages in the Muslim world." As even one Iranian commentator noted, Rafsanjani apparently wasn't concerned that "the destruction of the Jewish State would also mean the mass killing of the Palestinian population as well."[4]

Others present a similar argument as to why Iran would never launch a nuclear attack against Israel: because, as the old Sting song says about the Russians, the Iranians "love their children too." No Muslim leader would risk an Israeli counterstrike that might destroy them. In the days of the cold war we used to refer to this idea as MAD, or Mutually Assured Destruction. MAD doesn't work, however, if the Iranians believe there will be destruction anyway at the end of time. What matters, Bernard Lewis observed, is if the infidels go to hell and believers go to heaven. And if you believe that killing the nonbelievers will earn you a place in Paradise with 72 virgins, what difference does it make if you go out in a blaze of glory as a suicide bomber or in the shadow of a mushroom cloud?

Optimists also suggest the Iranians are driven more by rationality than theology and would not risk using nuclear weapons. Others believe they are irrational and therefore cannot be trusted to hold their fire. One does not have to believe the Iranians are irrational, however, to foresee the possibility of an attack on Israel with nuclear weapons. Rafsanjani, the president of Iran from 1989 until 1997, was just as adamant about destroying Israel as his successor. Contrary to the old aphorism that you can't win a nuclear war, he argued that Iran could achieve victory. He said that "Israel is much smaller than Iran in land mass, and therefore far more vulnerable to nuclear attack."[5] Since Iran has 70 million people and Israel only has 7 million, Rafsanjani believed Iran could survive an exchange of nuclear bombs while Israel would be annihilated. The rhetoric was bombastic, but he and other Iranian leaders might first consider the possibility that Israel could conceivably launch far more missiles, and the outcome might be very different than he imagined.

Rafsanjani is correct about Israel's vulnerability. Besides the population difference, the disparity in the size of the countries is such that it does not take a whole arsenal of ICBMS, like the old Soviet Union had, to destroy Israel; Iran need only have three crude bombs to attack Israel's three major population centers—Tel Aviv, Haifa, and Jerusalem—and it's goodbye Israel.

Iran will not have to use nuclear weapons to influence events in the region. By possessing a nuclear capability, the Iranians can deter Israel or any other nation from attacking Iran or its allies. If Iran had possessed nuclear weapons when Hizbollah attacked Israel in 2006, for example, it could have threatened retaliation against Tel Aviv for Israeli forces bombing Beirut. The mere threat of using nuclear weapons would be sufficient to drive Israelis into shelters and could cripple the economy. Will immigrants want to come to a country that lives in the shadow of annihilation? Will Israelis accept the menace? Israeli leaders will have to decide if they can risk calling the Iranians' bluff.

If Iran has nuclear weapons, it can also pose an indirect threat by sharing the technology or an actual weapon with other Muslim countries or terrorists. Iran is a signatory to the nuclear Non-Proliferation Treaty that allows the peaceful pursuit of nuclear technology, including uranium mining and enrichment, under oversight by the IAEA. Ahmadinejad raised worldwide concern about nuclear proliferation when he told the UN General Assembly in September 2005, "Iran is ready to transfer nuclear know-how to the Islamic countries due to their need." Ayatollah Ali Khamenei repeated the proliferation threat several months later when he told the president of Sudan, "Iran's nuclear capability is one example of various scientific capabilities in the country. The Islamic Republic of Iran is prepared to transfer the experience, knowledge and technology of its scientists."[6]

If Iran succeeds in getting a bomb, it will also create a potential arms race as Arab states will see the need to obtain weapons to deter the Iranians. Egyptian president Hosni Mubarak's son and likely successor, Gamal, proposed in September 2006 that Egypt pursue a nuclear option. Though he said Egypt's interest was purely in peaceful nuclear energy, the announcement was clearly a response to Iran. Similarly, in October Yemeni president Ali Abdullah Saleh said that his country, one of the poorest in the world, would develop nuclear energy for peaceful purposes. A month later, the IAEA said Algeria, Morocco, Tunisia, Saudi Arabia, and the United Arab Emirates were embarking on nuclear programs. King Abdullah subsequently suggested Jordan may also have to go nuclear. As Iran is demonstrating, however, it is not so easy to achieve a nuclear capability, especially with the whole world watching. Still, these are alarming developments that also reflect a dramatic shift in policy away from the Arabs' longstanding desire for a nuclear free Middle East.

Nuclear weapons are not the only danger Israel confronts; chemical and biological weapons are also threatening and Israel's enemies have been developing and stockpiling those as well. We saw a glimpse of what a nonconventional war might look like in 1992 when Iraq launched Scud missiles at Israel. At first the fear that these might have chemical warheads prompted the army to distribute gas masks to the entire Israeli population, which then was told to create safe rooms covered in plastic to shield them from whatever chemicals might be released. In those first terrifying strikes, Israelis feared that Jews would again be gassed by a genocidal maniac. Fortunately, Saddam either did not have the capability to launch a chemical strike or chose not to risk the inevitable retaliation that such an attack would have provoked.

The Iranians already have the ability to produce a variety of biological and chemical weapons. According to the CIA, "Iran may have already stockpiled blister, blood, choking, and possibly nerve agents—and the bombs and artillery shells to deliver them—which it previously had manufactured." In addition, the CIA says, "Even though Iran is part of the Biological Weapons Convention (BWC), Tehran probably maintained an offensive BW program. Iran continued to seek dual-use biotechnical materials, equipment, and expertise that could be used in Tehran's BW program. Iran probably has the capability to produce at least small quantities of BW agents."[7]

Should Iran fail to build a nuclear weapon, it would likely have the capability to produce a dirty bomb that combines a conventional explosive, such as dynamite, with radioactive material, such as uranium or plutonium from spent nuclear fuel. The explosive would kill people in the immediate vicinity like a typical bomb, but the radiation would spread beyond the blast zone and sow fear and panic. With the help of China and North Korea, the Iranians have developed a variety of ballistic missiles, said to have a range of 2,500 miles, that are capable of carrying nuclear warheads and reaching Europe, Israel, and U.S. bases in the Middle East. Iran also obtained cruise missiles from Ukraine that are capable of reaching Israel and carrying nuclear weapons. Iran's nonconventional weapons, therefore, are a threat not only to Israel, but to the United States and its interests around the world. The American people recognize this danger. According to a January 2006 Gallup poll, 19 percent of Americans see Iran as an immediate threat to the United States and another 65 percent said Iran is a long-term threat. Even the Europeans, who since George W. Bush became president have said that American belligerency is their biggest fear, have come to recognize that Iran is a danger since its long-range missiles can almost reach their capitals.

Iran's threats are not directed at Europe, however, but at Israel. If you're the prime minister, can you really take the chance that a country that openly expresses the desire to destroy you will obtain the means to do so? President Bush doesn't think so. "You've got to assume that the leader when he says that he would like to destroy Israel, means what he says," Bush told CNN on September 21, 2006. "If you say, 'Well, gosh, maybe he doesn't mean it,' and you turn out to be wrong, you have not done your duty as a world leader." Prime Minister Olmert agrees. "Under no circumstances," he said on January 17, 2006, "will Israel permit anyone who harbors evil intentions against us to possess destructive weapons that can threaten our existence."

The question of what to do about Iran may be the single toughest issue any political leader has to face today. An overwhelming majority of Americans favors diplomatic and economic sanctions over military action. A February 2006 Gallup Poll, for example, found that 68 percent of Americans preferred the use of economic and diplomatic efforts to get Iran to shut down its nuclear program; only 9 percent supported military action now, and 18 percent favored taking no action at this time.

The U.S. State Department has long clung to the delusion that the problem would go away by itself when the "reformers" retake control of the country from the Islamists. This has been the mantra of the diplomats for nearly 30 years. We've consistently been told the Iranian people really love Americans, that they are predominantly secular and chafe under the rigidity of the *Sharia,* that they identify with Western values, and that they hate the ayatollahs and want their country to be an enlightened democracy. All this may be true, but those Iranians who share this belief have been unable to shake the power of the theocrats—in the last election the "moderate" candidate lost decisively to the Islamist Ahmadinejad.

It is a mistake to believe that changing the regime would end Iran's pursuit of nuclear weapons. On the contrary, reformers have explicitly said they also support this strategy and would continue down this path for many of the same reasons as the present regime—the desire to demonstrate Iran's technological prowess, the interest in achieving regional hegemony, and the belief that Iran has the same rights to such weapons as the other members of the nuclear club. It is also worth remembering that for all the noise Iran makes about the "Zionist entity" and its patron, its principal strategic interest is regional domination, and the countries that are most concerned are its immediate neighbors. Iran wants to control the oil industry, to influence policy in the Middle East, and to become a major player in global politics. Again, this would likely be the case whoever ran the country.

Given the unlikelihood of a counterrevolution in Iran, more active measures are required to prevent Iran from acquiring nuclear weapons. Everyone desires a political solution. Because the United States has no diplomatic relations with Iran and the relationship is so hostile, the Europeans have taken the lead in trying to use carrots and sticks to persuade the Iranians to voluntarily abandon their nuclear ambitions. Iran agreed in a meeting with French, German, and British ambassadors on November 14, 2004, to immediately suspend its nuclear programs in exchange for European guarantees that it will not face the prospect of UN Security Council sanctions as long as their agreement holds. Iran's chief nuclear negotiator, Hassan Rohani, claimed a "great victory" after the UN said it would not punish Iran's nuclear activities with sanctions. Rohani said Iran would never give up its right to nuclear power and stressed during talks with European countries that Iran's freeze on uranium enrichment was only temporary. A few months later, Ali Agha Mohammadi, spokesman for Iran's Supreme National Security Council, said Iran would never scrap its nuclear program and that talks with the Europeans were aimed at protecting the country's nuclear achievements, not negotiating an end to them. This view was reiterated in March 2005 by Rohani, who said the country would never permanently cease enriching uranium.

In response to threats of sanctions from the West, the Iranians issued their own declarations that they would resume uranium enrichment, bar open inspections of their nuclear facilities, and forcibly halt oil supply via the Straits of Hormuz. They also issued a vague, ominous warning in March 2005 that "the security and stability of the region would become a problem."[8] Ignoring Iran's warnings, the five permanent members of the UN Security Council agreed on January 31, 2006, that the IAEA should refer Iran to the Security Council. The United States, Britain, China, Russia, and France reached a compromise whereby the Security Council would wait until March before discussing any resolutions or punitive measures to give Iran an opportunity to change its policy.

The IAEA reported on February 1, 2006, that they found evidence of links between Iran's nuclear program and its military work on high explosives and missiles. The report documented work Iran conducted on uranium processing, high explosives, and a missile warhead design, all of which contradicted Iranian claims that it was interested only in electrical power. Iran's reaction to international criticism was to announce that it had resumed uranium enrichment efforts and would no longer comply with voluntary measures designed to enhance international inspectors' access to its nuclear facilities.

The one remaining diplomatic option to avoid pursuing sanctions against Iran failed in March 2006, when Iran rejected an offer from Russia to enrich uranium on its behalf. Negotiations on the proposal were widely viewed as merely Tehran's tactical strategy to continue its program while staving off referral to the UN. The United States desperately wanted the UN to adopt a resolution imposing stiff sanctions on Iran; however, the most it could get was a Security Council request that Iran suspend its uranium-enrichment activities. The only way to get even this weak declaration passed was by eliminating language suggesting that Iran's pursuit of nuclear weapons was a "threat to international peace and security."

The Europeans continue to negotiate, offering a variety of incentives to Iran, including supporting a civilian nuclear program, if it will suspend uranium enrichment. The Iranians are happy to play along and keep talking. Hassan Rohani, who headed talks with Britain, France, and Germany until 2005, admitted that Iran played for time and tried to fool the West after its secret nuclear program was uncovered by the Iranian opposition in 2002. He revealed, for example, that while talks were taking place in Tehran, Iran completed the installation of equipment for conversion of yellowcake—a key stage in the nuclear fuel process—at its Isfahan plant.

The Iranians are very smart. They know that they can drag out talks as long as necessary to complete their work on a bomb. They know the West's options are limited. They are also well aware that even the strict sanctions placed on Saddam Hussein's Iraqi regime did not prevent him from finding ways to beat the system, and that years of cajoling and threatening did not prevent North Korea from going nuclear. Nonetheless, the Iranians are afraid of President Bush, whom they see as a reckless cowboy. They therefore have tried to keep the Europeans in the negotiations, and to give them enough hope for a diplomatic solution that they will restrain the United States from taking preemptive military action. The Iranians also know that Bush's days are numbered and hope to string out talks until a new president is elected who, they believe, will be far less likely to use force against them.

The Russians and the Chinese, who each have multibillion-dollar business deals with the Iranians, repeatedly raised objections to sanctions. These countries are motivated not only by their economic interests but also by their opposition to American hegemony. Each wields a veto at the UN Security Council and used the threat of one to prevent the adoption of any meaningful international sanctions.

Still, it was considered a diplomatic victory when the UN voted unanimously on December 23, 2006, to impose sanctions on Iran. Specifically, the Security Council resolution banned the supply of nuclear-related technology and materials and imposed an asset freeze on 10 key companies and 12 individuals involved in Iran's nuclear program. It also demanded that Tehran end all work on uranium enrichment. The resolution did not, however, authorize the use of force if Iran did not abide by the resolution.

Acting U.S. Ambassador to the UN, Alejandro Wolff, said after the vote that if Iran did not comply with the resolution, the United States would not hesitate to seek stronger sanctions from the Security Council. This threat was tempered by the knowledge that the resolution had been watered down after objections from both the Russians and the Chinese, who opposed a ban on international travel by Iranian officials involved in nuclear and missile development and a broader unspecified ban on materials that could be used for weapons. The Russians had also forced the removal of any mention of Bushehr and language that might have threatened their cooperation with Iran on nuclear energy. According to the *Washington Post* (December 24, 2006), Bush administration officials were concerned that Iran would use

Bushehr as a cover to smuggle goods for the weapons program, but the United States decided a weak resolution was better than nothing.

Iran's leaders have had their bluff called and we will see if they are prepared to take any of the measures they threatened to destabilize the region or to jeopardize the supply of oil to the West. The immediate reaction to the resolution was defiance. The government vowed to continue enriching uranium and foreign ministry spokesman, Mohammad Ali Hosseini, condemned the resolution as illegal. President Ahmadinejad threatened to reconsider relations with the countries that supported the resolution. The Iranians are now likely to accelerate their nuclear program. Sanctions also may further inflame public opinion in Iran and unite the country against outside intervention. In addition, it is likely the Iranians will continue to receive support from nations that are more interested in oil and in the large sums Iran will pay for technology than in nonproliferation.

Sanctions may also have negative repercussions for Israel. Already, the United Arab Emirates has called on the United Nations to make Israel cooperate with the IAEA and to submit to inspections. The argument will probably be made that no Middle East nation should have nuclear weapons and therefore steps must be taken to disarm Israel.

Other options are available for trying to stop Iran. It has been suggested that efforts could be made to either restrict foreign investment in Iran and/or interdict its gas supplies. In the case of investment, Iran needs $1 billion each year to maintain its current oil output; otherwise, it would have to import energy. By complicating the flow of investment, Iran could be forced to draw down reserves. In addition, while Iran is one of the world's largest oil producers, it must import about 40 percent of its gas from foreign sources. A gas embargo could wreak havoc on Iran's economy. Using these economic pressures might make it more difficult for Iran to continue to divert resources to develop nuclear weapons and might also cause such hardship to the Iranian people that they will finally take steps to change their government. For now, however, the Bush Administration has said it will not pursue such strategies because, according to Secretary of State Condoleezza Rice, the United States doesn't want to hurt the Iranian people.

One option remains: the use of military force. Experts debate whether a military option even exists, and if it is feasible, whether it could destroy Iran's nuclear program or merely slow it down. Americans are not averse to using force

against Iran. Though nonmilitary options are preferred, majorities are also start-
ing to favor targeted strikes according to a survey by The Israel Project in
September 2006, especially if the strikes were to be carried out by NATO or the
United States and its allies rather than just the United States or Israel alone.

The United States, in particular, faces a serious problem in mobilizing
support for a strike against Iran because of its experience in Iraq. Since most
Americans (and even higher percentages of the public in other countries)
believe that the Bush Administration was wrong about Iraq's nuclear capability and manipulated the intelligence for political purposes, it will be more difficult to convince people that Iran is really a threat to U.S. security. Some see
threats against Iran as just a continuing desire of the neoconservatives to push
America into war for the purpose of securing oil. The appeasement lobby that
always opposes military force will insist on pursuing diplomacy even as
the Iranians continue their program. A broader fear also exists that should the
United States go to war with Iran, we would face problems similar to those
we now have in Iraq.

Unlike U.S. policy toward Iraq, it appears that both inside and outside the
United States a much broader consensus exists that Iran has a dangerous
nuclear weapons program that must be stopped. That is why the Europeans
have been at the forefront of the diplomatic efforts. Since the Europeans have
shown little backbone in these negotiations, and even less willingness to con-
template the use of military force, the United States would likely have to go it
alone. We may not even be able to count on staunch allies in Britain because
of the public outcry there against the war in Iraq.

A war against Iran would also be a far more difficult undertaking than
the one in Iraq. The terrain is more mountainous, unlike Iraq's expanses of
open desert. The Iranians have a large, well-trained army that is likely to fight
with more dedication to defending the homeland than Iraqi soldiers who
knew they were primarily defending Saddam Hussein. While U.S. forces and
equipment are superior to those of Iran, it would undoubtedly be a costly war
in terms of both the economy and human lives.

Most analysts do not believe it is necessary to invade Iran to slow down
their nuclear program. The more likely scenario calls for air strikes on key
facilities. This will not be easy either. Unlike the case of Osirak, the United
States would not have the element of surprise. The Iranians expect to be hit
and have spread their facilities around the country, many of them hidden

below the ground, sometimes under civilian structures, and have strengthened their air defenses around the country. War planners may indeed know where the most important facilities are and may have "bunker buster" bombs and other munitions that can destroy labs built deep underground. It may also be possible to hit the sources of electricity needed to run labs. The use of cruise missiles and stealth bombers may allow U.S. forces to penetrate Iran's air defenses, but it may still be difficult to do enough damage to stop Iran from completing a bomb. Any attack must also take into account the possibility of collateral damage, civilian casualties, and the spread of contamination. Though public attention has focused on the possibility of a direct attack on Iran's nuclear facilities, other military options may exist, including targeting the country's leadership.

Israelis would prefer that the United States carry out any military attack. The United States has a greater capability for such a mission and it would reduce the risk of Israel being drawn into a wider war. Israelis are confident they can carry out the mission if necessary, but recognize it will be far more difficult than the surprise attack on Osirak. Before undertaking any military action, the United States and Israel will also have to take into account the possible Iranian reaction. Masud Yazaiari, spokesman of the Iranian Revolutionary Guards, warned against any Israeli efforts to stop their nuclear program. "Their threats to attack our nuclear facilities will not succeed," Yazaiari said. "They are aware that Tehran's response would be overwhelming and would wipe Israel off the face of the earth."[9]

World leaders face not only whether to use force against Iran, but how long the decision can be put off. If it is true that Iran is five to ten years away from building a bomb, it may be possible to pursue other options for a few years while closely monitoring Iran's progress. Israel believes that the red line is when Iran masters the nuclear fuel cycle and has the technical ability to produce weapons-grade uranium. Iran has enriched uranium to 3.6 percent but needs to get to 90 percent for a bomb.

While President Bush might have had the will before, he now has little political support, and few people believe we can afford to start a war with the Iranians while we've still got troops fighting in Iraq and Afghanistan. On the other hand, some people believe that Bush means it when he says, as he did in October 2006, that "the idea of Iran having a nuclear weapon is unacceptable," and that he will not trust a successor to do what needs to be done to stop them.

Israel is not sitting by idly, however, while its neighbors build up their nonconventional arsenals. Israel is acquiring a triad (air, sea, and land-based nuclear weapons) to give it a second-strike capability in the event nuclear war does come. Israel has also deployed satellites to spy on Iran (which is now seeking its own spy satellites) to provide as much advance warning as possible of any threat. Israel also has the Arrow, the world's most sophisticated antiballistic missile defense system, in place.

The world is rightly concerned with Iran's effort to covertly build a nuclear weapon and the possibility it will succeed within the next decade. But this is again short-term, Western thinking. The Muslims look at this in their wider historical perspective. Think 50 years into the future: Do you believe that no Muslim countries in the Middle East will have nuclear weapons? It's likely that several countries will have them, so this is a long-term threat.

Despite all of the dangers described above, Israel can survive. The president of Iran is a loose cannon whose rhetorical bombs have united most of the world against his country. In addition, he appears so incompetent in running the government, he may not succeed in producing a nuclear weapon. In fact, it appears the Iranians are probably still ten years away from developing a weapon. A lot can happen in that time. Iran may not succeed for technical reasons (the nuclear club is so small because it is very difficult to build a bomb), or because sanctions are eventually imposed and prove effective, or because a regime change in Iran results in a decision to accept a deal in exchange for abandoning its weapons program, as happened in South Africa. Iran is also unlikely to give terrorists whatever weapons it may build. It is likely to produce only a handful, and would be primarily for missiles that they can use for deterrence and/or a first-strike capability. They probably won't produce suitcase bombs or anything a terrorist could use, nor are they likely to give people whom they can't control that kind of power, especially since the use of a nuclear weapon by terrorists could produce a nuclear counterstrike against Iran. Even though some Iranians may believe they can win a nuclear war, they may not get the chance to start one. If Iran threatens the use of nuclear weapons or the imminent launch of a weapon was detected, it might trigger a first strike by the United States, Israel, or another nuclear power.

Throughout the Cold War, fears of nuclear confrontations gave rise to apocalyptic scenarios, yet not a single nuclear weapon was ever used. The Soviets did prove to be rational decision makers in the end. Similarly, the tensions between India and Pakistan have not led to a nuclear war. The fear of these weapons is such that a great inhibition exists against releasing that destructive power. On the other hand, one difference between Iran and the other nuclear powers is that the Islamists in Tehran do not recognize Israel's legitimacy. This was not the case for the United States and Soviet Union.

Still, Iran's leaders also will have to consider the possibility that any threats against the United States, Israel, or the gulf states might provoke a first strike by a country with more and better nuclear weapons. Israel could warn, for example, that if it had any indication Iran was preparing to use nuclear weapons, it would launch a preemptive nuclear attack.

Although it would be nice if Iran could be prevented from getting the bomb, we need to think more about how to live with a nuclear Iran and how to ensure it does not use its weapons.

Chapter 6

Dying of Thirst

"Water is life itself."

—Israeli Prime Minister Moshe Sharett

"The one issue that could bring Jordan to war again is water."

—Jordan's King Hussein

"Israel has no right even to a single drop of water in this region."

—Syrian Foreign Minister Farouq Al-Sharaa

"In Old Testament times, there were two ways of solving disputes over water, which has always been scarce in our region. One was to fight over it. The other was to jointly place over the mouth of the well a stone so large that five shepherds were needed to lift it, creating the need for cooperation."

—Israeli Agriculture Minister Yaacov Tsur[1]

"See to it you are always positioned upstream and your enemies downstream."

—American Indian proverb

As the quotations above suggest, the supply of water is a matter of life and death, war and peace for the peoples of the Middle East. This is not hyperbole. A few examples—

Israel and Syria clashed several times in the 1950s when Syria tried to stop Israel from building its National Water Carrier, an 81-mile-long pipeline completed in 1964 to bring water from the Kinneret to southern sections of Israel and other areas where it was most needed. They fought again in the prelude to the Six-Day War in 1965-66 when Syria tried to divert water from the Yarmuk River.

Iraq rushed troops to its border in 1975 when it believed Syria was cutting the flow of the Euphrates River.

In 1990, Turkey cut the flow of the Euphrates to fill the Ataturk Dam, provoking war threats from Iraq and Syria.

The World Bank highlighted the problem in a 1995 report, "From Scarcity to Security: Averting a water crisis in the Middle East and North Africa":

> The countries of the Middle East and North Africa (MENA) region are home to 5 percent of the world's people, but have less than 1 percent of the world's renewable fresh water. Inexorable population growth and associated water usage by farmers, firms and families have reduced the region's limited per-capita supply to only one-third of its 1960 level. Per-capita water availability is expected to halve over the next 30 years, exposing all but one or two countries to severe problems of water scarcity. Unless there are fundamental changes in the way water resources are managed and used, the region as a whole will experience a worsening crisis of water scarcity and economic decline. A vicious circle will set in whereby harsh water shortages adversely affect economic growth, and slower growth in turn constrains the investment needed to improve water availability. This downward spiral would spell disaster for the region.

The problem is most acute in Israel, Jordan, the West Bank, and the Gaza Strip. Egypt, Syria, and Lebanon also face potentially serious shortfalls in the near future. The situation is exacerbated by pollution and by the disproportionate use of water for low-value agriculture. For Israel, water is a key element of the peace process. A *Jerusalem Post* headline concisely stated the security threat, "The hand that controls the faucet rules the country."

Despite the voluminous literature on the peace process and the manifold proposals for territorial compromise, surprisingly little has been written about this crucial resource issue. Water is critical not only because it is a matter of dispute with Israel's neighbors, it is also vital to Israel's development and economic health, which are no less important to the nation's security. To maintain a standard of living that will allow Israel to continue as an advanced western country, it must have water for agriculture, industry, drinking and bathing, gardens, and recreational facilities such as swimming pools and parks. As living standards increase, so does water consumption.

The situation becomes more dangerous each year. As the population of the region continues to grow exponentially and thousands of immigrants arrive in Israel, the political disputes over existing water supplies become more pronounced, and Israel and the Palestinians must negotiate rights to the water in the West Bank and Gaza Strip.

The land God promised the Israelites may have been flowing with milk and honey, but it has no natural resources. Israel has little land and no great rivers, forests, or mineral deposits. It depends on scarce and erratic rainfall for its water supply. Its three main water sources are the coastal and mountain aquifers and Lake Kinneret (the Sea of Galilee). Each supplies approximately 25 percent of the total water consumed in Israel. Roughly 20 percent is derived from smaller aquifers; the remaining 5 percent comes from recycled sewage.

The coastal aquifer extends along Israel's Mediterranean shoreline between the southern approaches of Carmel in the north and the Gaza Strip in the south. Roughly 80 percent of Israel's population and most of its economic activity are concentrated in the coastal plain. The Kinneret basin is a little more than 1,000 square miles, about one-quarter of which is in Lebanon. The lake itself is 64 square miles, 15 miles long and 10 miles wide. It is fed by the Jordan River and its sources—the Hatsbani, Dan, and Banias rivers—as well as by streams and wadis in the Golan Heights that drain into the Jordan River and directly into the Kinneret. The mountain aquifer extends from the eastern approaches of the coastal aquifer under the hills of Judea and Samaria. Water flows westward from the highlands, where winter rainfall recharges the aquifer, and emerges at the surface through two outlets near the coast into the Yarkon and Taninim rivers, which empty into the Mediterranean Sea. This aquifer straddles the "Green Line" (the 1949 armistice line that separated Israel and the West Bank) and as much as 90 percent of its water originates from precipitation in the West Bank. It is Israel's principal source of high quality drinking water and supplies major population centers such as Jerusalem, Tel Aviv, and Beersheva.

All these water sources have delicate balances that have led Israeli water authorities to establish "red lines" below which the extraction of additional water can result in permanent damage from salting or other contamination that can render the water undrinkable. The water level of the Kinneret, for example, varies with rainy and drought years and, if the level is too low, it is necessary to reduce pumping to prevent salty water from neighboring springs to seep in. If the level rises too high, it may be necessary to allow water to drain out toward the Dead Sea to prevent flooding. Overpumping has already done severe damage to the coastal aquifer whose salinity has rendered nearly 20 percent of the water unusable.

The other major threat to the water supply is pollution caused by sewage infiltration, industrial spills and wastes, agricultural chemicals, and environmental blights typical of growing industrial nations.

This water crisis is not a result of Israeli wastefulness. Israelis are especially sensitive to the water scarcity and are relatively frugal in their usage, using only a small fraction of the amount of water that is consumed by people in an area with a similar climate, such as southern California. The government took control of water resources in 1959 when a law made water resources public property and has since regulated water resource exploitation and allocation.

Despite the awareness of the problem, water sources have been overused and contaminated, and water quality in some places has deteriorated. Numerous warnings have been issued over the last decade that Israel will face a shortage of water for drinking and for agriculture because of the recurrent droughts and the increase in consumption. The expectation is also that the amount of drinking-quality water will decline quickly to the point where reducing its use in agriculture will not make more water available for households.

Domestic (38 percent) and industrial (6 percent) needs comprise less than half of Israel's water consumption; the majority of water (56 percent) is used for agriculture. As a result, a great deal of research has been devoted to finding ways to reduce the amount of water required for growing fruits, vegetables, and other agricultural products. One innovation that succeeded in dramatically reducing water use in Israel and was subsequently exported around the world is drip irrigation—water (and fertilizer) is discharged from drippers uniformly and directly to the root system rather than to the total area of the field. This method allows for the use of lower quality water (saline water or effluents) and minimizes water loss from evaporation.

Israel's water balance is also affected by the supply and demand of its neighbors and by the conflict over lands that hold much of the water Israel needs to survive. As the quotation at the beginning of the chapter from King Hussein suggested, Jordan also takes the water issue very seriously. Part of its water supply problems are related to pollution and old and poorly maintained pipelines. A more serious issue for Jordan has been Syria taking more water from the Yarmuk River than it had agreed to in negotiations.

Israel and Jordan have managed their disputes over water very well over the years, even during wartime; nevertheless, the question of sharing water from the Yarmuk River, which adjoins the Israeli and Jordanian borders, was an important issue in the negotiations of the peace treaty signed between Israel and Jordan in 1994. Israel agreed to supply Jordan with 50 million cubic meters (mcm) of water a year, some of which would come from the Yarmuk River and the rest from the desalination of brackish springs around the Kinneret. Even after the treaty was signed, water quickly became an issue of contention, one of the few between the two countries, and Israel increased the allotment of water to 75 mcm.

Despite the agreements, Hussein's warning about potential conflict will remain a concern for Israel as Jordan's population continues to grow and its water consumption increases. Jordan could become tempted to satisfy its needs by taking aggressive action to gain access to the water resources in Judea and Samaria. Given Jordan's relative military weakness, and the ability of Israel and Jordan to negotiate even during the period before the peace treaty, the danger from this direction should remain small.

A far more serious problem is posed by Syria, which demands the full return of the Golan Heights in return for peace with Israel. If the Syrian border were redrawn closer to the 1967 border or to the international 1923 border, Syria would have the ability to affect the supply of roughly one-fourth of Israel's water. According to reports of secret negotiations in the 1990s between Israel and Syria, even hardline Likud prime minister Benjamin Netanyahu was prepared to give Syria territory that would approach the northern edge of the Kinneret. Given that starting point, it is unlikely that any Syrian leader would be satisfied with anything less. If Syria controlled the Golan Heights, it could severely compromise Israel's water supply even if its intentions were not malevolent. The expectation is that Syria would build up the area with perhaps as many as half a million people, who would produce sewage and other contaminants that could pollute the Kinneret. As one Israeli water specialist put it, "given the level of environmental protection and waste management in Syria," the Kinneret would become "an odious foul-smelling pond, unsuitable as a tourist attraction and certainly unable to supply drinking water without thorough and expensive treatment."[2]

It is also possible that the increase in Syria's overall population and/or the diversion by the Turks of water from the Euphrates River on the south side of Syria could produce a water shortage that would provoke the Syrians to divert water from the Golan. A belligerent Syria could purposely divert water to deprive Israel of water at any time. As noted at the beginning of the chapter, this was one of the causes of the 1967 Six-Day War.

Any peace treaty with Syria would have to ensure Israel's water rights, but can Israel afford to put one-third of its water supply at the mercy of a foreign power, especially one whose leaders have talked about denying Israel all "Arab water?" As Joyce Starr put it, "an Israeli government that concedes territory on the Golan without a guaranteed supply of Yarmuk waters, or a dedicated alternative source of water, would be committing national suicide."[3] Ultimately, Israel may have to choose between water and peace with Syria.

Israel's water security is further threatened by the fact that the mountain aquifer, which also supplies a quarter of Israel's water, including most of the drinking water for the major cities, is partially located in the West Bank. The Middle East Water Commission forecast in the 1990s that the West Bank and Gaza Strip will face a water deficit by 2020. According to Palestinian water authorities, as much as 50 percent of domestic water is lost because of old, inefficient supply systems. Today, the water Israel takes from the mountain aquifer is not sufficient for Israel to expand agricultural production, yet the Palestinians are demanding the right to expand their agricultural sector using the same limited water resources.

As in the case of Syria, even if a future Palestinian state had peaceful intentions, it could significantly reduce the water available to Israel because of the need to satisfy the needs of its own population, which could explode from more than two million to more than three million if the Palestinian refugees were resettled. Even today, unauthorized Palestinian drilling of wells in the West Bank has affected the quality of the aquifer. Without any other water source, the Palestinians will be tempted to pump more out of the aquifer to meet their growing needs and thereby could ultimately inundate it with sea water. There would be nothing Israel could do to stop them. Of course, the Palestinians see the situation in the reverse. If Israel's population and consumption increase, it will draw more water and reduce the amount available for them.

Also, as in Syria, the poor quality of Palestinian water treatment facilities, mismanagement, neglect, and the low priority placed on environmental issues increases the likelihood that the aquifer will be polluted and its quality reduced, perhaps to the point of being undrinkable. This has already occurred in the Gaza Strip where the sole aquifer is unusable because of contamination and salinity. Today, only five sewage treatment plants exist for the Palestinian population in the West Bank, and only one of these is functioning. That plant can handle sewage for up to 50,000 people, but the area's population exceeds two million. Israelis rightly ask, if the Palestinians cannot take care of the water for its own population, how can they trust them to protect the water that Israel depends on?

Regardless of treatment facilities, since water is crucial for the development of a Palestinian state, it is no surprise that the Palestinians argue that because the aquifer lies under the West Bank, it should come under their control. Prior to 1967, Israel used 95 percent of this water, the Arabs only 5 percent. Since then, the Arab share has increased to 17 percent and Israel has agreed to pump a negotiated amount across the Green Line to the Palestinian Authority.

The Palestinians maintain that Israel is stealing their water though most of the water Israel extracts is taken from within the pre-1967 border. Israelis also point out that Palestinian cultivation and agricultural output in the territories increased exponentially after 1967 because of the introduction by Israel of drip irrigation and other modern agricultural techniques. They also note that of 430 towns and villages in the West Bank, only 50 were connected to running water prior to the Six-Day War. Less than 25 years later, the figure was 260. Israel has long tapped the mountain aquifer while the Palestinians hardly used it; nevertheless, they now demand 100 percent of the water from the aquifer and compensation for water pumped since 1948, or at a minimum since 1967. Israel counters that it has a right to the water based on its prior use, its investment in development, and the water's natural flow inside the Green Line.

To secure its water future, Israel would need to maintain control over three West Bank regions comprising 20 percent of the land. These regions rest adjacent to the Green Line in northern and Western Samaria, and include the Jerusalem hills heading south past Gush Etzion. As in the case of the Golan, however, Israel has already offered territorial concessions that jeopardize the water supply. At Camp David in 2000, Israel was prepared to give up as much as 97 percent of the West Bank, and it is unlikely the Palestinians or the international community would be prepared to accept anything less today. To maintain the water supply would also require incorporating large numbers of Palestinians within Israel's borders—precisely what Israel seeks to avoid. Under most scenarios the areas that Israel would keep—that is, the major settlement blocks—do cover part of the mountain aquifer but would not give Israel complete control over its use.

The Oslo agreement signed in 1993 did not resolve the question of who would control the water resources, putting that off with the other contentious issues to the final status negotiations that never took place. Should the two sides discuss the water issue, a number of difficult questions would have to be resolved, such as who determines drilling sites, how much water can be pumped without causing damage, who makes decisions on treatment and disposal, and who will monitor treaty compliance.

In the end, the problem is similar to the one with Syria. If Israel gives up control of the mountain aquifer, as is implicit in the proposals made to date, it will depend on the goodwill of the Palestinians to protect the quality of the water and to ensure Israel continues to receive sufficient water to meet its needs. Israeli monitoring would increase but not assure the probability of a good outcome. A second possibility is for the two parties to have joint control for an interim period to give the Palestinians a chance to demonstrate their ability to manage the water supply. Another option would be to enlist a neutral third party to monitor water, but this might be resented by the Palestinians. The Palestinians might reject all of these options, however, as intrusions on their sovereignty.

One faint cause for optimism comes from the effort by Israel and the Palestinian Authority to protect the water supply during the Palestinian War. In 2001 the two parties issued a joint call to refrain from harming the water infrastructure and water supply to both Israelis and Palestinians in the West Bank and Gaza; it was upheld throughout the conflict. For its part, Israel also stuck to its obligations and resisted the temptation to use water as a weapon. Even when water allocations were cut within Israel, it continued to supply the water promised to the Palestinian Authority. After negotiating how much water Israel would supply to the territories, a formula was later agreed upon to increase the water allocation over the interim period outlined in the Oslo agreements.

Whether a final agreement on control of the aquifer is reached or not, Israel will face the dilemma of what to do if the water supply is threatened. Israel could detect any large-scale Arab efforts to target its water, such as the building of a dam or the diversion of water, but it will be more difficult to know if the mountain aquifer is being affected by activities that it cannot monitor, such as the drilling of wells in the West Bank. If it does see its water supply or quality endangered, Israel will have to decide whether to take military action to stop the drilling of wells, or the diversion of water, or to seize the water source. What level of provocation would the UN, the United States, or the international community in general find sufficient to justify Israeli action? What, if anything, would these parties be prepared to do to prevent the interdiction of Israeli water supplies? The historical answer to that question is not encouraging. Clearly, if Israel does not have control of its water sources, its future is threatened.

If Israel does not have control over the Golan Heights and/or the mountain aquifer in the West Bank, the need for alternative water sources will be essential. It will have to plan for the worst-case scenario of a cutoff of its water supply and ensure that it has enough water to make up for the loss of all its existing supplies. This would also mean increasing the infrastructure required for the additional supply, which in turn would require more energy and more investment. The ripple effect to the economy would be significant if not devastating. Even if Israel retains control over those areas, it will inevitably need more water to meet the demands of a growing population and thriving economy.

I like the idea I've read about of towing icebergs from the polar regions to the Middle East, but most proposals for alleviating the water shortage are more practical and realistic. Although improving water treatment, management, and infrastructure can make a marginal difference in the availability and quality of water, more drastic steps are required to ensure that Israel has the water it needs in the future. Israel's annual water consumption is approximately 580 billion gallons, and its water resources total only about 450 billion gallons. Israel is overconsuming its water resources by 25 percent.

This is reducing the water levels of the Kinneret and the aquifers to dangerous levels. To make up for the deficit, Israel is exploring and pursuing a
variety of options.

One possibility is to reduce the supply of fresh water to agriculture and
transfer it to urban and industrial use. Very little water can be diverted in this
way, however, because there is no way to bring much of the water from the
farm areas to the metropolitan urban centers. In addition, reduction of Israeli
agricultural production might lead to an increase in cultivation by Palestinian
farmers who would require water from the same sources for their crops and
probably use the water more inefficiently, resulting in a net loss to the water
supply. While reducing agriculture would save water, it would have other economic costs associated with the loss of revenue from that sector and would
have a number of other potentially damaging side effects, making it more difficult to sustain communities in arid areas such as the Negev.

A second option is to increase the use of recycled sewage water in agriculture. Reservoirs are being constructed by the Jewish National Fund to hold
recycled waste water and collect flood and runoff water, which the organization says will provide for the water supply of 1.2 million people. A high percentage of water used in agriculture, however, is already recycled (for example,
the cotton industry uses 90 percent recycled water), and the additional
amount that could be used may not significantly increase the amount of fresh
water available. Moreover, recycled water has some negative side effects such
as the potential of contaminants leaching into ground water supplies, salts
from the recycled water damaging the soil, and reducing crop yields.

A third possibility for increasing available water is to import it from
another country. This is logistically difficult, politically risky, and very expensive. The most popular ideas have been to either ship water from Turkey to
Israel or to transfer it via a pipeline. There has been discussion, for example,
of a Turkish "Peace Canal" that would bring water to Syria, Jordan, Israel, and
the Palestinians. This proposal seems unlikely given that it is expected to cost
more than $8 billion and take perhaps 15 years to build. The project is also
problematic because it assumes Turkey would not need the water for itself in
the future. Moreover, a pipeline would be a tempting target for terrorists. It is
also uncertain whether Israel would be included in the project; possibly
Turkey would choose to supply only Muslim nations. Relations between

Israel and Turkey have been very good, however, and prolonged negotiations were held to discuss an export deal. A deal was finally struck in August 2005: Turkey agreed to export 1.75 billion cubic feet of water from its Manavgat River to Israel each year for the next 20 years. The deal was expected to cost between $800 million and $1 billion. The cost of importing Turkish water is considerably higher than the price of desalinated or recycled water, so when the immediate need became less acute as more rain fell, Israel abrogated the deal.

Rather than a pipeline across countries, another suggestion has been to build one across Israel. Various proposals to take water from the Red Sea or the Mediterranean were considered too expensive and risked the contamination of fresh water aquifers by transferring salt water. One of the proposed canals would have also had to traverse the West Bank, which would have made it politically sensitive.

The most popular idea for alleviating Israel's water shortage, the one the government is now actively pursuing, is desalination—that is, the removal of salt from water to make it drinkable. Desalination is a proven technique with more than 7,500 plants in use in about 120 countries, 60 percent of which are in the Middle East (Saudi Arabia has the world's largest plant). Malta, for example, began desalination in the 1960s and by 1995 desalination supplied about 70 percent of its water needs. Israeli companies have been leaders in the field of desalination, supplying 30 percent of the world market with 300 plants in roughly 40 countries. One of the benefits of desalinated water is that it is a more predictable and reliable source than renewable water supplies. Although expensive, the cost is expected to fall as new technologies are introduced.

In 2000 Israel launched a Desalination Master Plan that envisioned the construction of a series of plants along the Mediterranean coast. The first of these was built in less than 30 months in Ashkelon and went online in August 2005. The $250 million plant is expected to provide between 5 and 6 percent of Israel's total water needs or around 15 percent of the country's domestic consumer demand. In theory, Israel could also sell desalinated water to the Palestinians, but for nationalistic reasons, they may reject the idea of depending on Israel for such a vital resource.

In February 2005 an agreement was signed for an $85 million sea water desalination plant in the Palmahim area, which was slated to be operational by 2007. Other facilities are planned for Hadera and Ashdod. In addition,

Israel signed an agreement in 2006 with Siemens to jointly develop water treatment technologies to solve challenges such as the supply of high-quality water.

Desalination is not an immediate panacea. It can ameliorate Israel's water problems but not solve them. The plants are expensive, take time to build, use a lot of energy, and will not supply as much water as Israel will need. They also make tempting targets for terrorists. The plant in Ashkelon, for example, is not far from where rockets fired from the Gaza Strip have landed.

There is a certain Chicken Little quality to the warnings about a water shortage that are similar to the inaccurate claims heard in the past about the exhaustion of oil supplies. The first warning about overpumping was issued by Israel's state comptroller in 1966. Dire forecasts throughout the 1990s suggested water would become more important than oil by 2000 and that, as early as 2005, Israel would not have sufficient water for household consumption. Water may yet become a threat to Israel's survival, but Israel has taken steps to improve its water security and this may turn out to be the least of the dangers described in this book. If nature does not play any nasty tricks on Israel, such as a prolonged drought, the combination of increasing the amount of recycled and desalinated water should meet Israel's needs for the foreseeable future.

Despite fears that water could become a flash point for conflict, Israel and its neighbors have for the last several decades been more successful in cooperating to resolve water disputes than other issues. Moreover, past negotiations and proposed peace plans have demonstrated that water will not be the principal factor in determining territorial concessions; strategic, economic, and political concerns will hold greater weight in the calculus of decision makers. The complexity of the issue led both sides to delay resolving it, but an agreement must be reached to avoid future conflagrations over water.

Chapter 7

Imperfect Peace

As the author of the book *Myths and Facts: A Guide to the Arab-Israeli Conflict*, I am often asked what the most persistent myth is about Israel or the conflict; my answer is the notion that Israelis don't want peace. It boggles the mind that anyone could seriously believe that Israelis want to live the way they do today, worrying about whether a public bus or cafe or discotheque might blow up. How can anyone believe that young men and women in their late teens want to serve in the army and go to terrible places such as Gaza or Jenin and carry out often unpleasant duties rather than enjoy sex, drugs, rock 'n' roll, and studying at a university like American kids the same age? And you can be sure that Israeli parents would much prefer to see their children in college rather than worrying about whether they will come back from some dangerous military assignment in the West Bank.

That said, the truth is that Israelis don't live in fear. They do not lock themselves in their rooms cowering. They act prudently, and though many are more cautious today than they were even six or seven years ago, Israelis live their lives. Citizens did not flee in the face of the five-year terror war the Palestinians waged from September 2000 until roughly the end of 2005. When an attack occurred, the area would be cleaned up, and it was usually only a short time before normality returned. Even during the recent short war with Hizbollah, when more than 4,000 rockets rained down indiscriminately on the heads of Israelis in the north, there was no widespread panic or exodus from the country.

Israelis desperately crave peace and that is why they have repeatedly devised peace plans and offered compromises in the hope of finding the haven from anti-Semitism that the Zionists imagined Israel would be. After the Zionists accepted the homeland they believed the British had promised them in the 1917 Balfour Declaration, the territory was arbitrarily mangled by Winston Churchill. In 1921, he decided to repay the Hashemite family for aiding the British effort to defeat the Ottoman Turks in World War I by giving them four-fifths of Palestine to create the new nation of Transjordan. In 1937 the British proposed dividing what was left of Palestine into a Jewish and Arab state. Though the Jews were now left with a small fraction of their original homeland, they were prepared to accept the deal; the Arabs refused. In 1947 the UN endorsed a similar division of the land into two states, this time taking the historic capital of Israel, Jerusalem, and internationalizing the city. Still, the Zionists accepted the partition decision, while the Arabs rejected it because they were not prepared to accept a Jewish state of any size in their midst. The Zionists ultimately declared independence in May 1948 in the area allotted to the Jewish state by the UN and then fought off the invading Arab armies to establish the State of Israel. The new state held parts of what were to have been the Arab state as well as the modern half of Jerusalem. Meanwhile, Jordan occupied the West Bank and East Jerusalem (including the Old City), and Egypt controlled the Gaza Strip.

After enduring years of terrorist attacks from Gaza and the imposition of a sea blockade along one of its major trade routes, Israel went to war against Egypt in 1956. President Dwight Eisenhower was upset by the fact that Israel, France, and Great Britain had secretly planned the campaign to evict Egypt from the Suez Canal. Israel's failure to inform the United States of its intentions combined with its ignoring American entreaties not to go to war sparked tensions between the countries. The United States subsequently joined the Soviet Union in a campaign to force Israel to withdraw. This included a threat to discontinue all U.S. assistance, UN sanctions and expulsion from the UN. American pressure resulted in an Israeli withdrawal from the areas it had conquered without obtaining any concessions from the Egyptians. Israel only briefly held onto the Gaza Strip and would have inherited the Palestinian problem at that time had it not acceded to Eisenhower's demands.

Until 1967 the Palestinians were not a major concern of Israel. The refugee issue did arise from time to time and, starting with the Arab League's creation of the Palestinian Liberation Organization (PLO) in 1964, terrorism was becoming a growing threat. Most of Israel's attention, however, was devoted to the Arab states. The Palestinians in Gaza were living under Egyptian rule, and those in the West Bank were living under Jordanian rule. Neither population expressed interest in statehood in those areas. In fact, the original PLO charter specifically ruled out exercising sovereignty in those areas. Then everything changed.

While Israel was fighting Egypt and Syria in June 1967, Jordan made the ill-advised decision to attack Jerusalem. Israel was forced to counterattack and in the process achieved the positive objective of reunifying the capital of Jerusalem. Israel had not set out to create "Greater Israel," that is, land that had once been viewed as belonging to the Jewish state, but in the course of the fighting, its forces captured Judea and Samaria, territory that became universally referred to as the West Bank (because of the area's position relative to the Jordan River). Along with the territory came a population of several hundred thousand Palestinians who became Israel's responsibility. Since then, Israel has literally become stuck with an area it captured in a defensive war from an enemy that wasn't willing to take it back as long as the price was peace. That's how Israel got into the mess it is in with the Palestinians today.

The situation was much the same in the south where Israeli forces expelled the Egyptians from the Gaza Strip and Israel was saddled with a tiny area that it had previously captured in 1956. At that time, David Ben-Gurion, who clearly understood the security threat posed by an enemy controlling the area said: "Gaza as part of Israel could be like a cancer. To take a small territory with a vast Arab population would be the worst possible exchange."[1] After 1967, that cancer returned and grew as Israel began an almost 40-year occupation, during which the Palestinian population grew to more than one million and Gaza became a terrorist base.

Israel held out hope for many years that Jordan would come around and agree to a peace deal that would allow Israel to live in security without the West Bank. In the meantime, however, Israel began to create outposts in the area, initially as forward positions for military purposes. Gradually, Jews started to move back to parts of the West Bank such as Hebron and Gush Etzion, where Jewish communities had once thrived before being driven out by Arab massacres. The Hebron community had existed for hundreds of years next to the tomb of the biblical patriarchs. In 1929, however, Arabs laid siege to the town and killed 67 Jews; the survivors were relocated to Jerusalem. Two days before the proclamation of the State of Israel, thousands of Arabs and

Arab Legionnaires attacked a group of settlements known as Gush Etzion, just outside of Jerusalem. Eventually, despite surrendering to the Arab army, 240 residents of Kibbutz Kfar Etzion were massacred, another 260 were captured, and the settlement was razed.

Israel's policy has changed very little since 1967. Almost immediately after the war, the government made clear its willingness to trade land for peace. This is not some slogan of the radical left: it has been the official policy of the government of Israel since the end of the 1967 Six-Day War. Israel never planned to administer all the territories it captured beyond the time it took to reach a peace agreement. The expectation was that most of the area won in the fighting would be returned. The Israelis believed, naïvely in retrospect, that having been routed so decisively, the Arab states would give up their dream of destroying Israel and negotiate an end to the conflict. The Arab answer came a few weeks after the war, however, when the Arab League formally announced at Khartoum that there would be no peace with Israel, no negotiations with Israel, and no recognition of Israel.

One thing Israelis did not fully appreciate was the psychological impact of the war. As noted in chapter 1, while the Israelis came out of the war beating their chests that they had proven themselves the toughest kids on the block, the Arabs were ashamed and their culture did not allow them to add to that sense of humiliation by negotiating with their enemy.

In an article that appeared in *Middle East Review* in 1975 and that remains no less relevant today, Harold Glidden, a former member of the State Department Bureau of Intelligence and Research, wrote: "All members of the Arab collectivity are bound to support the cause of their kinsman, the Palestinian Arabs, who demand the liquidation of Israel as a political entity, and the return to it of the refugee Arabs." The Arabs, Glidden added, feel it necessary to take vengeance "to restore to the Palestine Arabs what was wrongfully taken" and "eliminate the shame that had been visited on them and on the other Arabs by their defeats by Israel." While Israel believed that defeating the Arabs would encourage them to negotiate, Glidden said the adverse military balance "produces an emotional need for revenge, and this need is deepened rather than attenuated by each successive defeat." While a strong Israel helps to deter Arab aggression, Glidden explained why this potency is viewed threateningly by the Arabs. "The Arabs fear a strong Israel," he wrote, "because they cannot conceive that any strong state (whether Israeli or Arab) would not use its power and influence to dominate and control the others. This felt danger from Israel is what lies behind the long-reiterated fears of Israeli expansion and Israel's alleged desire to take over the Arab territory 'from the Nile to the Euphrates.'"

Westerners place peace high on their priority lists. But for Arabs, "the emotional need for vengeance to eliminate the ego-destroying feeling of shame" takes precedence. As an example, Glidden cited the Shiite chief Mujtahid of Iraq who said in August 1938—long before the creation of Israel—that a jihad (holy war) for Palestine was everyone's duty, and that if the Arabs lost they would suffer "humiliation, death and eternal shame."

While the Israelis slowly began to strengthen their hold on the West Bank, a growing Palestinian nationalist movement began to emerge. It was not entirely new—nationalist sentiments in the Middle East region can be traced to the late nineteenth and twentieth centuries—but it was not until after Israel took control of the West Bank that the Palestinians began to demand an independent state of their own rather than simply the liberation of Palestine. Throughout the 19-year Jordanian occupation, the Palestinians never demanded, nor did the international community support, the creation of a Palestinian state.

Many Israelis advocated the creation of a federation whereby the West Bank would be linked to Jordan, but the other Arab states never recognized Jordan's claim to the territory. The Palestinians would have been interested but only if they had self-rule, something the Hashemite family would not accept. Once the Jordanian option was taken off the table by King Hussein, the issue became how to reach an agreement with the Palestinians. Since the Palestinians and the rest of the Arab world had agreed that the PLO was its representative, Israelis faced the dilemma of how to negotiate with a group they considered terrorists. Their decision was not to talk to the PLO unless the organization renounced terror and recognized Israel's right to exist.

Trying to bypass the PLO, Israel attempted to work out a deal with Palestinians in the West Bank, in the belief that there was a split between those living in the territories, suffering under what Israel believed was a benign occupation (but the Arabs considered oppression), and the PLO leadership which was at that point in Tunisia, far from Israel, enjoying the freedom to jet-set around the world like celebrities. Israel's strategy failed, however, because the PLO ultimately controlled everything that went on in the territories, and no one dared cross Yasser Arafat and his henchmen.

Here the Israelis miscalculated by their failure to understand the nature of Palestinian political society. The simplest way to explain it is to think in terms of the movies. If you ask a group of older Jews what movie best represents the history of the Zionists, they will inevitably reply Exodus, the moving, idealized Leon Uris version of Israel's fight for independence. Now try to think of a comparable film about the Palestinian experience. Can't think of one? Well, the answer is The Godfather. If you understand that Palestinian politics is like the mafia and that Yasser Arafat was the godfather, then it is easy to understand why Israel's policy failed. It didn't matter that Arafat was in Beirut and later Tunis, his "family" still controlled everything that went on in the territories. Anyone who stepped out of line would have been whacked. This is also why later, after Arafat did return to the West Bank and Israel periodically threatened to expel him, to do so would have had no impact on the willingness of other Palestinians to step forward to negotiate.

Arafat was a mixed blessing as godfather to his people. Through terrorism he attracted the world's attention. He managed to win sympathy by his portrayal of Palestinians as victims. On the other hand, to win that sympathy, he had to keep the people in a state of victimhood. Thus, while the international community would eventually pour billions of dollars into his coffers—after he had spent decades accumulating a fortune through drug dealing, smuggling, robbery, and other illicit activities—most of the money went into his personal bank account, some was funneled to his wife in Paris, and most of the rest went to payoff gunmen, fellow members of Fatah, and to create monopolies in industries such as flour, oil, cigarettes, iron, and cement.

To his credit, unlike other Third World dictators, Arafat did not use the money for his own personal comfort; he didn't build himself palaces like Saddam Hussein. What he did do was buy guns and pay people to use them at his behest. He was the iconic figure in Palestinian life, but he was not popular because of his charm, good looks, or charisma. He was loved because he doled out the cash to his loyalists and he was feared because he ruthlessly punished his enemies. When continued terrorism caused the breakdown of the Oslo agreements, apologists for Arafat would often say he couldn't control the militants. It was nonsense; he controlled everything. When he really was concerned about someone's behavior, he took care of it godfather style. He'd usually have the person killed or he'd go through the charade of arresting and occasionally even trying someone before shooting them. The problem was not that he couldn't control the militants; it was that he did control them and wanted them to engage in violence.

An opportunity arose for the Palestinians to take a step toward independence when Menachem Begin and Anwar Sadat negotiated the Egyptian-Israeli peace treaty in 1979. The Palestinians were offered autonomy, a form of self-government that Begin saw as a way to forestall the creation of a Palestinian state. Seeing this as the purpose, the Palestinians rejected the idea. Had they accepted even this admittedly limited authority over their affairs, however, it would have been difficult for Israel to prevent the Palestinians from gradually expanding their power and eventually establishing an independent state. It was an example of Abba Eban's famous dictum: "The Palestinians never miss an opportunity to miss an opportunity."

Nevertheless, Israel had set a precedent in its willingness to grant the Palestinians the trappings of statehood and begin the inexorable march to independence. This is why Palestinians should one day put up pictures of Menachem Begin on their schoolroom walls and hail him as the father of their country, an incredible irony given Begin's reputation as a right-winger who led the militant Irgun and believed the Jewish state should have been established with its biblical boundaries.

So much for history. The question now is whether it is possible to achieve peace given all the challenges described to this point. To be fair, let's consider the options from the perspective of both the Palestinians and the Israelis.

Objectively, the lives of the Palestinians are miserable. As of late 2006, the economy is in shambles, unemployment has skyrocketed, the international community is withholding funds because the Hamas government refuses to recognize Israel or renounce terrorism, and basic necessities are becoming increasingly difficult to obtain. Israel bears some responsibility for the conditions. The imposition of occasional curfews, the use of checkpoints, and the periodic military operations against terrorists restrict the freedom of Palestinians, causes them humiliation, and sometimes results in casualties. Of course, none of these Israeli measures would be necessary if the Palestinian Authority prevented terrorists from threatening Israeli citizens. Following the Oslo agreements in the early 1990s, Israel had withdrawn its troops from the major cities in the West Bank and Gaza. The Palestinian Authority controlled the lives of about 98 percent of the Palestinians in the territories before the escalation of violence in September 2000 provoked Israel to take measures to defend its citizens. These actions, including the building of the security barrier, have contributed to the hardships of the Palestinians.

Much of the misery of the Palestinians, however, is self-inflicted. The Palestinian Authority, not Israel, governs the lives of almost all the Palestinians, and its leaders have adopted dictatorial methods that deny the people rights that Americans and Israelis take for granted. The rights denied include freedom of religion (non-Muslims face discrimination and the draft constitution makes Islam the official religion), freedom of assembly (you can only come together to express support for the authorities, to praise terrorists, or to condemn Israel and the United States), freedom of expression (you are free only to agree with the leadership; critics risk arrest or summary execution), freedom of the press (even those Arab journalists who aspire to a measure of objectivity complain that they are threatened and prevented from reporting anything other than what the authorities want to hear), women's rights (women are second-class citizens, their role is largely defined by Islamic custom, and "honor killing" is accepted), and gay rights (Islam considers homosexuality an abomination and gay Palestinians are so afraid that some have fled to Israel in hope of asylum). It is always ironic to hear American liberals who sympathize with the Palestinians try to explain how they support people who deny the rights they claim to hold dear and yet castigate Israel where these rights are cherished and vigorously upheld. The Palestinians actually are much more honest—they tell pollsters that the country they most admire is Israel because they see how their brethren are treated in Israel. In fact, while more than 80 percent of Palestinians praised Israel, only 20 percent expressed admiration for the corrupt Arafat regime in 2003. Israeli Arabs are even more adamant that while they believe their brethren should have a state, they have no desire to live in it, and they have vociferously opposed suggestions that in a future peace deal predominantly Arab towns in northern Israel would be exchanged for territory in the West Bank.

The Palestinian people have also been victims of their corrupt leadership. It was never any secret that Yasser Arafat and his cronies were crooks. Top Palestinian Authority officials run monopolies in a variety of key businesses such as cement and fuel. The International Monetary Fund found that Arafat stole $900 million of the assistance that international donors earmarked for the people. People living in refugee camps could not help but wonder how the Palestinian Authority could receive $6 billion in aid and still not tear down a single refugee camp or build even one house for a refugee. One of my favorite stories involved the speaker of the Palestinian legislative council, Ahmed Korei, who in 2002 suddenly vacated the villa he built for $1.5 million in Jericho after President Bush raised the issue of Palestinian Authority corruption. A sign posted on the door said the villa had become a welfare institution for the relatives of Palestinians killed in terror attacks.

Even after the Israeli disengagement from Gaza in 2005, the Palestinians failed to take advantage of the opportunity to improve their situation. The Israelis withdrew from all the towns they had created. At the Palestinians' request, the Israelis demolished beautiful homes. Many were lovely villas with views of the sea that would probably be worth millions anywhere else. At the time the Palestinians said they had no use for such single family dwellings because of the traditionally large extended Arab families and planned to build high-rise residences instead. A year later, however, not a single project had broken ground. The Israelis also left behind lucrative agriculture and flower businesses. In one of the great ironies, a number of wealthy Jews contributed millions of dollars to buy greenhouses from the settlers to transfer to the Palestinians so they could carry on these businesses and benefit from them. Instead, many of the greenhouses were vandalized, looted, and left unusable.

Palestinian frustration with the level of corruption was one reason why Hamas won its unexpected victory in the elections in 2006. The organization was considered more honest and more likely to act in the interests of the people rather than of individual officials' bank accounts. In the months after they came to power, Hamas only made the situation worse by provoking Israel to resume military operations in Gaza and the international community to withhold money from the Palestinian Authority. Moreover, order completely broke down as armed gangs turned Gaza, especially, into something resembling the Wild West.

Whatever blame one wants to assign for their plight, the reality is the same: the Palestinian people are suffering. But what can they do about it?

Most Palestinians would probably be happy to live in peace. A February 2006 poll, for example, found that 58 percent of Palestinians are prepared to accept a two-state solution. These Palestinians want to live normal lives, work, raise a family, send their children to school. They might prefer that Israel disappeared, but are willing to accept it as a fact of life as long as the Israelis don't bother them. The problem for these Palestinians is that they don't live in a democracy: Their leaders do not represent their views, and speaking out for peace, condemning violence, or criticizing the leadership is more likely to get you killed than to change policy.

Over the years, the Palestinians have adopted a series of failed strategies. One is simply to shout for all the world to hear, "End the occupation!" It's a nifty slogan. After all, who among us favors occupation? Unfortunately, the demand comes with no reciprocal obligations. Israel has no incentive to withdraw from the territory it holds, and the Palestinians have given them no tangible evidence that acceding to their demand will bring Israel peace or security.

A second strategy is to try to destroy Israel. The Palestinians have understood from the beginning that they do not have the capability, so they have relied on the other Arab states to do this for them. The strategy failed, however, when Israel defeated the Arab armies in 1948, 1967, and 1973. Afterward, the Arab states lost interest in sacrificing their soldiers and economies for sloganeering Palestinians who showed little inclination to fight for themselves. The Palestinians finally realized that the dream of being rescued by their brethren was over when Yasser Arafat was isolated by Israel in his headquarters in Ramallah during the Palestinian War and all his calls to Arab capitals for help went unanswered.

The repeated Arab defeats prompted the Palestinians to take matters into their own hands and to use terrorism in an effort to bomb Israel out of the territories and, eventually, out of existence. Believing that Hizbollah succeeded in bombing Israel out of Lebanon, the Palestinians decided in 2000 to adopt a similar strategy. The Islamist terror groups Hamas and Islamic Jihad, along with the PLO-affiliated Tanzim and Al-Aqsa Martyrs Brigade, killed more than 1,000 Israelis over the next five years. When Israel ultimately decided to evacuate Gaza, Hamas felt its strategy was vindicated.

The reality is that terrorism has achieved only marginal success for the Palestinians. The high-profile hijackings, murder of Israeli athletes at the Munich Olympics and other spectacular attacks helped raise their cause on the international agenda, but it has still failed to destroy Israel, to weaken Israeli resolve, or to win them statehood. The use of terrorism as a modus operandi also has reinforced negative stereotypes of Arabs and Muslims, attracted international condemnation, and torpedoed arrangements that would have long ago brought them independence.

Moreover, I would argue, the disengagement from Gaza had little to do with the terrorists and could have been achieved much sooner had the

Palestinians chosen to adhere to the Oslo peace agreements. Israel was not driven from the territories. It made a calculated decision to leave based on its own interests. The 8,500 civilians who lived in Gaza were viewed by the terrorists as targets, and Israel had to devote a great deal of its human and material resources to protect these innocent people. In addition, Sharon agreed with those who had concluded that it would make no sense for Israel to hold on to an area with a Palestinian population exceeding one million. By withdrawing, Israel's security was enhanced (though growing numbers of Israelis question this in light of the ongoing rocket attacks and weapons smuggling), and the Palestinians had the opportunity to govern themselves and to demonstrate that they could create a democratic society that can coexist with Israel—yet another opportunity they have wasted.

At the time of the disengagement, Israel had dramatically reduced the level of terror, and the security fence around Gaza had a nearly perfect record of preventing the infiltration of suicide bombers. Israeli forces had severely damaged the terrorist infrastructure and killed or jailed most of the leaders of the major terror groups. The disengagement took place after Israel subdued the Palestinian War; the withdrawal was implemented from a position of strength, not weakness. As Zakariya Zubeidi, the leader of the Al-Aqsa Martyrs Brigade terrorist group observed, "Not only was the intifada a failure, but we are a total failure. We achieved nothing in 50 years of struggle; we've achieved only our survival."[2]

Still, one incentive for the Palestinians to continue to pursue a violent course is that the international community has taught the Arabs that they have nothing to lose in the long run by going to war. After each loss, the international community has not pressured the Arabs to recognize Israel and to make concessions. Rather, it has turned the screws on Israel to give up captured territory, rewarded the aggressor with aid, and placed diplomatic pressure on Israel to make concessions to avoid a future war. In the most recent conflict in Lebanon, Israel was attacked but was forced to withdraw its troops before eliminating the threat to its citizens. The international community wouldn't enforce its own UN resolution calling for Hizbollah to be disarmed and the Israeli soldiers to be unconditionally released. To add insult to injury, international aid was raised for the Lebanese who started the war and nothing was given to the Israelis who had to defend themselves.

Yet another approach pursued by the Palestinians has been to repeatedly solicit the support of the international community to impose a solution on

Israel, one that invariably would require Israel to capitulate to Arab demands. The Europeans, the Russians, and the United Nations are enthusiastic participants in this effort, but none of them have any leverage over Israel because of their unwavering support for the Arabs. The Arabs have been successful in introducing numerous resolutions condemning Israel each year at the UN, and while most of these are adopted in the General Assembly where the anti-Israel bloc holds an automatic majority, the resolutions are nonbinding. Although the Arabs have had some success in raising issues in the Security Council, the United States has vetoed the most egregious ones and gives no indication that it will accept any punitive resolutions that would alter the status quo. The only party that has the power to coerce Israel is the United States and no American president since Eisenhower has been willing to use the full weight of his office to force Israel to withdraw from specific territory, stop building settlements or dismantle them, or to fulfill other Palestinian demands that Israel views as unacceptable threats to its sovereignty or security.

All of these strategies have been based, in part, on the view that the rational position of the Palestinians is to seek some immediate relief from their predicament. Many Arabs, especially Muslims, hold an equally reasonable view that it is not necessary to take any precipitous action today; it is better to be patient and to have faith that time is on their side. As noted in earlier chapters, people who hold this view see the expulsion of the Crusaders as the relevant precedent and are convinced that they can overwhelm Israel through the sheer weight of their numbers (the demographic bomb), or destroy the Jewish state with the atomic bomb. If you believe this, then why accept a crummy little state in the West Bank and Gaza Strip now when you can hold on a little longer and liberate all of Palestine?

Some Palestinians are prepared to compromise and to accept the creation of a Palestinian state in the West Bank and Gaza Strip beside Israel. Assuming these Palestinians ever assumed power, Israel probably would still question their motives. Are the Palestinians interested in real peace or are they simply making a tactical decision to achieve a base from which to pursue the ultimate objective of "liberating" all of Palestine? The Palestinians have not hidden their "strategy of stages." It was succinctly stated by Faisal al-Husseini, one of the well-known Palestinian "moderates": "If we agree to declare our state over what is now 22 percent of Palestine, meaning the West Bank and Gaza, our ultimate goal is the liberation of all historic Palestine from the River to the Sea. We distinguish the strategic, long-term goals from the political phased goals, which we are compelled to temporarily accept due to international pressure."[3]

From the Palestinian perspective, this is a plausible scheme that, paradoxically, could be modeled on the approach taken by the Zionists. The Zionists originally believed that a Jewish state should be created in all of the historic homeland, which included all of present-day Israel and what is now Jordan. Ultimately, however, they decided to accept a territory that was a fraction of the size. They could have tried to hold out for their maximal objective, as the Palestinians are doing, but the founders of Israel understood that the most important thing was to gain international recognition for a Jewish state in Palestine and then to build up that entity as a haven for the Jewish people. The Zionists were even willing to sacrifice their capital, Jerusalem, which was to be an international city according to the partition plan, because the size of the state was not as important to them as its existence.

Similarly, the Palestinians could accept whatever tiny, contorted state Israel is prepared to give them and then duplicate the Zionist enterprise by spending the next half century building it. Ideally, from their standpoint, they would mirror Israel's success in developing a first-world economy in a third-world region with virtually no resources. Though Israel will insist that the Palestinian state be demilitarized, the reality is that Israel is unlikely to have the ability to prevent the buildup of an army, just as they could not stop Hizbollah from acquiring a huge arsenal of sophisticated weapons. Then, perhaps in 50 years or so, the Palestinian state may have the capability to fight and win a war with Israel. The Zionists never aspired to destroy their neighbors, and David Ben-Gurion and the other Zionist leaders understood that even a seemingly unviable, checkerboard state was better than no state at all. The Palestinians, after all these years, still have not come to this realization.

The Palestinians could have done the same thing in 1947, and today they would be sharing with Israel the celebration of six decades of independence. Even now, it is not too late. If they had leaders with the vision and courage of Egypt's Anwar Sadat of Jordan's King Hussein, the Palestinians would negotiate a peace deal that would give them statehood in any part of the territories the Israelis are prepared to cede.

✡

Now, let's examine the situation from Israel's perspective.

First, what do Israelis see when they look at the Palestinians? To begin with, they see Islamists who say openly they will never accept a Jewish state in the Islamic heartland and declare their dedication to a jihad to destroy Israel. Hamas and Islamic Jihad make it clear that they will not cease their terror war even if Israel withdraws to the 1967 border (more accurately, the 1949 armistice line).

Israelis also see that the Palestinians are teaching their children to believe the Jewish people have no connection to Palestine, no history associated with Al-Quds (Jerusalem), and that no negotiations have been concluded between Israelis and Palestinians. Their textbooks often use anti-Semitic motifs and the entire curriculum appears aimed at indoctrinating youth with a hatred of Jews and Israel. While I could go into great detail about how problematic the textbooks are in Palestinian schools, literally the most graphic way to illustrate the problem is to note the fact that Israel does not appear on any maps in Palestinian textbooks. In every negotiation, Israel has highlighted the issue of incitement in the schools because everyone believes the greatest hope is that future generations will be more tolerant and prepared to live in peace. Palestinian education appears devoted to a very different future.

Israelis are further discouraged by the attitudes of Palestinians reflected in surveys showing that large numbers of Palestinians don't believe bombing restaurants and buses constitute terrorism; think it's a good idea to name a soccer tournament after a suicide bomber who killed 30 Israelis; believe the phrase "occupied territories" refers to all of Israel; say that Hamas and Islamic Jihad should not give up their armed struggle even if Israel were to withdraw from all the occupied territories and give the Palestinians a state; believe Israel planned the 9/11 bombings.

One of the most troublesome attitudes is reflected by the Palestinian commemoration on Israeli Independence Day of what they call Al Nakba ("The Catastrophe"). Had the Palestinians and the Arab states accepted the partition resolution in 1947, the State of Palestine would also celebrate its birthday, and Palestinians would not lament Al Nakba. Palestinians are understandably bitter about their history over these last six decades, but we are often told that what they object to is the "occupation" of the territories Israel captured in 1967. If that is true, then why isn't their Nakba Day celebrated each June on the anniversary of the Arab defeat in the Six-Day War?

The reason is that the Palestinians consider the creation of Israel the original sin, and their focus on that event is indicative of a refusal, even today, to reconcile themselves with the Jewish state.

As I noted in chapter 3, Israel lives in the Middle East and not the Middle West, and the presence of radical Muslims who will not accept a Jewish state in what they consider the Islamic heartland makes it unlikely that Israel can achieve the kind of peace that the United States has with its neighbors. This is not a revelation to Israelis. They understand their neighbors only too well. Though it is not what most people want to hear, what Israel therefore seeks is not perfect peace but, as economists would say, to maximize peace and minimize risk; that is, to get as much peace as it can with as little danger as possible.

So what can Israel do to maximize peace and minimize risk?

One option is for Israel to do nothing. Israel managed to survive holding the West Bank and Gaza Strip since 1967. It has now given up Gaza, but why go any further? Israel has a valid claim to Judea and Samaria on historical grounds and can justify holding the area to enhance its security. During the last 40 years, Israel has also created physical realities that now make it less likely it will give up as much territory as it might have if the Arabs had been prepared to make peace as recently as 20 years ago. At that time there were only 11,000 settlers in 80 settlements. Today, more than 260,000 Jews live in roughly 120 communities in the territories. Israel could continue along this path in the hope of either preventing the creation of a Palestinian state or further reducing its potential geographic size.

On the other hand, the cost of maintaining the status quo is enormous. The economic costs have been largely hidden, but the expense of building roads and other infrastructure, subsidizing mortgages, providing security, and all the other services to the settlers over the years is undoubtedly in the billions of dollars. Many Israelis believe that money could be much better spent on other societal needs. Israel has also paid a high political cost in opposition to its policies from the international community. The human cost has been high as well as hundreds of Jews living in the territories and traveling through them have been killed and injured, and the army has had to divert its resources from training and other military preparations to defend settlers and engage in counterterrorist actions against the Palestinians. The status quo has also taken a psychological toll on those who believe Israeli policies are immoral and on soldiers who have often had to do legal but very unpleasant things to defend their country. As a result, few Israelis advocate maintaining the current situation.

A small minority on the far right of the Israeli political spectrum advocates transferring the Arabs out of the disputed territories. If Israelis could make the Palestinians disappear, undoubtedly most would favor it, but they can't just be swept away. There is the practical matter of how one goes about forcibly moving more than three million people. Then there is the political issue of international opposition to such a move and the questions of where they would go and whether that would really make the security situation better. For example, if they all went to Jordan and radicalized that now peaceful country, wouldn't Israel be worse off? The real reason the idea is unfathomable, however, is rooted in morality. Jews are not going to load another people into trucks or other conveyances and ship them off. Just imagine the TV image of Jewish soldiers herding Palestinian mothers and children with their bundles onto transports. What would that remind you of? It's not going to happen.

Israel could annex the territories. At any time in the last 40 years Israel could have simply announced that the West Bank and Gaza are now Israel (as it did with Jerusalem and the Golan Heights). Israel never did that because of the demographic problem, described in chapter 4, that makes it impossible for Israel to remain both a democratic and Jewish state if a majority or even a significant minority of its population is not Jewish.

Another possibility is a military option. Israel has fought and won multiple wars, and it has achieved formal peace agreements with two Arab states and de facto peace with the rest. The real battle, now, however, is with Islamists who are fighting a nonconventional war. Commentators like to say that Israel can't win that type of war with force. It's not true; Israel can win, but it is just not prepared to do what is necessary. Time and again we've seen Israel flagellate itself in public over the deaths of innocent civilians. Yet, the terrorists don't care about civilians. That's why they use them as shields and targets. When an Arab is killed in error, Israel launches an investigation, and there is often a great public outcry when a military operation goes awry and injures innocents. By contrast, when Jews are murdered by terrorists, the Palestinians and other Arabs hold celebratory parades.

During the conflict with Hizbollah, Israel was vilified by the Lebanese government and many Europeans for using what they labeled "disproportionate" force in response to the terrorists attacking and kidnapping its soldiers and unleashing an indiscriminate barrage of thousands of rockets at Israel's civilian population. Since Hizbollah's stated objective is the destruction of Israel, isn't the appropriate response the destruction of Hizbollah? Wouldn't random missile strikes on Lebanese cities be proportionate to Hizbollah's rocket attacks on northern Israel? Can you imagine any of Israel's critics accepting those responses?

A more salient question is who decided that one side must respond proportionately in a war? The United States certainly doesn't believe this. Imagine if terrorists based in Cuba had 10,000 rockets pointed at Miami, would U.S. officials sit by and wait for them to be fired at Florida? And once they were launched, would any American call for a proportionate response? Americans went through a version of this with the Cuban missile crisis, when President Kennedy made clear that the presence of missiles pointing at the United States was intolerable and that he was prepared for a nuclear war if they were not removed.

Americans believe in Colin Powell's doctrine, which holds that "America should enter fights with every bit of force available or not at all." General Powell, for example, insisted on deploying overwhelming force before going to war against Iraq in the first Gulf War. The allied force of more than half a million troops demolished Saddam Hussein's army at a cost of fewer than 200 American lives, while approximately 35,000 Iraqis were killed, including many civilians. He also oversaw the invasion of Panama, which required the deployment of 25,000 troops. Thousands of Panamanian civilians were injured and displaced and at least 100 killed. He said later, "Use all the force necessary, and do not apologize for going in big if that is what it takes. Decisive force ends wars quickly and in the long run saves lives."[4] In reaction to an attempt to assassinate President Bush in 1993, the United States launched 23 cruise missiles at Iraq's intelligence headquarters and hit a civilian neighborhood in the process. Powell later said this was an "appropriate, proportional" response.[5]

The United States uses overwhelming force against its enemies, even though the threats are distant and pose no danger to the existence of the nation or the immediate security of its citizens. The accomplishment of U.S. military objectives is also routinely accompanied by errors and collateral damage that results in civilian casualties. The threat Israel faces, in comparison, is immediate in time and physical proximity, and poses a direct danger to Israeli citizens. More than a thousand rockets fell on Israel's cities—not its military installations but its civilian centers. Approximately one million Israelis fled south or were living in bomb shelters. Still, Israel did not used its full might as the Powell doctrine dictates.

It is difficult for Israel to win a war with the terrorists because it is fighting from the moral high ground and its enemies have no morals whatsoever. The situation reminds me of the scene in The Untouchables when Eliot Ness, the honest cop who wants to play by the rules, becomes frustrated with his inability to stop Al Capone. He asks a tough old cop named Malone how to get Capone. "Here's how," Malone explains, "they pull a knife, you pull a gun. He sends one of yours to the hospital, you send one of his to the morgue. That's the Chicago way, and that's how you get Capone! Now do you want to do that? Are you ready to do that?"

In the case of Israel, the way to get Hamas and Hizbollah is to play by what Tom Friedman called "Hama rules." This refers to how Syria dealt with the problem of Islamic fundamentalists threatening the regime in 1982, namely, wipe out an entire city and kill as many as 20,000 people. You can search the UN archives for a record of any condemnation of that massacre. No Arab or European leader spoke out against this atrocity. And remember in all-out war even the powers that adhere to moral standards, such as the United States and its allies, have not hesitated to use whatever force they believed necessary to defeat their enemies. Remember Dresden, Nagasaki, and Hiroshima? If Israel carpet-bombed southern Lebanon and the Gaza Strip and killed 10 or 20 thousand Palestinians and Lebanese it could stop the terror. Israel would, of course, be pilloried everywhere. But would the condemnation for thousands of deaths be much different than what Israel customarily receives for the deaths of a few dozen people?

Israel would never resort to Hama rules because its leaders operate according to a moral code that seeks to minimize harm to innocents. Israel blows up empty buildings and launches pinpoint attacks; sometimes civilians are killed and Israelis are usually the first to decry the tragedy. Israel could just as easily bomb the same buildings when they are full of people, but Israel's answer to Malone's question to Ness is that it is unwilling to do it the Chicago way. Still, Ariel Sharon proved that by taking tough measures, which include assassinating terror leaders and building a security fence, it is possible to dramatically reduce the level of terror.

✡

While the Islamists are patient, the Israelis are not. They want peace now. It is not a slogan of left-wing activists, it is what every Israeli desires. This is why Israel eschews the military option and has persistently offered compromises that it hoped would satisfy Arab demands. Israelis know the agenda of the Islamists, and they are equally aware that some Palestinians believe in the strategy of stages, but they still are prepared to negotiate because they are confident they can survive. The Palestinians can say whatever they want—for example, that they will return to Jaffa and Haifa—but that does not mean Israel has any intention of allowing them to achieve their irredentist goals.

The Oslo negotiations were a good example of Israel's willingness to take risks for peace. Unlike many people who believe they were a great mistake, I think they were a calculated gamble to maximize peace and minimize risk based on the precedent, set in the talks with Egypt, for successful negotiations with an Arab state. In that case, Egypt maintained a state of war with Israel for more than 25 years before Anwar Sadat seriously talked about peace. Bloody conflicts were fought in 1948, 1956, 1967, 1968-70, and 1973. The anger, heartache, and distrust of a quarter century did not dissipate overnight. The process began after the 1973 war when Henry Kissinger facilitated the negotiation of a disengagement agreement in which both sides made significant concessions. Egypt had demanded that Israel make a substantial withdrawal from Sinai and commit to abandon all its territorial gains from 1967, but Israel gave up only a tiny area of the Sinai. Rather than resort to violence, the Egyptians engaged in more negotiations.

The first agreement was signed in January 1974. It took about a year and a half before a second agreement was reached. It wasn't easy. Israel was criticized for inflexibility, and the Egyptians were no less difficult. Anwar Sadat agreed to limit anti-Israel propaganda in the Egyptian press and to end his country's participation in the Arab boycott. Yitzhak Rabin also made difficult territorial concessions, giving up oil fields and two critical Sinai passes.

After Sinai II (the 1975 agreement whereby Israel withdrew from part of the Egyptian areas it captured in 1973), Egypt still had not recovered all of its territory. Sadat was dissatisfied and was excoriated by the other Arabs for going as far as he did toward peace with Israel. Nevertheless, he did not resort to violence. There was no unleashing of terrorists, as Nasser had done in the 1950s. Instead, he continued talking. It took three more years before the Camp

David Accords were signed and another six months after that until the final peace treaty was negotiated. It took five years to work out issues that were, in many cases, as complex as those in the current impasse.

In return for its tangible concessions, Israel received a promise of a new future of peaceful relations. Israel could take this risk because Egypt had demonstrated over the previous five years that it would resolve disputes with Israel peacefully, and that it no longer wished to destroy its neighbor. Egypt still wasn't completely satisfied. Sadat demanded a small sliver of land that Israel retained in the Sinai. It took another nine years before international arbitration led Israel to give up Taba. Rather than using this dispute as a pretext for violating the peace treaty, Egypt negotiated.

Israel tried a similar approach with Arafat. After he agreed to Israeli conditions and renounced violence, recognized Israel, and expressed a willingness to negotiate over their differences, peace talks began. No one had any illusions about Arafat; they believed he was a murderer and a liar, but Israel decided to put him to the same test as Sadat. Israel subsequently withdrew from part of the Gaza Strip and the West Bank with the expectation that the Palestinians would keep the peace and that more difficult outstanding issues would be addressed in continuing negotiations. Instead, Palestinian terrorists launched a wave of violence. Still, Israel continued to give up land. After withdrawing from about 80 percent of the Gaza Strip and 40 percent of the West Bank, however, the attacks continued. Israel traded land, it turned out, for terror rather than peace.

The final straw for most Israelis came in 2000 when Prime Minister Ehud Barak decided to jettison the incremental approach and sit down with Arafat and resolve all the outstanding issues at once. President Bill Clinton was a willing host as he hoped to achieve a great diplomatic breakthrough that would cement his place in history. During the course of talks at Camp David and the White House, Israel agreed to withdraw from about 97 percent of the West Bank and all of Gaza. Barak was prepared to demolish the isolated settlements. He also agreed to a partial division of Jerusalem in which the Arab neighborhoods in East Jerusalem would be part of Palestine and the Jewish neighborhoods part of Israel. The Palestinians would also gain limited sovereignty over the Temple Mount. Israel accepted an unlimited right of Palestinians to return to a Palestinian state, agreed to participate in a compensation fund to resettle the refugees, and offered to admit a limited number of refugees to Israel on the humanitarian basis of family reunification.

Arafat rejected the deal. Not only that, he refused to offer any counter proposal. It was not as though he said, you've offered 97 percent, I want 99.9 percent. He simply said no. One of the telling moments in the talks occurred when Arafat questioned the Jewish connection to Jerusalem, suggesting that no Jewish Temple ever existed on the Temple Mount. At that point the president recognized that Arafat was so caught up in his own mythology, he couldn't sign an agreement. Contrary to revisionist histories that insist the problem was that Israel offered a lousy deal, the truth was evident to Clinton who blamed Arafat for the breakdown of the talks. Chief U.S. negotiator Dennis Ross said the PLO chairman simply couldn't give up his identity as a revolutionary. "For him to end the conflict," Ross said, "is to end himself."[6] In retrospect, many Palestinians now admit they made a grave error, and for the seventh time missed an opportunity to achieve independence.

Why was Arafat unwilling to accept a deal? Psychology again played a key role. As Ross observed, Arafat could not make the psychological leap that Sadat had made before making peace with Israel. He had spent his whole life as a revolutionary, and his personal and political esteem stemmed from the pursuit of his goal of liberating Palestine. After spending his adult life with that objective, he couldn't say, "I didn't really mean all of Palestine, just part."

It is this psychological view that may be the principal impediment as long as Arafat's generation is in power. His successor Mahmoud Abbas was, after all, the number three man in Arafat's organization, had advocated the same positions and been just as much a part of the terror infrastructure. Some may argue he has changed—the Israelis see him as a moderate with whom they can negotiate—but it is more likely Israel will have to wait for the younger generation of Palestinian leaders. Many of this next generation appear even more militant than Arafat and the PLO, having grown up under the occupation, spent time in and out of Israeli jails, and become convinced from the actions of Hizbollah and Hamas that resistance may be the best option. On the other hand, unlike Arafat's generation, who spent little time actually living under the Israelis—they were based in Tunis after their expulsion from Jordan and Lebanon—those who grew up in the West Bank and Gaza understand their adversaries better and have greater incentive to do what they can to end the occupation. It will free them of the Israelis without bearing the burden of appearing to have abandoned the ideology of liberation.

For Israel, the rejection of Camp David was a repudiation of the left's belief that dismantling the settlements and ending the occupation would bring about peace. Of course, the left tends to have a short memory (as when some well-known leftists said they would never feel the same sympathy toward the Palestinians after seeing them cheer for Saddam Hussein as he fired Scud missiles at Tel Aviv); so it would not be long before they would return to this theme. In the short run, however, most Israelis concluded that if they offered the Palestinians everything they thought they wanted and it still wasn't enough, what more could they do?

When Arafat unexpectedly died in November 2004, many people believed a new opportunity for a negotiated peace was at hand. His successor, Mahmoud Abbas (a.k.a. Abu Mazen) was a familiar interlocutor and the Israelis considered him a moderate whom they could talk to. He immediately proved a disappointment because he was unable and/or unwilling to take the necessary steps to prove that he was serious about peace, namely by arresting the terrorists, confiscating their weapons, preventing violence and ending incitement. He signed the road map for peace, championed by the United States, Russia, the European Union, and the United Nations, that required these steps, but he has failed to meet his obligations (which, incidentally, were the same as those Arafat first promised to fulfill at Oslo 12 years earlier).

Since Hamas won the Palestinian Authority elections, Abbas's already feeble power has been further diminished. He is unable to govern because the Hamas members of the government oppose his agenda and continue to compete for money and influence. The West Bank and especially Gaza have become lawless as his security forces have been unable to enforce order. He has tried to get Hamas to agree to recognize Israel and abide by past agreements to restore international support for the Palestinian Authority, but Hamas has repeatedly rejected his overtures and has reiterated its commitment to destroy Israel. Rather than acknowledging Abbas's impotence, Israel is blamed by those who believe Abbas is a credible peace partner for not doing enough to help him. But why should the burden of Palestinian leadership fall on Israel?

Though it has no obligation to do so, Israel has taken steps to show its goodwill, including facilitating the Palestinian elections, releasing prisoners, and withdrawing troops from parts of the West Bank. More important, Israel evacuated all of its civilians and soldiers from the Gaza Strip. Even so coexistence is impossible unless Palestinian violence stops. There can be no attacks on Jews anywhere, no mortars or rockets fired into Israel, and no incitement to violence. This is not a case of giving extremists a veto over negotiations;

Israel has not said that Abbas must stop 100 percent of the incidents before it will talk, but Israel does insist that he demonstrate a 100 percent effort to stop them. To date, he has not done so.

After Israel evacuated Gaza in 2005, nothing prevented the Palestinians from creating the infrastructure of statehood there. They could have spent the time since Israel's departure peacefully, demonstrating to Israelis that they will indeed receive peace in return for land. Instead, the Palestinians have done the exact opposite and continued their attacks, have engaged in extensive smuggling of weapons, and have given no indication that they are any more willing to live in peace with Israel than they were before the disengagement. For years the Palestinians claimed they were only engaged in terror because of the occupation, but there is no occupation in Gaza and they continue to shoot rockets into Israeli towns.

A popular slogan says that you have to make peace with your enemies. This is the mantra of those who believe that negotiations are the only way to end conflict. Israel would love to sit in a room with its adversaries and hash out a settlement of all their respective grievances. Israel has engaged in many such discussions. The problem with the snappy slogan is that it assumes the enemies are interested in peace. In truth, you can only make peace with enemies who are prepared to make peace. This is not the case with the Islamic terrorists and it has not been true to date of other Palestinian leaders. Even if Abbas is sincere about wanting peace, negotiators are still faced with the same difficult issues that were left unresolved in the Oslo process—borders, settlements, refugees, and Jerusalem. Though each of these issues have proved daunting so far, the resolution to each is clear.

✡

The question of where to draw the border between Israel and the Palestinian state has largely been determined. Israel has already withdrawn from Gaza and the existing border of the Gaza Strip should be the final frontier between that part of the Palestinian state and Israel.

In the West Bank, Israel has consistently said it is willing to withdraw to the 1949 armistice lines with modifications. What does that mean? Israel is prepared to move very close to the pre-1967 lines with the aim of keeping as much territory as it can and incorporating as many Jews and as few Palestinians as possible. If you look at a map of where the security fence is being built, that is roughly the future border of Israel and Palestine. Israel cannot afford to give up much more territory without returning to the insecure borders it had before the 1967 war, and Israel will not dismantle the larger Jewish communities established in the West Bank. This is consistent with UN Security Council Resolution 242, the internationally recognized basis for resolving the conflict, which said Israel must withdraw from "territory," not "all the territories." The drafters understood that it was unreasonable to expect Israel to return to the 1967 lines because they had proven insecure. The second part of the resolution, moreover, says that every state, including Israel, has the right to live within secure and recognized boundaries.

President George W. Bush endorsed the Israeli position in his April 14, 2004, letter to Prime Minister Ariel Sharon in which he acknowledged that given "new realities on the ground, including already existing major Israeli populations centers, it is unrealistic to expect that the outcome of final status negotiations will be a full and complete return to the armistice lines of 1949, and all previous efforts to negotiate a two-state solution have reached the same conclusion."

Israel has already withdrawn from about 94 percent of the territories it captured in 1967, so the area that is still in dispute is quite small (about 1,200 square miles). Still, any new evacuation from the West Bank will involve another gut-wrenching decision that most settlers and their supporters will oppose with even greater ferocity than the Gaza disengagement. Nevertheless, Sharon acknowledged that "not all the settlements that are today in Judea and Samaria will remain Israeli." This view is supported by the majority of Israelis, who have no opposition to withdrawing from small and isolated communities (about half of the settlements today have fewer than 500 residents).

A general consensus also exists to preserve the larger communities in five settlement blocks near the 1967 border where approximately two-thirds of the settlers live. Sharon repeatedly said the large settlement blocks would "remain in our hands." These are towns with thousands of residents comparable to such American cities as Annapolis, Juneau, and Augusta. On a proportional basis, compared to the total population of the country, these areas would be the equivalent of U.S. municipalities with populations ranging from a half million (e.g., Boston, Denver, Seattle, Washington, D.C.) to 1.7 million (e.g., Philadelphia and Houston).

At Camp David, Israel insisted that 80 percent of the Jewish residents of the West Bank would be in settlement blocks under Israeli sovereignty. President Clinton agreed and proposed that Israel annex between 4 and 6 percent of the West Bank, which included three settlement blocks to accomplish this demographic objective, and swap some territory within Israel in exchange. Even Arafat said he was prepared to allow Israel to retain some settlements. Nevertheless, Palestinians complain the incorporation of settlement blocs would prevent the creation of a contiguous Palestinian state. A look at a map shows this is untrue. The total area of these communities is only about 1.5 percent of the West Bank. A kidney-shaped state linked to the Gaza Strip by a secure passage would be contiguous. Some argue that Israel's proposed project (known as E1) to link Ma'ale Adumim to Jerusalem would cut off East Jerusalem, but even that is not necessarily true as Israel has proposed constructing a four-lane underpass to guarantee free passage between the West Bank and the Arab sections of Jerusalem.

Meanwhile, the Palestinians and their supporters contend that settlements are an obstacle to peace; they blame Israel's continued expansion of the population of the territories for the failure of the Oslo accords and everything that happened since. But, the historical evidence shows that settlements are not an impediment to peace.

From 1949 until 1967, a period when Jews were forbidden to live on the West Bank, the Arabs refused to make peace with Israel.

From 1967 until 1977, the Labor Party established only a few strategic settlements in the territories, yet the Arabs were unwilling to negotiate peace with Israel.

In 1977, months after a Likud government committed to greater settlement activity took office, Egyptian President Sadat went to Jerusalem and later signed a peace treaty with Israel. Israeli settlements existed in the Sinai and those were removed as part of the agreement with Egypt.

One year later, Israel froze settlement building for three months, hoping the gesture would entice other Arabs to join the Camp David peace process. None did.

In 1994 Jordan signed a peace agreement with Israel and settlements were not only not an issue, but the number of Jews living in the territories was growing.

Between June 1992 and June 1996, under Labor-led governments, the Jewish population in the territories grew by approximately 50 percent. This rapid growth did not prevent the Palestinians from signing the Oslo accords in September 1993 or the Oslo 2 agreement in September 1995.

In 2000 Prime Minister Ehud Barak offered to dismantle dozens of settlements, but the Palestinians still would not agree to end the conflict.

In August 2005 Israel evacuated all of the settlements in the Gaza Strip and four in Northern Samaria, but terror attacks continued.

Settlement activity may actually stimulate peace talks because it forces the Palestinians to reconsider the view that time is on their side. "The Palestinians now realize," said Bethlehem Mayor Elias Freij, "that time is now on the side of Israel, which can build settlements and create facts, and that the only way out of this dilemma is face-to-face negotiations."[7] Many Israelis nevertheless have concerns about the expansion of settlements. Some consider them provocative; others worry that the settlers are particularly vulnerable and note that they have been targets of repeated Palestinian terrorist attacks. To defend them, large numbers of soldiers have been deployed who would be otherwise occupied. Some Israelis also object to the amount of money and the special subsidies that have been provided to make housing in those communities more affordable. Still others feel the settlers are providing a first line of defense and developing land that rightfully belongs to Israel.

According to every Israeli peace plan under consideration a significant number of Jews, perhaps 60,000, will find themselves literally on the wrong side of the fence. Given the Gaza precedent, we know these settlers will either have to move voluntarily to one of the settlement blocks that are retained, move within the Green Line (the 1949 armistice line) or be forcibly evacuated. The Sharon government complicated the task of a second withdrawal by promising the Gaza settlers who left voluntarily generous compensation packages and warning those who resisted that they would not receive the same amount of money. Ultimately, however, the government gave money to everyone, even those who had to be dragged from their homes, thereby sending the message to West Bank settlers that they aren't likely to be penalized for defying an evacuation order and might be able to negotiate better terms the longer they hold out. In the end, the Gaza disengagement cost Israel nearly $1 billion to compensate just 8,500 settlers; the price tag for evacuating 60,000 from the West Bank will be upward of $10 billion.

The second major issue to be resolved in negotiations is the disposition of Palestinian refugees. The Palestinians insist they have a right of return to their homes. Most Palestinians already live in historic Palestine, which includes the Palestinian Authority areas and Jordan. When Palestinians speak of the right to return, however, they don't mean just to Palestine, but to the exact houses they lived in prior to 1948. These homes are now either gone or inhabited by others. From Israel's perspective, it has no obligation to accept people who, for the most part, chose to leave in the hope that they would return to a land devoid of Jews. From a purely practical standpoint, the idea is a nonstarter. The current Israeli population is approximately 7 million and 5.3 million are Jews. If every Palestinian was allowed to move to Israel, the population would exceed 11 million and the Jewish proportion would shrink from 76 percent to 48 percent. The Jews would be a minority in their own country, the very situation they fought to avoid in 1948, and which the UN expressly ruled out in deciding on a partition of Palestine. Even Israelis on the far left are unwilling to accept this suicidal formula.

The Palestinian position also makes no sense from a nationalist perspective. If the Palestinians are entitled to and achieve a state in the West Bank and Gaza Strip, how can they want 4 million of their people to live in another state? Even respected Palestinian leaders have begun to acknowledge that it is a mistake to insist that millions of refugees move to Israel. Palestinian intellectual Sari Nusseibeh, for example, said the refugees should be resettled in a future Palestinian state, "not in a way that would undermine the existence of the State of Israel as a predominantly Jewish state. Otherwise, what does a two-state solution mean?"[8]

In the context of a peace settlement, Israel could be expected to accept some refugees, as Ben-Gurion said he would do more than 50 years ago. If and when a Palestinian state is created, however, most, if not all of the refugees should be allowed to move there. The Palestinian leadership has expressed little interest in absorbing these people, a huge problem that they haven't even begun to address.

The last of the final status issues is Jerusalem. Often described as the most intractable issue of all precisely because of one of the central premises of this book—the dispute over the city is not purely political. If it was just a political problem, it would be simple: most of the Jews live in West Jerusalem and most of the Arabs live in East Jerusalem, so divide the city roughly in half. That can't be done because East Jerusalem includes the Old City, which brings the element of religion into the equation. The Western Wall, Judaism's holiest place, is in Jerusalem. For Christians, it is the site of the death, burial, and resurrection of Jesus Christ. Muslims believe that Muhammad made his night flight with the angel Gabriel to the throne of god from Jerusalem (though Muhammad never physically set foot in Jerusalem). Geography also matters because the Temple Mount where the Dome of the Rock and al-Aqsa Mosque sit is literally on top of the Western Wall and the Church of the Holy Sepulcher is around the corner. History matters as well. Jews know that for the 19 years that Jordan controlled the Old City they were denied access to their shrines (as were Israeli Christians). The Jordanians also desecrated Jewish synagogues, used tombstones from the holy Mount of Olives cemetery for paving stones and buildings, and generally showed no respect for the Jewish connection to the city. Few Israelis are prepared to trust another authority to protect their rights in the city.

It is sometimes suggested that the city be internationalized on the ground that it is holy to the three major religions and should be under no one faith's control. Again, history matters because Israel has seen the way its interests are treated by the United Nations and it is hard to imagine any other international overseer that would be acceptable to all the parties. And why should Jerusalem, alone among all the cities of the world, be under outside authority?

Critics protest that freedom of religion and access must be insured. Of course it must. And the only time in history when all people and faiths have had such freedom is in the years since Israel took control of the city. Consider the story you didn't read in the fall of 2006, the one about Muslims observing the holy month of Ramadan. More than 100,000 of the faithful gathered to pray on the Temple Mount, but you probably didn't hear about it because there were no violent incidents, no stones were thrown, and no Israelis acted improperly, so there was nothing negative for the media to report. This is an annual example of how Israel administers the city.

The Palestinians say that Jerusalem must be their capital, but is there a reason to accept this just because that is their demand? Jerusalem was never under their control and was never the capital of any state other than Israel in its 3,000-year history. Still, Ehud Barak offered to allow the Palestinians to establish their capital in part of the city. Arafat rejected the proposal and Barak was subsequently defeated by Ariel Sharon in the next election in what was seen as a referendum on Barak's willingness to divide Jerusalem. Sharon's landslide victory suggested that most Israelis were not prepared to accept such a compromise.

Israel may refuse to give up any part of what it considers its eternal capital, and the wall currently being built around Jerusalem is further cementing its hold on the city. Nevertheless, the contours of a future agreement were laid out in prior negotiations that would allow the Palestinians to establish their capital in a suburb of Jerusalem known as Abu Dis. In fact, the Palestinians have already constructed a building for their parliament in the city and the Israelis carefully constructed the Jerusalem wall so that Abu Dis is just on the other side. It is a reasonable compromise because the Palestinians can still claim their capital is in Jerusalem and the Israelis can keep their existing capital without sacrificing any part of the city that holds real significance for them. Is it a great solution? No. The Palestinians will still be unhappy because they dream of flying their flag over the Temple Mount. And it's not ideal for Israel because that area of the city is literally a stone's throw away and it will be risky to give up the area. Still, it is the most plausible compromise offered to date.

✡

Israel would like to reach agreement on these issues through negotiations, but it has become increasingly clear that no Palestinian has the power or the will to negotiate such a deal. The conclusion that Israel had no partner for peace combined with the serious demographic imbalance led Sharon to make the momentous decision to act unilaterally and evacuate all of the Jewish civilians and soldiers from Gaza. His successor, Ehud Olmert subsequently ran for prime minister on the platform of additional unilateral steps in the West Bank, which he referred to as "realignment." According to this plan, Israel would withdraw from most settlements while holding onto five settlement blocks if no agreement can be negotiated with the Palestinians.

Shortly after Olmert's election, however, the Palestinians decided to instigate new hostilities. For the previous 10 months following disengagement, the Palestinians had fired rockets from the Gaza Strip at civilian targets in Israel. Despite this incitement, Israel responded with great restraint, sending no troops into Gaza and focusing most of its counterstrikes on terrorists responsible for the ongoing violence. When the Palestinians took the additional belligerent steps of killing several soldiers on Israel's side of the border and kidnapping a young soldier, it was no longer possible to wait for the Palestinians to act responsibly and put an end to the provocations. The decision was made to launch an operation to secure the release of the soldier and stop the rocket attacks.

The situation was further exacerbated by Hizbollah's attack and kidnapping of two more Israeli soldiers a few months later, an act of aggression that once again had occurred after Israel had unilaterally withdrawn from territory. The promise of land for peace once again proved to be an illusion. The end of occupation brought only more terror. This turned Israeli public opinion against the idea of further unilateral steps and Olmert shelved his plan. Yet again, the Palestinians blew an opportunity to improve their lives and move closer to independence.

A unilateral approach remains Israel's best option, a view I've held since April 1988 when I wrote in *Commentary* that Israel should unilaterally withdraw from the territories. At the time, it was a heretical idea that few voiced. Many Israelis, Sharon, and Olmert, still opposed the creation of a Palestinian state, and the argument that Jordan was the Palestinian state was prevalent. I argued that "Israel would be ridding itself of the need to rule over another people, with all the degenerative effects that such a policy entails" and that it would "remain strong enough to counter any threat." This is still true.

It is not surprising that unilateralism has fallen out of favor given what followed the withdrawals from Lebanon and Gaza. The chaos in Gaza, the rampant arms smuggling, the ongoing terror and rocket attacks, and the prospect of the Palestinians obtaining more sophisticated weapons, such as those used by Hizbollah, have increased the risks to Israel's security.

Israel cannot avoid choosing among bad alternatives, which remain the same as before—annexation, transfer, negotiation, status quo, or unilateral action. I would argue that none of those options are better than unilateral action. By acting unilaterally Israel can define its borders in a way that creates greater security than it has today and that would inevitably be more favorable than any the Palestinians would accept in negotiations. Israel should immediately complete the security fence, which is taking years longer to finish than expected, and then evacuate all Israelis behind it. As it is, the fence actually creates two classes of Israelis, those who are protected inside the fence and those outside it.

Curiously enough, given the international outcry over the fence, it was actually Jews who were the first to complain about its construction. When I spoke to pro-Israel groups, people would ask, "How can you build a fence? It's impractical. It's unfeasible. It won't protect anyone." I would point out that Israel already had similar fences along its borders with Lebanon, Syria, and Jordan. In the years since their construction, these barriers have proved very effective in preventing infiltrations. One danger the fence cannot stop, as Hizbollah demonstrated in Lebanon, is rockets. The threat from the West Bank would be particularly acute because the major population and industrial centers, as well as the capital and the international airport, would be in the line of fire. Since no defense exists against short-range rockets, Israel will remain susceptible to aerial bombardment. On the other hand, the war in Lebanon also demonstrated that missiles fly in both directions and that Israel has far more powerful and accurate weapons with which to respond to provocation.

While the construction of the fence generated international opprobrium, there is nothing unusual about a fence demarcating a border and providing security. Similar fences exist all over the world, including countries that were most outspoken in criticizing Israel's fence. Spain built a fence, with European Union funding, to separate its enclaves of Ceuta and Melilla from Morocco to prevent poor people from sub-Saharan Africa from entering Europe. India constructed a 460-mile barrier in Kashmir to halt infiltrations supported by Pakistan. Saudi Arabia built a 60-mile barrier along an undefined border zone with Yemen to halt arms smuggling and announced plans to build another fence along the frontier with Iraq. Turkey built a barrier in the southern province of Alexandretta, which was formerly in Syria and is an area that Syria claims as its own. In Cyprus, the UN sponsored a security fence reinforcing the island's de facto partition. British-built barriers separate Catholic and Protestant neighborhoods in Belfast. And, lastly, the United States is building a fence to keep out illegal Mexican immigrants. Ironically, after condemning Israel's barrier, the UN announced plans to build its own fence to improve security around its New York headquarters.

The more serious argument was not over whether to build the fence but where to put it. Critics have said that Israel has no right to build on disputed land, that the fence should be along the Green Line. This also would have been problematic, because it would have suggested a future border that is unacceptable to the Israeli government. To put the fence on that line would also have contradicted the Israeli position that the barrier was being constructed for security rather than political reasons. To be an effective deterrent to terror, the fence route had to be based on where it would save the most lives, not on where it would create the least political uproar. Still, Palestinians and Israeli Arabs have had recourse to the courts to protest the route and the Israeli Supreme Court has ruled that a balance must be struck between security needs and harm to the civilian population. The court subsequently ruled that the fence had to be rerouted in some locations. This has slowed construction and led the government to take the court's ruling into account as it planned the final stages of the project.

Israelis themselves never wanted a fence. It's a blight on the landscape and an admission that their dream of open borders with friendly neighbors remains a fantasy. Still, they waited 35 years before taking such a drastic step, and then only after suicide bombers had killed and maimed thousands of innocent people. Even now, the fence does not mean that peace is impossible. If the Palestinians break with their past and seize the opportunity to reach an agreement, the fence can be moved, opened, or torn down.

While calling for a unilateral withdrawal that would allow the Palestinians to create a state, I am under no illusions about the prospects for coexistence. The Palestinians may build up their state, as suggested earlier, to increase the chance of confronting Israel down the road. It would be in their interest, however, not to provoke Israel to return to the West Bank or Gaza. Unfortunately, history shows the Palestinians may not behave in the way others consider rational. Following disengagement, for example, they acted against their political and economic interests by continuing their terror campaign and compelling Israel to resume military operations in Gaza.

Even in the best case, Israel has to assume a Palestinian state could turn hostile. Leftists who long ago called for the creation of a Palestinian state naively believed that it could be demilitarized. There is little chance the Palestinians would accept such a severe restriction on their sovereignty or that they would fulfill such a commitment even if they did accept it. Israel and Jordan will have to use whatever means they can to prevent the Palestinians from building up a credible military capability. Jordan will be just as concerned that the Palestinians might turn their guns to the east as the Israelis are that they might turn west.

Another leftist delusion is that once the Palestinians have a state, the two states will be viewed as equals and any aggressive move by the Palestinians would be rightly viewed by the international community as a violation.

Rather than a state fighting a stateless people, the argument goes, two equal states will be at war and then Israel's actions will be legitimate. Sounds good in theory, but in practice it will never happen. The Israelis learned from their recent Lebanon experience that even when the whole world acknowledges it has been wronged, the weight of international opinion will ultimately turn against them.

This chapter has focused on the dispute with the Palestinians. Israel also would like to reach agreements with Syria and Lebanon. Because Syria still influences Lebanon, it is unlikely that country can negotiate with Israel before Israel and Syria make peace. I discussed in earlier chapters the geographic and water issues related to the Golan Heights; the fact is several Israeli prime ministers have laid out the details of a peace agreement with Syria. They have expressed a willingness to meet the Syrian demand for a return of most, if not all, of the Golan but only in exchange for a full peace. Neither Bashir Assad nor his father were prepared to make that commitment. Consequently, unless Assad has a change of heart or a new leader emerges, it is unlikely any treaty will be signed. From Israel's perspective, this is not such a bad thing because the Syrians have kept the border quiet since 1973 and Israel remains on the strategic high ground with its water supply reasonably assured. The downside remains Syria's continued support for terrorists in the Palestinian Authority and Lebanon, which would be expected to cease once peace was achieved. For now and for the foreseeable future, Israel can live with the status quo on its northern border.

Nothing Israel does is without risk, and there is no perfect peace. Israelis will ultimately have to decide if they agree with my view that they can get more peace with less risk by acting unilaterally than by hoping for the emergence of a negotiating partner or maintaining the status quo. It is the Israelis who serve in the army and send their children to serve who must ultimately make the decisions and live with the consequences, so I will not be offended if they do not heed my advice.

Chapter 8

A Civil War

FOR YEARS JEWS USED TO SPECULATE THAT IF THERE WERE EVER PEACE IN THE Middle East, the Arabs would probably resort to killing each other because of their religious, political, and historical rivalries. In recent years, however, it has been more common to worry that it is the Israelis who might tear themselves apart if peace was achieved with their neighbors. Strains within Israel have been growing between Israelis on the right and left of the political spectrum, between Arabs and Jews, and between religious and secular Jews. As Israeli scholar Maoz Azaryahu noted, "In Israel, Jews are not 'tolerated,' but asked to be tolerant of others."[1]

When asked in 2006 about the source of internal divisions in Israel, 42 percent of Israelis blamed politicians, 39 percent the media and 9 percent the rabbinical establishment. When asked which events most influenced society's polarization, 48 percent said the disengagement and 39 percent Rabin's assassination. The disengagement probably was rated first because the memory of the rawness of emotions in the period before and during the evacuation from Gaza was still fresh. When I arrived in Israel in August 2005, tensions had been building for months as the disengagement approached. Few Jews living in the Gaza communities had left because they still thought that either Prime Minister Ariel Sharon would change his mind or the opposition of their supporters would force the government to back down. Rallies were being held and Jews from other parts of the country were infiltrating Gaza to prepare for a possible showdown with the army.

Thousands of journalists from around the world landed in the country to join the already large existing pool of reporters based in Israel. They came expecting to see a blood bath. For months, hyperbolic reports had suggested that Israel was on the verge of a civil war and the international press wanted a front row seat to the implosion of the Jewish state. But no civil war occurred.

On the contrary, what I saw was the triumph of democracy and an example for people in the Middle East and throughout the world. The democratically elected government of Israel had made a painful and risky decision to disengage from Gaza. It did so with the approval of the popularly elected parliament and the support of a majority of the public. The minority exercised its right to protest and tried to change the decision by petitioning their representatives in the Knesset and lobbying members of the cabinet. They took their case to the independent judiciary and were heard by the nation's highest court. The opponents of disengagement used their rights of free speech and assembly to demonstrate. Thousands of people exercised their freedom of religion at the Western Wall and tried to go over the head of the government to a higher authority.

When it was time to implement the disengagement, it was carried out with professionalism and sensitivity. Instead of taking two months, as the original plan called for, it took less than a week. The operation went remarkably smoothly with the exception of a few instances, most of which involved agitators from outside Gaza who ignored the wishes of the residents and engaged in activity that crossed the line of legitimate protest.

The settlers literally had made the desert bloom with flowers, fruits, and vegetables in areas where the Arabs have produced little more than discontent. And the settlements themselves were beautiful. I went to a place called Miami Beach, and if I showed you a picture of it, you'd think it was in Florida—except for the armored personnel carriers the army had moved into the beach-front hotel. In the northern settlement of Elie Sinai, I went into the home of a man who had been evicted from Yamit in 1982. He lived in a magnificent house with a spectacular view of the sea. Anywhere else, it would probably be a multimillion dollar villa, but in Gaza it was a target. Around the corner was a woman who had lived in the settlement for 18 years in a house she and her husband had built with their own hands. She was packing all her possessions. The Keren Kayemet took one of her trees—each family was allowed to have one tree transplanted to Israel—and she was now trying to figure out what to do with her birds. She had an aviary with dozens of birds and no idea what to do with them.

In Netzer Hazzani, I spoke to a grandmother who had come to Gaza 30 years earlier, when there was nothing there but sand dunes. She couldn't understand why she should have to leave.

In Neve Dekalim, I spoke to two young women who assured me they wouldn't have to move because the messiah was coming. It reminded me of the scene in *Fiddler on the Roof* when the residents are leaving Anatevka and one man asks the rabbi if it would be a good time for the messiah to come, and the rabbi tells him they'll have to wait for him somewhere else. Down the road was the cemetery with the graves of 48 Israelis, including several terror victims. They had to be dug up and moved into Israel, and the families of the dead had to go through a new period of mourning.

I'm not sure Americans fully appreciated how traumatic it was for Israelis to uproot Zionist pioneers. In a country as small as Israel, nearly everyone had some connection to the settlers; they were friends, relatives, comrades in arms. It was surprising to find that Jews who never thought the settlements should be there in the first place sympathized with people who had been encouraged by their government to live in one of the most dangerous places on earth. Every Israeli was aware that the Jews in Gaza were at risk for one reason—because they were Jews.

Though the withdrawal of Jews from Gaza (and four small settlements in the West Bank) went more smoothly than most people expected, it required 50,000 Israeli soldiers and police officers to evacuate 8,500 Jews. What will happen when Israel attempts to remove some of the more than 60,000 Israeli settlers on the "wrong side" of the security fence?

This question highlights the political chasm between Israelis on the right and the left.

Settlers should not be lumped in a single category but rather three separate ones—security, economic, and religious. Many of the Jews were encouraged by the state to settle in the territories because of a belief that strategically located outposts were needed to protect the borders against future attack. Most Jews who moved to the territories in the last three decades did so more for economic reasons. The government offered fiscal incentives, such as low-cost mortgages, and most of the towns these Jews moved to were essentially bedroom communities just beyond the Green Line within easy commuting distance to jobs in the major cities. The third group of settlers, those who moved primarily for religious reasons, are the ones who have created the greatest internal threat to civil society; some feel alienated from the state, reject its legitimacy, and believe they answer only to divine authority. For the more extreme religious settlers, what is important is the *land* of Israel rather than the *state* of Israel. They do not believe any government has any right to give up territory promised to the Jewish people by God. And even among this already zealous group, many of the youth have become even more radicalized and, in some cases, violent. They were among the Jews who went to Gaza to fight the disengagement and who fight soldiers trying to remove illegal settlements; they also sometimes attack Palestinians or their property. Most of the settlers are not violent but have now lived in their homes for decades and will be particularly resistant to removal.

In addition to the settlers (and including some of them), Jews on the far right of Israel's political spectrum advocate the expulsion of the Palestinians in the territories and, in the most extreme cases, they also advocate the transfer of Israeli Arabs. These Israelis believe Israel's future is threatened by the weakness and indecisiveness of leaders on the moderate right who fail to recognize that the Arabs only understand force. They have no doubt Israel can prevail over its enemies by military action. Jews from this school of thought dismiss those on the left as hopeless romantics and appeasers whose policies would hasten Israel's destruction.

On the opposite pole are Israelis who believe it is the Jews in the territories who need to be expelled from their homes and forcibly, if necessary, brought within the borders of the state. The Israeli left sees the militant settlers as people who behave as though they are above the law and who have often been treated that way. According to these Israelis, the settlers unnecessarily provoke the Palestinians and are the principal obstacle to peace. Furthermore, the far left sees the entire occupation as immoral and having a corrosive effect on the values of the nation and, especially, on soldiers who must carry out what they see as often brutal and humiliating policies that dehumanize the Palestinians and the soldiers. Some Israelis have risked going to jail by refusing to perform their army service in the territories; few have actually been prosecuted and all express a willingness to do their duty elsewhere. The leftists tend to ignore the reality of Palestinian terrorism and Islamism and the lessons of past failed negotiations.

The political divisions are sometimes portrayed as particularly acute, but they are not really new. Long before Israel controlled the West Bank, Zionists such as David Ben-Gurion and Ze'ev Jabotinsky disagreed over the boundaries of a Jewish state, with Jabotinsky insisting that Jews fight for the entire historic homeland and Ben-Gurion accepting a diplomatic compromise. A civil war nearly did erupt in the first months of statehood when the armed paramilitary force inspired by Jabotinsky and led by Menachem Begin resisted Ben-Gurion's call for all forces to be united under the new Israel Defense Forces. Begin's Irgun tried to bring a shipload of arms aboard the *Altalena* into Tel Aviv and Ben-Gurion ordered his forces to stop them; a fierce gun battle ensued that left 16 Irgun fighters and 3 IDF soldiers dead. Israel survived the trauma of Jews fighting Jews in 1948 and Ariel Sharon was prepared to risk a civil war as well when he agreed to the disengagement. Fortunately, the desire of the Jewish people for unity and security in their homeland proved stronger than the impulses to divide the nation.

Parallel to the political divisions in the country, Jews have also found themselves at odds over whether Israel should be a Jewish state or a state of the Jews. "For centuries before this one, the Torah is what united Jews everywhere," Adam Garfinkle observed. "In Israel today, the Torah is what divides Jews."[2]

When the state was founded, the Zionist leadership and the religious leaders of the community could not agree on a constitution for Israel. The former wanted a document similar to that of the United States, which was based on the rights and laws derived by men and women, and the latter insisted that the Jewish people already had a code of laws known as the Torah. That basic disagreement has remained the impediment to the adoption of a constitution to this day. The compromise that was struck at the outset, which remains in effect, was that the status quo in religious affairs would be maintained whereby religious courts would be responsible for matters of personal status—marriage, divorce, conversion, adoption—and the state would make laws to govern the nation. To avoid a split in the community that might have prevented the establishment of the state, the Zionist leaders also agreed that government institutions would operate according to the Jewish calendar and observe religious holidays, as well as financially support religious schools and exempt religious women and yeshiva students from military service.

As in the territorial compromises Israel accepted for statehood, Ben-Gurion recognized that it was more important to achieve a state with the

Jewish people united than to allow divisions to delay independence or weaken the nation. The compromises were acceptable to most Jews who understood that Israel must be a Jewish state and that meant adopting at least some religious symbols and traditions. In reality, a consensus exists that Israelis should be familiar with Jewish religion, customs, and history.

Extreme secularists favor the complete separation of religion and state while the religious extremists would like the state to be governed by *halacha* (Jewish law). Unlike Muslim countries that insist that all Muslims conduct their personal and public lives in accordance with Muslim law, the religious Jews are concerned with the observance of *halacha* in public life, though this often has implications for private life as well. For example, the Orthodox have successfully managed to restrict the sale of pork (pigs cannot be raised on Israeli soil, so they are raised on platforms so their hoofs don't touch the ground) and the use of public transportation on the Sabbath. Given the choice, they would eliminate the discretion municipalities have to decide their own rules about the Sabbath, would strengthen the rabbinical courts' role in matters of personal status, would require all restaurants to be kosher, and would change the definition of who is a Jew for the purpose of the Law of Return (which grants automatic citizenship to Jews) so that only Jews converted according to Orthodox conventions would qualify. For these religious Jews, adherence to Jewish law is a prerequisite for having a Jewish state.

Secular Jews object, however, to what they see as religious coercion. They believe they should have the right to make their own decisions as to how to behave and what to believe. Author Amos Oz observed that secular Israelis dream of an "enlightened, open and just country, not in some messianic, rabbinic monarchy, and not in the whole land of Israel." He added, "To be a free people in our land . . . means each person decides which parts of Jewish tradition are important to him, and which to leave behind. It means to have the freedom to run our country according to our free will, rather than rabbinic dictates."[3]

The secular Israelis also resent the fact that a small minority of the country have the power to impose their religious beliefs on the nation. Together, the number of religious Jews is roughly equal to the number of Arabs (a little more than one million), and only about 25 percent of all religious Jews are ultra-Orthodox (called *haredi* in Israel, which literally means fearful, as in a person who fears the word of God), which is approximately 5 percent of the entire population of Israel. *Haredim* believe they have a special relationship with God and strictly interpret Jewish law. Unlike religious Zionists who support the state, the ultra-Orthodox do not believe a Jewish state can be established until the coming of the messiah. They live in Israel for religious, not political, reasons and usually seek exemptions from military service to allow the men to spend their time studying in a yeshiva.

According to an October 2006 poll by the Gesher organization, 37 percent of Israelis consider *haredim* the most hated group in Israel, compared with 15 percent who said new immigrants from the former Soviet Union and 13 percent who said settlers.[4] Secular Israelis do not like the idea that they are risking their lives for the state, which also protects the ultra-Orthodox, while the *haredim* not only sit in their yeshivas praying, but also receive government services and subsidies, often without working, paying taxes, or making any other contribution to society. From the religious perspective, the *haredim* are helping to preserve the Jewish people by their study of Torah and by their prayers for those who do fight. The army serves as a melting pot to bring Israelis of all backgrounds together, but this is precisely what the *haredim* fear will corrupt their youth. While secular Israelis see westernization and progress as a positive development, the ultra-Orthodox view it as a source of evil influences.

The hatred between secular and ultra-Orthodox Jews is mutual, as the *haredim* see non-*haredim*, which includes Jews who may be religious but not religious enough to meet their standards, as the cause of Israel's misfortunes and the catalysts for assimilation and the ultimate destruction of the Jewish people. The most extreme elements of the *haredi* community, the Neturei Karta, oppose the existence of the state, compare Zionism with Nazism and frequently ally themselves with Israel's enemies. Aharon Rose, a researcher on *haredim* at Hebrew University, said many *haredi* leaders do not mind that they are hated because it helps them "keep their society separate from the general culture." It also makes it "easier to keep the kids inside haredi society."[5]

Unlike the *haredim*, who wear black hats and long coats, speak Yiddish, avoid army service and isolate themselves in closed communities, most religious Israelis are modern Orthodox Jews who dress in western clothes, wear knitted yarmulkes, serve in the army and integrate with other Israelis. Ultra-Orthodox women usually don't work outside the home, and the married women shave their heads and wear wigs. Modern Orthodox women cover their hair in public but don't wear wigs, and many work outside the home.

Secular and modern Orthodox Jews rarely conflict with one another because they are not very concerned with imposing their values on each other. Most secular Jews also have religion as a part of their lives. They are usually born, circumcised, bar mitzvah'd, married, divorced, and buried according to Jewish religious law. In school, they study Jewish history, traditions, culture, philosophy, and literature, so even the most secular Israeli is typically far more knowledgeable about their heritage than American Jews. While this level of connection to Judaism is acceptable, they do not want rabbis telling them what they can do on the Sabbath, where and what they can eat, and when public transportation will be available.

Most secular Jews are respectful of the sensitivities of observant Israelis, and do not care if restrictions are enforced in religious neighborhoods. Problems arise when the two live in close proximity and values clash. For example, when the mayor in the town of Petah Tikvah decided the movie theater in the town could stay open on the Sabbath, religious Jews mounted demonstrations that were sometimes met by usually smaller numbers of secular counterdemonstrators. Hyperbolic warnings of civil war were heard even though the rest of the country was unaffected by the uproar. The demonstrations continued for more than three years, but the cinema remained opened and the threats proved groundless.

For the most part, extremists on both sides avoid contact with each other. Totally secular neighborhoods are rarely penetrated by the *haredim*, with the exception of Jerusalem where ultra-Orthodox families are purchasing more and more property and expanding their presence into areas where the population is predominantly nonreligious. This has sparked fears that the city will one day become completely religious and that the types of restrictions observed in *haredi* neighborhoods such as Mea Shearim (e.g., prohibitions on the use of cars and buses on the Sabbath and expectations that women will dress modestly) will spread. Secular Israelis increasingly feel uncomfortable in their own capital.

A separate issue involves divisions between Jews in Israel and in the diaspora, which some may argue also threatens Israel's survival, that are sparked only occasionally when the "Who is a Jew?" question is raised and when public slights are directed at American Reform and Conservative Jewish leaders by (secular and religious) Israelis. Rank-and-file American Jews seem less concerned and are only marginally affected by the religious debates. The movements, however, have been engaged in long struggles to obtain recognition in Israel. Reform and Conservative schools, seminaries, and synagogues have been established, but relatively few native Israelis have joined them. The split in Israel is typically between those who are observant and those who are not; the gradations common in the U.S. do not exist in Israel. The conflict with diaspora Jews is an issue for Israelis only insofar as it reflects the intolerance and appetite for power of the Israeli religious authorities.

The proportion of secular to *haredi* Jews shifted even further over the last 15 years as one million mostly secular Jews arrived from the former Soviet Union. In addition, the majority of religious Jews do not have extreme beliefs and have little conflict with secular Israelis. Similarly, most secular Israelis recognize and even want the state to have Jewish religious elements. The divisions are also minimized by the overarching security dilemma. As a result, most Israeli Jews live in relative peace and should continue to do so.

A more serious question is whether Israeli Jews and Israeli Arabs will continue to live in peace. This has only become an issue in the last few years after decades of relative harmony. In the early days of the state, some suspicion naturally existed that the Arabs who chose to stay in Israel during and after the 1948 war would become a fifth column. The other Arab states believed at the time that is exactly the role the Israeli Arabs would play. Instead, Israeli Arabs proved to be extremely loyal citizens who did not engage in any subversive activities, even during wartime, that threatened the nation's security.

By law, Arab citizens of Israel are treated equally with Jews, with the lone exception of their exemption from military service that all but the Druze and a handful of other Arabs accepted. Although the Israelis may have been worried about Arab loyalty in war, the reason given for exempting them from the army was to spare them the possibility of fighting against their brethren. The positive side for the Arabs was that exemption allowed them to work or go to school while Jews were doing their compulsory service. On the other hand, military service is an important socializing experience to bring Israelis of all walks of life together, and it is a catalyst for imbuing a sense of responsibility to the nation. Army service also has historically influenced careers because employers routinely look at their applicants' military records, and personal relationships developed in the military often provide networking opportunities. Former soldiers are also eligible for certain government benefits that are denied to those who do not serve.

Because they live with Jews, the Israeli Arabs generally have more moderate opinions toward Jews than other Arabs. Israel's Arabs have benefited from living in a democracy where they have rights that are denied to their fellow Arabs under the Palestinian Authority and elsewhere in the Arab world. They can become members of the Knesset and other political bodies. Israeli Arab women have equal rights under the law, something unheard of in Muslim countries. The national languages of Israel are Hebrew and Arabic, and Arabs have their own schools where they learn about their history and culture in Arabic. Many individual Arabs have been successful in business, politics, and entertainment. Arabs, for example, have been appointed to the Supreme Court and have won the Miss Israel contest. They also have a better standard of living than most Arab citizens of other countries. Christian Arabs, in particular, recognize that they have freedom to practice their religion and much more secure lives in Israel than they would anywhere else in the region. Israel allows them to use their own schools and books, something unlikely elsewhere. The Christian Arabs also see Israel as a one of the last lines of defense against militant Islam in the region.

Most Israeli Arabs are not proud of their citizenship (56 percent) and are not ready to fight to defend the state (73 percent), according to the 2006 Herzliya Patriotism Survey. The number of Arabs who are proud of the social welfare system (53 percent), however, is three times higher than the percentage of Jews (17 percent). And the percent of Arab Israelis who believe Israel is better than most other countries in the world (77 percent) is among the highest in the developed world.[6]

For all these reasons, it is not surprising that Israeli Arabs vehemently oppose suggestions that any of their towns be included in any exchange of territory with the Palestinian Authority. Much like American Zionists, the Israeli Arabs believe in the importance of the establishment of a state, but much prefer the comfort of the one they live in to any new "homeland."

While all this is true, it is also the case that Israeli Jews and Israeli Arabs live largely segregated lives. With the exception of a few mixed cities, such as Haifa, and the universities, most Arabs do not live, work, or go to school with Jews. And both communities prefer this. Jews and Arabs want to retain their cultural values and uniqueness and neither are pressing for any type of desegregation.

Many Jews do want to increase lines of communication and promote tolerance and coexistence, and a large number of projects exist to advance these goals. I studied several of them a few years ago and one of the most interesting findings was that not one of the programs was stimulated by the Arabs; they were all created by Jews. This is a fairly consistent theme in relations between Jews and Muslims, not only in Israel but elsewhere. The Jews crave peace and are desperate for acceptance, while the Arabs and Muslims may be willing to go along with a program but will not initiate any themselves. The other conclusion I drew from my research was that the most successful projects did not involve head-on discussions of political issues; rather, they brought people together for activities that allowed them to get to know each other so that they would develop personal relationships, which made it easier to discuss controversial issues.[7]

Rather than grow closer, other signs point to growing alienation among Israeli Arabs. Israeli Jewish intellectuals tried to work out a shared vision of the future with Israeli Arab leaders but discovered the Arabs were unwilling to recognize Israel as a Jewish state. Instead, at the end of 2006, a group of Israeli Arabs produced a document titled, "The Future Vision of Palestinian Arabs in Israel," which laid out a radical agenda to eliminate or minimize the Jewish and Zionist character of Israel and create what amounts to a binational state. According to this vision, Israeli Arabs would have the right to veto decisions on domestic issues that concern them as a group and to exercise greater autonomy over their affairs. The state would also be stripped of its symbols—the flag with the Star of David and the "Hatikvah" anthem, which expresses the Jewish yearning through the ages for a return to Zion.

Under the Israeli Arab scenario, after the Palestinians achieve statehood in the West Bank and Gaza, they will effectively have one-and-a-half states while the Jews have only half a state. Given the demographic dilemma, it is conceivable the Palestinians could ultimately have two states while the Jews have none (to add to the absurdity, given the Palestinian majority in Jordan, it could be argued the Palestinians would go from stateless to three states).

After building up goodwill over the years by their loyalty, the Israeli Arab community provoked new fears during the years of the Palestinian war when violence broke out in a number of Israeli towns and some Israeli Arabs were arrested for assisting Palestinians in terrorist activities. Jews in some mixed towns were especially traumatized when they saw that neighbors, whom they had spent a lifetime living and working with, rioted and expressed sympathy for attacks against Israel. The trust that had been established will be difficult to restore.

Signs of the growing Islamization of Israeli Arabs is also alarming. As in Gaza, the Islamic organizations are winning hearts and minds in Israeli Arab towns by providing services the government, and Arab Knesset members, have failed to supply. This social welfare behavior is coupled with increasingly hostile rhetoric. For example, Sheikh Reed Salah, head of the northern faction of Israel's Islamic Movement, told a rally of 50,000 people at Umm el-Fahm in September 2006, "Soon Jerusalem will be the capital of the new Muslim caliphate." If this type of rhetoric is followed by action, the probability of terrorism from within Israel increases as will the possibility of Muslim extremists winning seats in the Knesset.

The increasing identification of Israeli Arabs with the Palestinians in the territories also worries Israeli Jews who have to wonder what will happen as the demographic balance tilts more in the Palestinians' favor. The Israeli Arabs, who already represent 20 percent of the population, could take advantage of Israel's democracy to gain a significant share of power in the government if they were to ever vote as a bloc and form a single Arab or Islamic party list. Instead of winning a handful of seats that are spread across multiple parties, a single party might win 15 or 20 seats, which would make it one of the larger parties in the Knesset and potentially make it a partner in a governing coalition.

The prospect for radicalizing the Israeli Arab population is exacerbated by the inequalities that exist between Jews and Arabs, particularly in funding for municipalities. During the war with Hizbollah, when Arab towns in Israel came under attack, it was learned that many did not have shelters or sirens or other means of civil defense available to Jewish towns (in Nazareth, where two Arab children were killed in a Hizbollah rocket attack, sirens were in place, but had been turned off so the mostly Arab townspeople would not be disturbed when they sounded to commemorate Israel Memorial Day and Holocaust Remembrance Day). With the exception of a handful of statements by some of the more radical Arab leaders, including Kresset member Azmi Bishara, who led a delegation to Lebanon and Syria to express solidarity with Israel's enemies, most Israeli Arabs again demonstrated their loyalty to the state by their behavior. They also shared in the suffering as almost half the civilian deaths were Arabs. If the Arab minority becomes more embittered about their treatment by the Jewish majority, the internal security situation in Israel could take a dramatic turn for the worse. Israeli Jews recognize the problem and have increasingly, if belatedly, focused on it. Greater efforts are being made to equalize the funding for Jewish and Arab towns, schools and infrastructure, and to create more economic, employment and educational opportunities for Arab citizens. Everyone recognizes much more needs to be done.

The poll cited earlier placed the most responsibility for the divisions in Israel on the politicians. While overwhelming majorities of Israelis take great pride in their security forces (86 percent) and their scientific and technological achievements (97 percent), only 38 percent of Israelis have faith in the way their democracy works. On my last trip to Israel, the theme that was most prevalent was that the country's leaders were corrupt, incompetent, and uninspiring, and that no new visionary politicians were on the horizon. With Shimon Peres, the last of the founding generation of politicians, leadership has been turned over to a group viewed as mediocrities. Politics has become so unattractive that the best and brightest in Israel are going into business rather than sully themselves in the political arena.

Granted, Israel had just come out of a traumatic war with Hizbollah when the poll was conducted, but the feeling that the country's leadership is not what it should be has been steadily growing after what were considered the disastrous tenures of one-term prime ministers Benjamin Netanyahu and Ehud Barak. Interestingly, those two individuals were the first leaders to come from the second generation of Israelis after the founders who fought for independence. Both had also come to office with high expectations. Netanyahu had gained prominence on the international stage as Israel's premier spokesperson and proved himself a savvy politician within Israel while Barak was known for his intelligence and his reputation as Israel's most decorated soldier. Not surprisingly, the man who came to the rescue was from the old guard, Ariel Sharon, who Israelis believed would protect the nation at all costs. Equally important was the fact that whether they agreed with him or not, Israelis were confident he could get things done.

Sharon proved this by carrying out the disengagement, but when he became incapacitated by illness, he was replaced by another of the young guard, Ehud Olmert. Meanwhile, the leader of the Labor Party was a political neophyte, Amir Peretz, a successful union organizer who burst on the national scene by placing socioeconomic issues ahead of security concerns in his campaign. Having no experience in national affairs, Peretz had an opportunity to implement his societal vision as a member of Olmert's government but chose instead to try to advance his personal ambition to be prime minister. Lacking experience in security issues, a vital component for any Israeli leader's resume, Peretz looked to burnish his credentials by becoming defense minister. This decision upset many Israelis, particularly those who supported him in the hope that he would do more for the welfare state. The strategy backfired when Israel battled against Hizbollah; the unsatisfactory outcome was blamed in part on Peretz's inexperience and poor leadership.

In addition to the perceived military failures of Olmert and Peretz, a number of political scandals were swirling around the government. By the end of 2006, the president was being investigated for charges of sexual misconduct and rape and being pressured to resign; the justice minister resigned in response to allegations of sexual harassment (and was later convicted); the prime minister was accused of corruption; the IDF chief of staff made questionable stock deals on the day that Israeli soldiers were captured in Lebanon and resigned under pressure; a prominent politician was prevented from becoming a minister and was accused of cronyism while in an earlier assignment as minister of the environment; and several senior police officers were accused of a range of misdeeds.

With no visionary or charismatic leaders on the horizon, Israelis increasingly say they would like to see technocrats enter the government to clean up the corruption and to simply make the government work. On the other hand, one of the lessons of the war of 2006 was that Israel cannot afford to have leaders who lack experience in military affairs at the top of the government. Following the war, 70 percent of Israelis said they could not count on the state-military leadership and 65 percent thought Israel could be surprised again as it was in 1973. Still, barring a disastrous miscalculation in dealing with security issues, Israel can survive bad leadership, but it will not achieve the peace and prosperity Israelis crave.

For some Israelis, the decay in political leadership is a reflection of a broader decline in the moral fiber of the nation. Israelis today, the argument goes, do not have the same commitment to the nation and are not prepared to make the type of sacrifices required to insure the country's survival. This was reflected in Olmert's reluctance to send ground troops into Lebanon to fight Hizbollah. While in the past Israel would have deployed the force necessary, Olmert was too afraid of casualties and did not think the nation would sustain support for the campaign if large numbers of soldiers were killed.

No one wanted to suffer casualties, but the sense was that today's Israelis, or at least their leaders, did not have the will to fight that their parents and grandparents had. This is further reflected in the perception of army service as being less important than it once was. In the old days, every Israeli (with the exceptions of some women, most Arabs, and many yeshiva students) enthusiastically served in the IDF because they understood it was part of their responsibility to defend the nation. A stigma was attached to those who did not serve, and careers were heavily influenced by one's army record.

The impression has been created that today careers are less dependent on army service and many Israelis opt out and suffer no social antagonism, though they are still viewed as missing an important social and cultural experience. Actually, much of the image of Israeli patriotism and commitment to the army is based on nostalgic myths. Even in 1948, when Israel was fighting for its independence, young Jews could be found in the coffee shops of Tel Aviv rather than the Negev desert. Today, more than 20 percent of the potential soldiers are not enlisted: 8 percent because of "religious reasons" and the rest because of psychological or medical reasons, because they are the children of people who left Israel, or because of pacifism and insubordination. Israel is not suffering from a shortage of soldiers though; in fact, the army does not need as many conscripts and does not mind the current number of dropouts.

More telling, however, may be the fact that 85 percent of Israelis said they're willing to fight for their country and that the percentage of volunteers for combat units has actually grown during the last five years, a period coinciding with the war with the Palestinians. While it is true that thousands of yeshiva students receive exemptions from service—many more than originally envisioned by Ben-Gurion when he first agreed to them to gain the support of Orthodox leaders for the original government—it is inaccurate to suggest that religious Jews do not serve their country. Setting aside the argument that the yeshiva students do their part by studying and praying, the highest percentage of combat soldiers (30 percent) is modern Orthodox and secular Sephardim while secular Ashkenazim comprise 20 percent of the forces and Russians another 20 percent. If Israelis are going soft, it's not reflected in their willingness to fight and die for their country.

Perhaps the best indication of Israel's health and true unity was the response of Israelis to the attacks by Hizbollah. For all the talk about disenchantment with the army and the reluctance of a new generation to serve and sacrifice, the response of young and old was remarkable. More than 100 percent of those called to duty reported, which means that people who did not have to fight showed up anyway to volunteer.

A look at the profiles of those soldiers who made the ultimate sacrifice also offers a window into the strength of the society. Among the 117 active and reserve soldiers who died, 12 were religious (half from settlements); 12 were immigrants from the former Soviet Union; 15 were from kibbutzim, 15 were from *moshavim* (cooperative agricultural settlement); 9 were from cities with difficult socioeconomic populations; 3 were immigrants from Ethiopia; and 3 were from Tel Aviv. In addition, 5 immigrants from the West (United States, Australia, France, and South Africa) were casualties. One of those casualties was U.S. Staff Sgt. Michael Levin. Levin had been visiting his family in Philadelphia, hanging out with his twin sister and making plans to study medicine when he finished his tour of duty with the IDF in the fall. He was hardly the stereotype of an Israeli paratrooper, the elite of Israel's soldiers. He weighed a scant 118 pounds and was so light that his comrades had to tie weights onto his pack so he could control his parachute. When Hizbollah started the war, he cut short his vacation and went to join his unit. His father saw him off from the airport in New York and Michael said: "Please don't worry about me. I'm going exactly where I want to be and doing exactly what I want to do." Michael Levin was killed on the 21st day of the war. He was 22 years old.

Perhaps 117 deaths do not seem like a large number for so short a war, but, on a comparative basis, Israel suffered the equivalent of 5,000 American dead in just three weeks of fighting. After nearly four years of war in Afghanistan and Iraq, the United States has had just over 3,000 casualties. Israel is also a tiny country where each death is felt by the nation. While Americans were fed media reports that focused mostly on what Israeli forces were doing to Lebanon, Israelis were watching funerals on their nightly news. The entire country was also united in supporting the troops and doing whatever was possible to assist the civilians under fire. People brought food, medicine, and water. Citizens who had to evacuate their homes were put up in hotels and the homes of friends, relatives, and strangers. Kids were sent to special camps in the south. Those who stayed endured living for as long as a month in a bomb shelter. Not only did people not flee the country, many Israelis returned to be with their countrymen or to join military units even if they had not been recalled. It may be argued this patriotism would dissipate if the conflict ended and Israel had to focus all its energy and attention on its internal problems, but I don't see the evidence for this occurring.

Israel is only 60 years old; it's in a postrevolutionary period. No one should expect it to have solved all its problems in six decades when the United States has not ameliorated many of the same problems in more than 230 years. Still, Israel has already made great strides, exemplified by the improvement in relations between Ashkenazi (Jews of European descent) and Sephardi (Jews of Spanish descent) and Mizrachi (Jews from Arab countries), which in the first two decades of Israeli history was a source of internal friction. By the 1980s, however, while 44 percent of Israelis said they were concerned with the secular-religious conflict, only 5 percent were worried about "ethnic" conflict.

Israel will continue to have its share of internal challenges, but the Israeli people, Jew and non-Jew, religious and secular, have proven they can live together and be a source of strength to guarantee Israel's survival.

Chapter 9

Silicon Wadi

ISRAEL IS OFTEN PERCEIVED SOLELY IN THE CONTEXT OF ITS CONFLICT WITH its neighbors, but its strength and ultimate survival will depend not just on its military might but on its economic and intellectual output. A small country of barely seven million people with no natural resources located in a region that is relatively undeveloped and closer to the third world than the West, Israel has proven that people are the ultimate source of a nation's wealth. Its people are Israel's greatest resource. In less than half a century, that resource built a modern nation that is the envy of the developing world out of what literally were malarial swamps and desert.

The Jewish pioneers of the early twentieth century created the foundation for the modern high-tech state of today. They had to be resourceful to survive in the harsh conditions of Palestine and learned how to make the deserts bloom. They created collective farms, the *kibbutzim*, to produce food, and began a program of afforestation that enabled Israel to end the century as the only country in the world with more trees than it had when the century started. As Helen and Douglas Davis noted in *Israel in the World*, "Israel is probably the only country in history to have had a world-class university, sophisticated medical, scientific and agricultural research institutes, and an internationally acclaimed philharmonic orchestra even before it became a state in 1948."[1]

Paradoxically, it is the economic success of the Zionists in that pre-state period that also contributed to the conflict with the Arabs. The population of Palestinian Arabs was 643,000 in 1922 (compared to 84,000

Jews), but increased 120 percent after the Jews began to settle in large numbers and set about improving health care, sanitation, agricultural techniques, and the overall standard of living. While the British were placing tight restrictions on the numbers of Jews who could enter the country, a policy that would ultimately have devastating and deadly consequences during the 1940s, Arabs from neighboring states were allowed to freely enter the country; these nonnatives and their descendants form a significant proportion of the population that today call themselves Palestinians.

Even an Arab nationalist like Sherif Hussein, the guardian of the Islamic holy places in Arabia, noted that the Palestinians had historically shown a lack of rootedness to the country, while the Jewish immigrants saw the land as sacred and were bound to improve the country. In 1918 an Arab newspaper, *Al Qibla*, quoted Hussein:

> The resources of the country are still virgin soil and will be developed by the Jewish immigrants. One of the most amazing things until recent times was that the Palestinian used to leave his country, wandering over the high seas in every direction. His native soil could not retain a hold on him, though his ancestors had lived on it for 1000 years. At the same time we have seen the Jews from foreign countries streaming to Palestine from Russia, Germany, Austria, Spain, America. The cause of causes could not escape those who had a gift of deeper insight. They knew that the country was for its original sons, for all their differences, a sacred and beloved homeland. The return of these exiles to their homeland will prove materially and spiritually [to be] an experimental school for their brethren who are with them in the fields, factories, trades and in all things connected with toil and labor.

As Hussein foresaw, the regeneration of Palestine and the growth of its population came only after Jews returned in large numbers. This was further reflected by the fact that the Arab population increased the most in cities where large Jewish populations had created new economic opportunities. From 1922 to 1947, the non-Jewish population increased 290 percent in Haifa, 131 percent in Jerusalem and 158 percent in Jaffa.

In the early years of statehood, Israel was inundated with new immigrants. The population doubled between 1949 and 1951. The burden of absorbing so many people, particularly the hundreds of thousands who had fled with little more than the shirts on their backs from the Arab countries, could have crippled the economy, but it did not. Instead, the newcomers continued the process of nation building. As in America, immigrants to Israel have tried to make better lives for themselves and their children. Some have come from relatively undeveloped societies, such as Ethiopia or Yemen, and arrived with virtually no possessions, education, or training and become productive contributors to Israeli society.

Even in the 1950s, when it was still in its infancy, Israel was so confident of its economic prowess, it felt compelled to share its knowledge with the less developed nations of Africa. Future prime minister Golda Meir was the driving force behind the project because she believed the lessons learned by Israelis could be passed on to Africans. "Like them," she said, "we had shaken off foreign rule; like them, we had to learn for ourselves how to reclaim the land, how to increase the yields of our crops, how to irrigate, how to raise poultry, how to live together, and how to defend ourselves." Israel could provide a better model for the newly independent African states, Meir believed, because Israelis "had been forced to find solutions to the kinds of problems that large, wealthy, powerful states had never encountered."[2] This tradition of assistance to other developing countries continues today through MASHAV, Israel's Center for National Cooperation. In 2005 MASHAV was active in 108 countries and offered courses in a wide range of disciplines, including agriculture, education, economic and social development, community development, rural and urban development, medicine and public health, and science and technology.

It is not surprising that so many nations around the world are interested in learning from Israel. Today, Israel is recognized as one of the world's leading emerging economies. More Israeli companies are listed on U.S. stock exchanges than any other country's, except Canada. More than 10,000 U.S. companies do business in or with Israel, including McDonald's, Baxter International, and Ben & Jerry's. Because of its pool of top scientists and researchers and the largest concentration of high-tech companies outside Silicon Valley, Israel has become known as Silicon Wadi. Companies with subsidiaries, research and development, or production facilities include most of America's high-tech giants—IBM, Motorola, Cisco, AOL, Intel, and Microsoft. Israel is at the forefront of developing new technologies not only in computers but in telecommunications, lasers, optics, and other high-tech industries.

Why do so many companies do business in Israel? Because they're Zionists? Of course not. American business has learned that Israel is a great place to make a profit, to tap into a large pool of extraordinary talent, and to serve as a gateway to the European market. Investors loathe instability and yet, despite ongoing violence in and around Israel, U.S. companies have made huge investments in Israel. In July 2005, for example, Intel announced that it would invest $4.6 billion in its Israeli operations; in 2006 Google announced plans to open a research and development center in Tel Aviv; IBM established a new software lab and legendary investor Warren Buffet announced he was paying $4 billion for an 80 percent stake in Iscar, a maker of precision cutting tools. "When you invest in Israel, you have to take into account a certain risk," Buffett said. "We live in a dangerous world as it is and in the long term, the risk premium in Israel will not be different from the U.S."[3]

Buffett is not the only one who feels positive about his investments in Israel. Despite the security situation, international ratings agencies consistently maintain Israel's high credit ratings and express confidence in the Israeli economy. In 1992 total foreign investment in Israel was $537 million. In 2006 the figure should approach $18 billion. While Israel's detractors have attempted to mount a campaign to delegitimize Israel and call on communities, church groups and universities to divest from Israel, American have instead continued to pour money into Israel. Individuals, states, universities, and other institutions invest more than $600 million in Israel Bonds alone.

The United States is Israel's largest trade partner after the European Union, importing nearly $17 billion worth of goods from Israel and exporting nearly $10 billion. New York alone exported almost $4.4 billion worth of goods to Israel, making it the Empire State's second leading trade partner. The United States also established the first Free Trade Agreement (FTA) with Israel in 1985. The FTA eliminated all duties and virtually all other restrictions on trade in goods between the two countries. The overall volume of trade between the two countries has risen 471 percent in the last 20 years. Israel is now America's nineteenth leading trade partner. The FTA gives American companies exporting to Israel an advantage over competitors by virtue of the elimination of all tariffs on American exports to Israel. In addition, as one of only three countries (Jordan and Mexico are the others) with free trade agreements with both the United States and the European Community, Israel can act as a bridge for international trade between America and Europe. In addition to the U.S. and EU agreements, Israel also has bilateral trade agreements with many countries, including Turkey, Canada, Mexico, Bulgaria, India, and Taiwan. Trade is especially booming between Israel and China, as volume topped $3 billion in 2005.

Israel's economic success is all the more remarkable when you consider the external conditions under which Israelis work. Israel has fought eight wars and conflicts, and over the years devoted roughly one-fourth of its national budget to defense (today the figure is around 17 percent). Israel ranked 17 on a list of the world's top 25 defense spenders (based on total dollars spent) in 2005, with more than $9 billion in expenditures. This is a huge sum for such a small country and it could be spent far more productively if Israel did not have to constantly maintain such a high level of military readiness. Moreover, most men who are in the workforce have to spend nearly a month every year doing reserve duty until the age of 45 (the two Israelis taken hostage in Lebanon in 2006 were reservists). During wartime, large numbers of people must leave their jobs to join their units, depriving the economy of their input.

The Arabs have also engaged in a more than 60-year campaign of economic warfare that began even before Israel declared its independence. In 1945 the Arab League imposed an economic boycott that prohibited direct trade between Israel and the Arab nations. A secondary boycott was directed at companies that do business with Israel, and a tertiary boycott involved blacklisting firms that trade with other companies that do business with Israel. The refusal of the Arab states to trade with Israel deprived it of its most natural market and also discouraged foreign firms from doing so.

In 1977 the United States passed legislation prohibiting U.S. companies from cooperating with the Arab boycott, and while the boycott technically remains in force, most Arab countries have stopped actively enforcing it. Egypt became the first country to formally end the embargo when it signed the peace treaty with Israel. Jordan followed after it signed its treaty with Israel. Most Gulf states announced they would no longer boycott Israel after the Oslo agreements in the 1990s. Saudi Arabia remained one of the most committed to the boycott but promised to rescind its participation as a condition of entering the World Trade Organization in 2005. The Saudis subsequently said they would continue to boycott Israeli products. Even with the crumbling of the boycott, however, trade with the Arab world is minimal (although some of the belligerent states trade with Israel under the table). Overall, the boycott hurt Israel but did not prevent its economy from ultimately thriving.

While Israel today is again enjoying an economic growth spurt, it is subject to the vagaries of its security situation. The war with Hizbollah in 2006, for example, cost more than $5 billion and diverted scarce funds that were targeted for many urgent social and education needs. It also devastated the tourism industry, which had just begun to recover after five years of war with the Palestinians. The economy rebounded remarkably quickly, however, with the Tel Aviv stock market reaching an all-time high less than three months after the fighting in Lebanon ended; exports rose sharply, productivity improved and capital continued to flow into Israel at record levels. The unemployment rate is at its lowest level in a decade (though still high at 8.4 percent). Per capita gross domestic product has surged from $15,000 a year six years ago to $18,000 today. Overall economic growth was projected to be nearly 5 percent in 2006, just below prewar estimates.

The situation bears no resemblance to 1984 when years of shouldering the enormous defense burden, the dependence on imported raw materials and fuel, and the cost of absorbing waves of destitute immigrants led the country to the brink of economic disaster. Israel carried a huge foreign debt, its foreign reserves plummeted, unemployment was at an 18-year high, and inflation raged at 450 percent per year. Israel requested economic assistance from the United States, but Secretary of State George Shultz insisted on economic reforms that included budget cuts, tighter control of the money supply, and devaluation of the shekel. When Israel took these and other steps, President Ronald Reagan approved a $1.5 billion emergency aid program, helping to save the Israeli economy from collapse and to stimulate the recovery that reduced inflation from triple digits to the low double digits, and this laid the groundwork for Israel to have one of the world's fastest growth rates just a decade later. This also contributed to the gradual movement of Israel away from a mixed economy that combined capitalism with socialism along the British model, toward a free market system analogous to that of the United States.

U.S. economic and military assistance has also played an important role in promoting Israel's growth. The foreign aid program is premised on the notion that a strong Israel can bolster American interests in the region and can also take risks for peace. Thus, starting in 1949, the United States began to provide Israel with various types of assistance. The aid has been crucial to Israel's development, as it has freed up financial resources to pay for the absorption of immigrants and other social needs. The military aid has been critical to maintaining Israel's qualitative edge over its enemies, who benefited in the past from generous subsidies from the Soviet Union and now use oil revenues to finance the purchase of some of the world's most sophisticated weapons. U.S. assistance allows Israel to purchase a quantity and quality of weaponry that would otherwise be impossible to obtain, in part because of the cost but also because of the unwillingness of most other countries to sell arms to Israel. The Israeli purchases have also benefited the United States because roughly 80 percent of the military aid is paid to American contractors—the increased sales of high-priced items such as fighter planes help lower the overall unit costs to the U.S. military. More than 1,000 companies in 47 states, the District of Columbia and Puerto Rico have signed contracts worth billions of dollars through this program.

The bulk of the economic aid to Israel prior to the 1973 war was in the form of loans. Since 1974, however, Israel has received nearly $100 billion in aid, only part of which was loans that Israel is still repaying. Starting with fiscal year 1987, Israel annually received $1.2 billion in all-grant economic aid and $1.8 billion in all-grant military assistance. In 1998, Israel offered to voluntarily reduce its dependence on U.S. economic aid. According to an agreement reached with the Clinton Administration and Congress, the $1.2 billion economic aid package will be reduced by $120 million each year so that it will be phased out in ten years. Half of the annual savings in economic assistance each year ($60 million) will be added to Israel's military aid package in recognition of its increased security needs. In 2005, Israel received $360 million in economic aid and $2.22 billion in military aid. In 2006, economic aid is scheduled to be reduced to $240 million and military aid will increase to $2.28 billion. A variety of other smaller assistance-related programs actually push the total Israel receives higher.

Israel also received $3 billion in special assistance as part of the 1978–79 Camp David agreements ($2.2 billion in high-interest loans), $1.5 billion in emergency economic assistance to stabilize the Israeli economy in 1985–86, and $10 billion in loan guarantees (spread over five years) in 1992. In 2003, Congress approved another $9 billion in loan guarantees over three years. As with the earlier guarantees, Israel was required to use the funds within the pre-1967 borders and the amount of the guarantees could be reduced by an amount equal to Israel's expenditures on settlements in the territories. The first package of guarantees was intended primarily to assist Israel in absorbing immigrants from Ethiopia and the former Soviet Union, while the second one was meant to aid Israel's economic recovery and compensate for the cost of military preparations associated with the war in Iraq. Guarantees are not grants—not one penny of U.S. government funds is transferred to Israel. The United States simply cosigns loans for Israel that give bankers confidence to lend Israel money at more favorable terms. These loan guarantees have no impact on U.S. taxpayers unless Israel were to default on its loans, something it has never done. In addition, much of the money Israel borrows is spent in the United States to purchase American goods.

Israel also receives U.S. funds for joint military projects such as the Arrow antitactical ballistic missile (for which Israel has received more than $1 billion in grants since 1986), which are provided through the U.S. defense budget. These programs are meant to develop new weapons systems for both nations.

Though the totals are impressive, the value of assistance to Israel has been eroded by inflation. On the other side of the coin, Israel does receive aid on more favorable terms than other nations. For example, all economic aid is given directly to the Israeli government rather than allocated under a specific program. It may be argued that U.S. assistance is critical for Israel's survival, but today it actually comprises a tiny proportion (less than 5 percent) of the Israeli budget. Moreover, aid can also adversely affect Israel's survival, as was the case when Eisenhower threatened to cut off aid to Israel if it didn't withdraw from the territory captured in 1956. By coercing Israel to give up territory without pressuring Egypt to negotiate peace, the U.S. action contributed to the next war. The fear of becoming too dependent on the United States and susceptible to such pressure is one reason, along with the growing strength of its economy, that Israel negotiated a gradual phase-out of economic aid (though it remains heavily dependent on military aid).

By bolstering Israel's economy, the United States has also helped it become more competitive. In 2005 Israel jumped from twenty-third to fifteenth place in the World Economic Forum's Global Competitive index, a leap made possible, in part, by Israel's commitment to innovation. Today Israel devotes almost 5 percent of its GNP to research and development, most of which goes toward electronics, its leading industrial sector. As a proportion of its population, Israel has more university graduates than any other country, and its researchers publish more papers per capita than other countries. Israel has 135 engineers per 10,000 employees, compared with 70 in the United States and 65 in Japan. As a result, Israel has become a leader in a wide range of high-tech fields, such as image processing, optics, digitization, and computer-based education. In 2004 two chemists, Aaron Ciechanover and Avram Hershko of the Technion, became the first Israelis to win the Nobel Prize in science for their investigation of the mechanism by which the cells of most living organisms remove unwanted proteins, research that has potential implications for the treatment of diseases such as cystic fibrosis.

Given Israel's particular strengths in computer technology, it is not surprising that the first research and development facility that Microsoft built outside the United States was in Israel. Cisco's only non-American research and development facilities are in Israel and Motorola's Israel plant is that company's largest development facility in the world. Some of Intel's fastest microchips—such as the Pentium and the Centrino used in most laptops today—were created in the research and development center in Israel and many are fabricated in one of the two production facilities there. Other innovations largely or totally developed in Israel include firewall and antivirus software for computer security, the technology for instant and text messaging on computers and cell phones, voice mail, and compression technology that makes it possible to transfer pictures and movie clips to cell phones.

The government also encourages individual entrepreneurs and small companies to pursue new and innovative ideas through incubators, which were established in 1991 as large numbers of immigrants began to arrive from the former Soviet Union. These incubators provide new immigrants and veteran Israelis with financial support, expert business advice, subsidized office resources, and exposure to interested investors.

One indication of Israel's technological prowess is its membership in the exclusive club of nations with a nuclear capability. Another is its development and launch of satellites, a feat accomplished by only eight other nations. Israel maintains an active space program in partnership with NASA and its European and Russian equivalents. The pride of all Israelis swelled in 2003 when Israel's first astronaut, Ilan Ramon, flew on the ill-fated Columbia shuttle that disintegrated just before landing. A year later, Israel and the European Union agreed to cooperate on the Galileo project to produce a European satellite navigation system.

Israeli researchers are also leaders in the health sciences, developing new drugs and treatments for a variety of illnesses including multiple sclerosis and AIDS. Hebrew University ranked twelfth in the world in the number and quality of patents it registered in 2005 in biotechnology, and on these criteria ranked first among universities outside the United States and the United Kingdom and placed higher than Yale, MIT, and Oxford. In 2006 Shulamit Levenberg, a biomedical engineer at the Technion, was named one of the world's top 50 scientists by *Scientific American* for her work in creating lab-manufactured tissues and organs for transplant with the hope of one day creating synthetic organs.

Israeli biotechnology products and procedures have been developed to monitor, protect, improve, or restore human health. Among the country's many scientific achievements, Israeli researchers have transferred functioning human bone marrow cells to mice to create laboratory animals that can produce human antibodies, found the damaged muscle protein that leads to Myasthenia Gravis and isolated the gene responsible for Gaucher's disease. Because of the quality of its research facilities and scientists, Israel is the site of many clinical trials for medicines while Teva is the world's largest generic pharmaceutical company.

Israel also has been an innovator in diagnostics, producing a variety of computerized imaging systems, including a nuclear magnetic resonance imaging device that is four times faster than existing systems and is sensitive enough to detect very small tumors. Israel also developed a revolutionary diagnostic capsule, equipped with a miniature video camera, that a patient ingests. The capsule films the small intestine as it travels through the body and may become useful for other procedures that now require more invasive procedures. Researchers have also been pioneers in the field of cloning and other types of genetic engineering, producing monoclonal antibody-based test kits and methods for producing a human growth hormone and interferon.

From the earliest days of Zionist settlement in Palestine, Jews have been pioneers in the field of agriculture. By draining the malarial swamps and finding new ways to use scarce water supplies to irrigate crops, farmers produced oranges and other fruits. Today they export fruits, vegetables, flowers, and wines. Many agricultural innovations of the last three decades have been developed in collaborative projects with American researchers supported by the United States-Israel Binational Agricultural Research and Development Fund (BARD), created in 1978 with contributions of $40 million by both the

United States and Israel. BARD-sponsored research has led to new technologies in drip irrigation, pesticides, fish farming, livestock and poultry production, disease control, and farm equipment.

Farmers have always faced the dilemma of how to protect their crops from pests and diseases; protection has become more difficult as environmental concerns have led Israel and other nations to ban the use of certain pesticides and treatments. Israeli researchers, often with American collaborators, have designed delivery systems that reduce the amount of pesticide needed to protect crops. More than 25 percent of harvested fruits and vegetables are lost to postharvest decay. Health and environmental concerns also prompted the development of alternatives to chemical control in Israel. New biocontrols have been created for use on greenhouse, turf, and row crops. Products derived from Israeli projects are used to promote disease resistance in plants, ornamentals, apples, tobacco, potatoes, and grapes. Other innovative research has helped control viral diseases in plants and animals. For example, an Israeli test for Rift Valley fever has improved detection of a virus that infects cattle, sheep, and humans in many developing countries.

Israeli agriculturists have found ways to improve dairy cow productivity, plant fertilization, tomato crop yields, wheat production, and farm efficiency. Researchers, for example, have developed techniques to stimulate growth in broiler chickens and turkeys. Their approach increases feed efficiency and reduces fat in the birds, saving the farmer money on feed and giving the consumer a leaner bird. Israel has also become a major flower exporter, but growers lost money because flower quality deteriorated during the shipping process. Israeli research provided the first safe and effective means of inhibiting shoot bending to preserve flower quality.

In addition to joint research in agriculture, the United States and Israel also engage in cooperative research in basic science. The Binational Science Foundation (BSF) was created in 1972 to promote research cooperation between scientists in the two countries. Each government initially contributed $30 million and in 1984 added another $20 million each to create a $100 million endowment used to fund projects. Since then, BSF has awarded more than 3,000 grants, involving scientists from more than 400 institutions located in 44 states and the District of Columbia. The benefits to the United States from BSF-sponsored studies include the extension and elaboration of research to achieve milestones that might not have been reached otherwise; the introduction of novel thinking and techniques that led American researchers to move in new directions; confirmation, clarification, and intensification of research projects; access to Israeli equipment and facilities unavailable elsewhere; and early access to Israeli research results that have sped up American scientific advances. BSF has documented no fewer than 75 new discoveries that probably would not have been possible without foundation-supported collaboration. These advances included the development of new methods and techniques, the discovery of new phenomena, and major theoretical breakthroughs.

In addition to promoting science, the United States has created institutions to stimulate joint research and development. The Binational Industrial Research and Development Foundation (BIRD) was established in 1977. Both countries provided equal contributions to create a $110 million endowment that funds joint U.S.-Israel teams in the development and subsequent commercialization of innovative, nondefense technological products from which both the Israeli and American companies can expect to derive benefits commensurate with their investments and risks. Most grant recipients are small businesses involved with software, instrumentation, communications, medical devices, and semiconductors. Since its inception, BIRD has funded more than 600 joint high-tech research and development projects through conditional grants totaling more than $210 million. Products developed from these ventures have generated sales of $5 billion, tax revenues of more than $700 million in both countries, and have created an estimated 20,000 American jobs.

To encourage economic cooperation as a pillar of the peace process, the United States, Jordan, and Israel created TRIDE (Trilateral Industrial Development) in 1996. Modeled after BIRD, TRIDE supports joint venture projects by private sector firms from the three countries.

Another institution created to stimulate cooperation is the U.S.-Israel Science & Technology Commission (USISTC). The USISTC was established in 1993 to encourage high-tech industries in both countries to engage in joint projects, to foster scientific exchanges between universities and research institutions, to promote development of agricultural and environmental technologies, and to assist in the adaptation of military technology to civilian production. Israel has some similar agreements for cooperative research with other nations, such as Germany, but the principal partner for most projects remains the United States. The result of all of these initiatives is to multiply the impact of the research in Israel and to create a broad international network for the development, commercialization, and marketing of products.

For a single indication of the confidence Israelis have in their survival, just travel around the country and see the construction boom. Roads and railways are being built. Cranes dot the skyline of several cities. The Shalom Tower was built in 1957 and was, for many years, Tel Aviv's only skyscraper and Israel's tallest building (433 feet). Today it is dwarfed by the Azrieli towers and many other high-rises being constructed. The country's tallest building today, Migdal Shaar Ayir in Ramat Gan, is nearly twice the height of the Shalom Tower. Real estate, particularly in Jerusalem, is at a premium. Irreplaceable homes near the Old City and newer luxury apartments bought largely by wealthy foreigners who want second homes in Israel are sold for prices in the millions. The king of the luxury builders, Donald Trump, announced in 2006 his intention to build a 70-story Trump Plaza Tower on the site of the Elite candy factory in Ramat Gan that will become the tallest building in Israel. He also agreed to build the first Trump hotel in Israel as part of a tourism project in Southern Netanya.

Booms do not go on forever, and Israel may suffer the type of busts that have caused other economies to decline. Like the United States, Israel enjoyed a real estate and a high-tech boom in the 1990s that may not have completely burst but certainly slowed during the Palestinian war. Living with terror and war has a steep financial and psychological price. It affects productivity, investment, trade, and consumer confidence, but Israelis have not let the external threats deter them from achieving the Zionist dream of a strong and secure Jewish state. It would be misleading, however, to present the Israeli economic picture as a paradise. Among the serious problems that still exist are industries that have not been completely privatized, inequalities in the distribution of wealth, a suffocating personal tax burden and a high unemployment rate. The poverty rate has become particularly shocking as more than 20 percent of Israelis, including one-third of the children, have slipped below the poverty line. These problems are not unique to Israel. They are a worldwide problem exacerbated in part by globalization. In Israel's case, economist Howard Wachtel explained, the participants in globalization, such as those in the high-tech industry, are feeling the positive effects while the older, socialist remnants of the society, such as the Histadrut (Israel's labor federation), the *kibbutzim*, and publicly owned industries, have been left farther behind.

Still, Israel is ranked twenty-third on the UN's Human Development Index, which measures the average achievements in a country in three basic dimensions of human development: a long and healthy life, knowledge, and a decent standard of living. These statistics include life expectancy, literacy, and gross domestic product per capita. To get a sense of how Israel compares with Western nations, Norway is ranked number 1, the U.S. is 8, the U.K. is 18. Germany is only two places higher than Israel, and no one is questioning whether it will survive. Incidentally, the highest ranked Arab country is Bahrain at number 33 while, for example, oil-rich Saudi Arabia is ranked 76.

In the days of high inflation, a prevalent joke was that the best way to make a small fortune in Israel was to bring a large one with you. Today, inflation is under control (averaging less than 1 percent annually for the past five years), and many people in Israel have accumulated tremendous wealth, but the degree of concern average Israelis have about their economic security is only slightly less than for their physical well-being. That is why people tell pollsters that their worries about the economic situation are second only to the danger of Iranian nuclear weapons.

Israelis still cite their scientific and technological achievements as their main source of pride in their country. While Israelis account for just one-thousandth of the world's population, they enjoy a standard of living comparable to many Europeans. As in any society, Israel has people living at different strata of society, but overall, most Israelis enjoy a good life in Israel and do not need to leave the country for economic reasons.

Israel's future will continue to depend on the growth of its economy, and the past suggests that this will be a continuing source of strength. Israelis have great faith in their ability to overcome challenges because of the quality of their education, the inventiveness of their researchers and the determination of their workforce. The country's prosperity will grow even faster if Israel normalizes relations with its neighbors. Shimon Peres has often talked about his vision of a Middle East in which all the nations have the type of normal trade and tourist relations as the European Union. Such a Middle East would benefit all the people of the region, yet that prospect appears far off. In the meantime, Israel has proven it cannot only survive but thrive.

10

Does Media Bias
Threaten Israel?

THE OLD CLICHÉ IS THAT FOR EVERY TWO JEWS, THERE ARE THREE SYNAGOGUES, four opinions, and five political parties. In speaking to Jewish audiences around the country for nearly 20 years, however, I found one issue on which seemingly every American Jew agrees: the media is irrevocably biased against Israel. This chapter will offer examples to support this belief, but the more important question is whether it really matters. Most American Jews intuitively believe the answer is "yes." Actually, it's not so much intuition as paranoia. American Jews have an almost pathological fear that the media will turn the American people against Israel and the public will then demand that the United States government change its policy toward Israel in a way that will lead to its destruction. While Henry Kissinger's remark that it's not paranoia if people are really out to get you has a ring of truth here, the evidence suggests that the media's bias has not had the malevolent impact the pro-Israel community fears.

To get a sense of how Israel's friends view the media, consider how four of the most important newspapers might cover the biggest possible news story—the end of the world:

New York Times: "World Ends. Third World Countries Hardest Hit"

Wall Street Journal: "World Ends. Dow Jones Industrial Average Hits Zero"

Washington Post: "World Ends. White House Ignored Warnings, Unnamed Sources Say"

USA Today: "We're Dead. State-by-State Demise, pg. 8A. Final, Final Sports Scores, pg. 6C"

John Quinn, the first editor of *USA Today* told this as a joke, but for people who follow media coverage of the Middle East, the humor is lost, because they believe each of these publications as well as other media have very definite biases that generally reflect badly on Israel.

Perhaps every interest group looks at its own cause with an equally keen eye, but supporters of Israel see coverage of Middle East stories differently than others. They have a myopia that focuses on how Israel is portrayed and they perform a talmudic analysis of each word of a report or frame of a broadcast to see whether it is accurate and fair to Israel, and whether any alternative interpretation unsympathetic to Israel can be detected. For example, there have been newspaper reports about terrorist attacks in Israel that have put more emphasis on the family of the suicide bomber than the victims of the atrocity. Media watchdogs will immediately jump on the publication for showing more sympathy for the killer's family than for the victims or their families out of fear that readers would not appreciate the fact that this was a heinous act of violence against Israelis.

I don't believe the average American looks at the story the same way. Most readers do not have a special interest in a particular article on the Middle East and have no reason to critique its objectivity. They are not as likely to see the nuances a partisan detects. Rather, they will likely see the description of the bomber's family in the broader context of the complete story of terror committed against Israel, which also fits into the stereotypes reinforced in news and entertainment.

A similar case occurred with the Steven Spielberg film *Munich,* which attracted many filmgoers who were curious to find out if the Jewish director who so moved us with *Schindler's List* really produced a film that was as hostile to Israel as some amateur critics were saying. Even before the film was released, Spielberg invited opprobrium by hiring a vocal critic of Israeli policy, Tony Kushner, to write the screenplay based on a book that was discredited years before. Given Spielberg's resources, it was shocking that he rejected offers to talk to people directly involved in the operation to track down the terrorists responsible for the Munich Massacre. In fact, according to journalists Yossi Melman and Steven Hartov, writing in the *Guardian,* "During shooting, numerous offers to provide the production team with the

facts of the case were rebuffed. More than 30 years had passed . . . and participants on both sides were ready to talk. Yet the men who held the secrets were
never contacted."[1]

While some critics believe he created a moral equivalence between the
Israelis and the terrorists, I didn't see it that way at all. The Israelis were
clearly distinguished by their displays of ethics and conscience, such as when
they abort a bombing after they realize the terrorist's daughter is in the room
with him, and when one member of the team refuses to participate in a
killing that he does not believe is justified. The scene that many critics found
the most disturbing was an absurd one in which the Israelis and the terrorists
end up in the same safe house and one of the Palestinians proceeds to give a
speech to the Mossad agent rationalizing his actions. Many people didn't like
the idea of giving the terrorist a platform, but I thought this was perhaps the
most important and honest moment in the film. The terrorist says, in effect,
that the Palestinians will fight for the next hundred years to destroy Israel,
and this is a message Americans need to hear. The character expresses the
view that I have tried to convey many times in this book: Many Palestinians
believe that time is on their side and that they will drive the Jews into the sea.

Scenes that portray Israel unflatteringly can be picked apart, but the
overall feeling of the film is that the Arabs were savage murderers who
deserved to be assassinated. It is hard to imagine many people coming away
from the film feeling more sympathetic toward the Palestinians and less so
toward Israel. *Munich* was a work of art, not a documentary. The news, in
contrast, is supposed to reflect reality, and it is easy to demonstrate the
media's repeated failure to accurately portray events in the Middle East.
Coverage of the Lebanon war during the summer of 2006 was so scandalous
that one photographer was fired for obviously doctoring photographs (e.g., to
exaggerate the effect of an Israeli attack), and *Washington Post* reporter
Thomas Ricks was rebuked by executive editor Leonard Downie for outra-
geously suggesting that Israel intentionally left Hizbollah rocket launchers
intact because having Israeli civilians killed would help Israel in the public
relations war. These were examples of the media acting responsibly when
confronted with obvious mistakes.

In other cases, however, journalists presented incomplete reports, including CNN's Nic Robertson. Early in the war he was taken to an area of Beirut
and told that the rubble of buildings was a result of Israeli air strikes on civilian targets. He repeated the allegation as fact, although it wasn't the full story.

Robertson later admitted on CNN's Reliable Sources on July 23 that although there was civilian damage, his report had been influenced by his Hizbollah guide. He acknowledged that he had been told what to film and where. He also acknowledged, "there's no doubt that the bombs there are hitting Hizbollah facilities." Robertson's CNN colleague, Anderson Cooper, one of the journalists who was consistently fair, did not hesitate to point out Hizbollah's mendacity. He said in an August 8 CNN interview on the war coverage that the group was "just making things up."

The press sometimes immediately reported whatever statistics they were fed by Lebanese officials. Front page stories around the world said that 57 civilians were killed when Israel bombed a building in Qana it believed to be empty. While still tragic, the actual casualty figure was only 28. Moreover, most accounts failed to mention the building was in an area where 150 rocket attacks on Israel had originated. Over the years, the Arabs have learned one sure-fire way to get media attention is to scream "massacre" when Israelis are in the neighborhood. On August 7, 2006, news outlets repeated Lebanese prime minister Fouad Siniora's claim that Israel had committed a "massacre" by killing 40 people in an air raid on the village of Houla. Later, it was learned that only one person had died.

The dread provoked by media bias has spawned an industry of media watchdog organizations, which grew significantly after Israel became the focus of negative reporting in September 2000 following the outbreak of the Palestinian war. Millions of dollars have been spent to monitor and react to the press, but no one asks whether this investment has had any real impact on the media. The watchdogs document media failings on almost a daily basis, so what exactly has been accomplished? After years of complaining, boycotting, meeting editors, writing letters, and demanding corrections, CNN, the *New York Times*, and National Public Radio (often referred to by some wags as National Palestinian Radio), continue to be criticized for the same types of bias they were accused of before they became targets of the monitors.

NPR is an especially good example. Israel's supporters have complained for years about the irresponsible coverage, and some even initiated boycotts to try to use the network's reliance on public funds to influence their editorial decisions. WUBR, Boston's NPR affiliate, for example, said it lost at least one million dollars in funding because of a boycott initiated by donors unhappy with NPR's coverage. International news is generated, however, at the national rather than the affiliate level, so reporting was unaffected by local boycotts. As Eric Rozenmann of the Committee for Accuracy in Middle East Reporting in America (CAMERA) noted in a column about NPR's bias, the $225 million bequest of McDonald's heiress Joan Kroc and a $15 million grant from the John D. and Catherine T. MacArthur Foundation was worth two years of the network's operating budget and helped make the network largely immune to financial coercion.

The media monitors can claim small victories here and there in getting stories corrected, but always after the initial impact. Occasionally, they've had some influence on the decision to run a story or its slant, but the best the watchdogs can say is that without them the coverage might be even worse. Doing something, no matter how futile, makes many of Israel's supporters feel better than doing nothing. A bigger problem is that the examples occasionally cited by the watchdogs to prove the media has made a difference demonstrate their own impotence, because they couldn't do anything to prevent the most problematic reports.

One of the best examples of how correcting a story after the fact cannot undo the harm involves the most vivid image of the Palestinian War, in which a Palestinian father tried unsuccessfully to shield his son from gunfire. The French TV reporter's edited footage of the incident on September 30, 2000, was shown repeatedly on television broadcasts around the world and photographs made the front page of newspapers. Israel was universally blamed for the death of 12-year-old Mohammed Aldura, but subsequent investigations found that the boy was most likely downed by Palestinian bullets. Efforts to correct the record came too late to erase the misperception that Israeli soldiers had killed a child in front of his father. As horrifying as that case was, it is not clear it did any real lasting damage to Israel's image or had any impact on U.S. policy. Israel got a black eye, but, like the damage from a physical beating, it too would pass.

An example of an image that is said to have had an impact on policy was the case of a *Washington Post* photograph published during the 1982 Lebanon War that showed a baby who appeared to have lost both arms. The UPI caption said that the seven-month-old had been severely burned when an Israeli jet accidentally bombed a Christian residential area. The photo disgusted President Ronald Reagan, and his anger was one reason he subsequently called for Israel to halt its attacks. It turned out the photo and the caption were inaccurate. The baby had not lost its arms, and the burns the child suffered were the result of a PLO attack on East Beirut. So did this media distortion cause a shift in U.S. policy? No. While Reagan mentioned the photo upsetting him, he was angered more by Israel's overall policy and the fact that he no longer trusted Israeli prime minister Menachem Begin. He did not express his outrage and demand an Israeli cease-fire when the *Post* photo appeared on August 2. The policy change came more than a week later, on August 12, after the media accurately reported Israeli warplanes bombarded Beirut and killed more than 300 people. And even then, overall U.S. policy toward Israel remained supportive and subsequently improved.

The Lebanon example also illustrates a fallacy in the thinking of media monitors who act as though decision makers get all their information from the press. The president, especially, has independent sources and would typically have ample information about an incident without having to rely on the press.

Still, for those who are convinced the bias is universal and irrevocable, I have two words for you: Fox News. Actually, let me add three more: *Wall Street Journal.* While the media exhibits an overall anti-Israel bias, is it possible to demonstrate that NPR has greater influence on policy or opinion than the pro-Israel editorial page of the *Journal?* Are Pat Buchanan's screeds on Israel more persuasive than sympathetic columns by the likes of George Will, Charles Krauthammer, and Mort Zuckerman?

It is also debatable whether the confrontational approach toward journalists adopted by many watchdogs is productive, since it is likely to alienate the people they are trying to convince to be more fair minded. Reporters have told me they are only angered by attacks. An educational approach that seeks to help them do their job better seems more likely to affect reporting.

I am reminded of the old joke about two Jews sitting on a park bench. The first one is reading an Israeli newspaper and the second is reading an anti-Semitic paper. The first Jew asks, "How can you read such a publication?" The second Jew says, "I used to read the Israeli paper and the news was all bad, but the anti-Semitic paper says we own the banks, control the media, we run the world. Wouldn't you rather read good news?"

While it may be heretical to say, at one level we should be glad a bias exists, because it is a reflection of the free and open societies that exist in the United States and in Israel. After all, if you want to read the most vicious criticism of Israeli policy, all you have to do is read the Israeli press. Now that several of the papers are translated into English online, it's very easy for foreign correspondents to learn about every wart in Israeli society.

Most people get their news from television, and here the bias is far more extreme. Journalists regularly report from Jerusalem, Tel Aviv, or other locations in Israel. But when was the last time you saw a TV correspondent reporting live from Cairo, Riyadh, or Damascus? Those closed authoritarian societies usually do not allow Western journalists to enter at all, let alone roam freely, and since few reporters speak Arabic, it is not surprising that so little news emanates from the Arab world. On those rare occasions when a correspondent does get into one of these countries, they often consciously pull their punches. When asked to comment on what many viewers regard as CNN's bias against Israel, Reese Schonfeld, the network's first president explained in 2001, "When I see them on the air I see them being very careful about Arab sensibilities." Schonfeld suggested the coverage is slanted because CNN doesn't want to risk the special access it has in the Arab world. Reporters also know that saying the wrong thing could lead them to be kidnapped, killed, or expelled. As *Time* magazine contributor Christopher Albritton noted during Israel's war with Hizbollah: "To the south, along the curve of the coast, Hizbollah is launching Katyushas, but I'm loath to say too much about them. The Party of God has a copy of every journalist's passport, and they've already hassled a number of us and threatened one."[2]

Some journalists are simply ignorant of the subject they are reporting on and pass on information that sounds newsworthy but would not be if they understood the context. For example, CNN managed to get a reporter into Syria during the Lebanon war in 2006 who would report how the Syrians at the border and the Lebanese fleeing the violence were supportive of Hizbollah—without explaining that this was to be expected since Syria was Hizbollah's patron and that the Lebanese he was interviewing were probably from Hizbollah strongholds. He and other reporters throughout the fighting would paint the false impression of widespread support for Hizbollah based on interviews with people who knew their lives would be in danger if the terrorists ever learned they had said anything against them.

Print reporters have gained more access in recent years to parts of the Arab world, but they have not done as much to enlighten us about those societies as an organization that has simply made available translations of what is regularly said in the Arab press. The Middle East Media Research Institute (MEMRI) has given Americans a window into the Arab world that has affected the political environment by exposing the true views of people in the region, views that are otherwise customarily filtered through translators, spin doctors, and publicists. Thanks to MEMRI, it is no longer possible for Arab leaders to say one thing to an American reporter and something entirely different in Arabic, as Yasser Arafat was famous for doing. We now know exactly what Arab officials, intellectuals, and religious leaders are saying to their fellow Arabs. Similarly, Palestinian Media Watch has exposed the truth about Palestinian society by translating textbooks, crossword puzzles, commercials, and television shows. And much of that material is frightening. To give just one example, a Palestinian children's television show called the "Children's Club" uses a "Sesame Street" formula involving interaction between children, puppets, and fictional characters to encourage a hatred for Jews and the perpetration of violence against them in a jihad. In one episode, young children are seen singing about wanting to become "suicide warriors" and taking up machine guns against Israelis. Another song features young children chanting a refrain, "When I wander into Jerusalem, I will become a suicide bomber."

NBC's Tel Aviv bureau chief Martin Fletcher acknowledged that the Palestinians manipulated the Western media during the first intifada by casting themselves as David against the Israeli Goliath, a metaphor used by Fletcher himself in a 1988 report. "The whole uprising was media-oriented, and, without a doubt, kept going because of the media," he said in an August 5, 1991 interview with *Near East Report.* Fletcher openly admitted accepting invitations from young Palestinians to film violent attacks against Jewish residents of the West Bank. "It's really a matter of manipulation of the media. And the question is: How much do we play that game? [We do it] in the same way that we turn up at all those Bush or Reagan photo opportunities. We play along because we need the pictures."

I'm actually happy that a bias exists against Israel because it proves that Israel is a democracy that is open to criticism. So long as Israel remains the region's sole democracy, it is inevitable that it will receive disproportionate attention and, since most reporters focus on bad news, it is not surprising that the coverage will be primarily negative. Because it is a democracy, Israel is typically held to a higher standard than other countries. Americans generally have little interest in the Arab world and don't have high expectations for the conduct of the Arab states, often viewed as backward and hostile bases for terrorists. Arab transgressions merely reinforce the already negative views most Americans have of these dictatorships.

One approach taken by those who hope to divert the media's attention from the battlefield is to produce positive reports about Israel. While there is no shortage of such stories about the beauty of Israel, its unique archaeological sites and the achievements of its doctors and scientists, the public relations effort to focus the media beyond the conflict is doomed to fail as long as there is a conflict that will generate the front page stories and the bulk of the news headlines. One of the problems is that marketing Israel is not like selling soap—consumer products generally don't have religious and political dimensions. America's security and broader foreign policy is not affected by choices of cleansers.

One organization with a different approach is The Israel Project, which is trying to "sell" Israel as if they were promoting a political candidate. This involves conducting surveys and focus groups to determine public opinion and, more important, testing arguments and phraseology to determine what is effective in moving opinion. This is a quantum leap in thinking about the problem of Israel's image and has significantly improved the quality of pro-Israel communications; nevertheless, this approach also has its limitations, principally, that Israel is *not* like a political candidate. In a political campaign, there is an outcome at a predetermined time; that is, if it is effective, the campaign will influence a voter to cast a ballot for a particular candidate on election day. When it comes to Israel, however, most respondents in polls will give an answer, but this answer does not necessarily translate into any action. I'd suggest that it rarely does. Many people answer questions because they don't want to look stupid, see no harm in expressing an opinion, or just want to make the surveyor happy. Most Americans don't feel that strongly about Middle East issues; in fact, polls indicate that they wish the whole mess would just go away. In the end, it makes little or no difference if someone expresses views hostile to Israel or is moved by a TV ad campaign to change their opinion, because they are not likely to vote for a particular candidate based on their position on Israel or call their member of Congress to lobby them to support or oppose particular legislation affecting Israel.

In addition, other than foreign aid, most Israel-related issues are not decided by Congress. At best, public opinion has a marginal impact by shaping the climate in which a president makes foreign policy decisions. I'm not aware of any evidence, however, that suggests President George W. Bush's position on the road map, the security fence, or settlements is determined by poll data on those specific questions.

The assumption of those who fear anti-Israel media bias is that it will affect public opinion, which in turn will cause a shift in U.S. Middle East policy. The general perception is that Americans once loved Israel, particularly in the wake of the dramatic victory in the Six-Day War, but that public support has gradually eroded over time because of Arab propaganda and the anti-Israel media bias (some would also blame Israel's "bad behavior").

The data tell a different story. American public support for Israel has consistently exceeded that of the Arabs and Palestinians by huge margins, and the overall trend over the years has been in Israel's favor. Large majorities of Americans also view Israel as a friend and reliable ally. In June 1967, 56 percent of Americans supported Israel, compared to only 4 percent who said they sympathized with the Arabs. Despite all that has transpired in the last 39 years, the latest Gallup poll, taken in February 2006, found that 59 percent of Americans still sympathize with Israel. Support for the Palestinians (Gallup changed the question wording from "Arabs" in 1993) was only 15 percent. Overall, support for Israel has been on the *upswing* since 1967. Meanwhile, support for the Arabs/Palestinians has actually declined in the last two decades. On average, Israel is favored nearly four to one. The percentage of Americans with a favorable opinion of Israel in 2006 was 68 percent. This is the most positive rating for Israel in a Gallup poll other than a 79 percent favorable rating in February 1991 during the first Gulf War. By contrast, just 11 percent of Americans have a favorable opinion of the Palestinian Authority, while 78 percent have an unfavorable view, the most negative Gallup has found since it began asking about the Palestinian Authority in 2000. On a list of 22 countries, the PA was ranked second from the bottom—only slightly more positively than North Korea.

In mid-August 2006, while Israel was viewed by many of its supporters as being unfairly pilloried for "indiscriminate" attacks against civilians and the "disproportionate" use of force in its campaign against Hizbollah, Pew reported that 52 percent of Americans sympathized with Israel while 11 percent backed the Palestinians. A month earlier, before the largely critical coverage of Israel's Lebanon campaign, support for Israel was 44 percent, but it was still lower, 9 percent, for the Palestinians.

Polls also indicate the public views Israel as a reliable U.S. ally, a feeling that grew stronger during the gulf crisis. A January 1991 Harris Poll, for example, found that 86 percent of Americans consider Israel a "close ally" or "friendly." This was the highest level ever recorded in a Harris poll. The figure in 2006 was 75 percent.

One of the other keys to understanding attitudes toward the Middle East, a factor that no one likes to say aloud, is the stereotypical feeling many Americans have toward Arabs and Muslims. A 2006 Gallup poll found, for example, that when asked what they admire most about the Muslim world, the most common response was "nothing" (33 percent) and the next most common answer was "I don't know" (22 percent). As horrible as coverage about Israel may be, it is much worse for the Arabs. In fact, journalists usually justify their anti-Israel bias by claiming they get just as many complaints from the Arabs as the Jews, which they rationalize as an indication their coverage is balanced. The difference, some may argue, is that the coverage of the Arabs is accurate.

Arab-Americans, for example, complain that Arabs are too often portrayed as terrorists, but the reality is that Norwegians and Swedes are not blowing up themselves and civilians in suicide attacks. Every terrorist attack reinforces stereotypes of Arabs as barbarians. While the situation in Iraq may not help President Bush's political standing, it also does nothing to reverse the perception of the barbarism of Arabs who have beheaded and dismembered their enemies. They are seen as religious zealots who have no interest in democracy and share none of our values. These images are further reinforced by popular media in which, for example, terrorists portrayed on TV are typically Arabs or Muslims. Protests from Arab-American groups, seeking to tap into Hollywood liberals' desire to be politically correct, have led to some changes to balance or sanitize movies and television, to offer more sympathetic Arab characters or provide justifications for their behavior. One of the most extreme cases in recent years was the film adaptation of Tom Clancy's book, *The Sum of All Fears,* in which the antagonists were transformed from Muslims in the book to neo-Nazis in the movie.

By contrast, for all its flaws, Americans still understand that Israel is a democratic society whose citizens enjoy the same freedoms that we do. Yes, Israel gets a black eye every time there is a story about house demolitions, civilians killed inadvertently during military operations, or some other action that seems particularly unfair, disproportionate, or injurious to the average Palestinian, but these stories are powerful mainly because they conflict with the generally positive image most Americans hold of Israelis. If the media has grown progressively more anti-Israel since 1967 and impacts policy, we would expect a deterioration in U.S.-Israel relations. But by any measure, the relationship has grown progressively stronger. Today, whatever else one may think about President Bush, he is regarded even by his detractors as perhaps the most pro-Israel president in history.

It is also important to recognize that while the assumption is that public opinion affects policy, the reality is often the reverse. A president is far more likely to influence opinion on the Middle East than public attitudes are to influence policy. Historically, major shifts in the polls are associated not with media coverage but with presidential statements and actions associated with the conflict. Look at the correlation between policy and opinion over time. Public sympathy for Israel, on average, was lowest during the Carter and Clinton administrations. Carter is generally viewed as relatively unsympathetic to Israel while Clinton was considered the most pro-Israel president in history to that point. By far the highest level of public support for Israel was recorded during the administration of George H. W. Bush, who was considered perhaps the least friendly president toward Israel. Of course, the data during his term is largely skewed by the record high level of support for Israel during the Gulf War.

By far the low point in public opinion toward Israel occurred during the Lebanon war in 1982. Though Ronald Reagan is remembered as a great friend of Israel, he had a bitter fight with the pro-Israel lobby over the sale of sophisticated radar planes to Saudi Arabia, suspended arms shipments to Israel after the annexation of the Golan Heights, and condemned the Israeli strike on the Iraqi nuclear plant. The day Reagan launched a peace initiative, Begin called it the saddest day of his life. During the Reagan period, however, the U.S.-Israel strategic relationship was formalized, the amount of aid to Israel increased, a free trade agreement was signed, and the informal alliance between the two nations strengthened.

In March 2002 Israel decided to mount a large-scale military operation in the West Bank to root out the terrorist infrastructure that was sending suicide bombers into Israel. The United States, to the chagrin of the Arabs, said nothing and appeared satisfied that Israel was responding appropriately to the threats to its population. Suddenly in April, President George W. Bush publicly demanded that Israel withdraw its troops immediately from the West Bank. During the week that Israel continued its operations, the media led nearly every report by saying that Israel is defying the president of the United States. Based on the coverage, if you believe in the omnipotence of the media, you would have expected public sympathy for Israel to plummet and Congress to take punitive action against Israel. Instead, public support for Israel was at 47 percent, below the historical average (just below the 50 percent recorded earlier in the month), but still above the 43 percent documented the month before. Congress voted to give $200 million more in aid to Israel and to impose new restrictions on support for the Palestinians.

On matters pertaining to Israel, Congress pays little attention to public opinion or the media and has not wavered in its support. Occasionally, a particular issue arises that generates congressional concern, such as the charges during the 1982 war in Lebanon that Israel was using American-made cluster bombs. (This allegation was repeated in the 2006 war and led several pro-Israel members of Congress to introduce legislation to ban sales of the munitions, which was defeated 70-30.) These are isolated incidents that haven't affected the overall support of Congress for Israel or broader policy. More often, Congress takes the opposite tack, sending letters to the president and passing legislation that is even more supportive of Israel than public opinion and contrary to what one would expect if media bias had any impact.

One obstacle to changing media coverage is that there is little that anyone can do to make Israel look good as long as the situation on the ground is in upheaval. Israel had a honeymoon during the peace process with the Palestinians in the 1990s, especially under Labor Party leaders, because it was clear that they were making every effort to resolve the conflict. It was not difficult to market the idea at that time that Israel was interested in peace. Although Israel still has that interest and it should be obvious that the other side is the obstacle, it is much more difficult to sell a positive image of Israel by castigating the Palestinians. This was the pre-Oslo situation, and it is no coincidence that a lot of the old propaganda is being dusted off. Negative campaigns may work in electoral politics, but it has never been that effective in the Mideast public relations war. Israel does best when it has a positive message about itself.

The other impediment to any public relations strategy, especially one that focuses on criticizing the Palestinians, is that nothing will have as much impact as a single incident shown repeatedly on TV, such as the killing of the boy being shielded by his father in Gaza. Journalists use those pictures because they make great TV, and as long as Israel is in armed conflict, the dominant image is going to be heavily armed Jews fighting Arab children with rocks. Because Israelis have no interest in martyrdom, the casualty figures will always be lopsided and every story will mention the disproportionate number of Palestinian fatalities. Events can be placed in context; one can, for example, talk about Palestinian children being cynically used as cannon fodder, but it doesn't change the statistics or the drumbeat of coverage about Palestinian suffering. Fratricidal violence among Palestinians that leaves innocents dead is viewed as par for the course, and goes largely unreported, but if Israelis are involved headlines are generated.

Israel's enemies have also become very sophisticated at manipulating the media. In the war with Hizbollah, for example, an Arab woman was shown in one picture wailing about the loss of her home to Israeli bombs and then later shown in another picture in another place again wailing about the loss of her home. Anderson Cooper said he was given a tour in which Hizbollah had lined up some ambulances. They were told to turn on their sirens and then the ambulances drove off as if they were picking up wounded civilians when, in fact, they were simply going back and forth. Boston University professor Richard Landes has put together a web site with raw video footage he calls "Pallywood," which documents how the Palestinians fake everything from shoot-outs with Israeli troops to funerals. The classic scene shows a group of mourners carrying a body on a stretcher. Suddenly, the stretcher falls to the ground and the "corpse" gets up and runs away.

Coverage also tends to be detrimental to Israel because of the asymmetry of Israel's battles with terrorists. This was readily apparent in 2006 when Israel's powerful military inflicted heavy damage on Lebanon and killed hundreds of civilians. The pictures, especially the doctored ones, were dramatic and the stories compelling. By contrast, Hizbollah's weapons were inaccurate and, fortunately for Israel, caused comparatively little death and destruction. Hizbollah's cynical and ruthless use of civilians as shields also insured that Israel would be unable to attack them without also hitting civilians. One cartoon captured the distinction between the combatants by showing an Israeli soldier holding a rifle and kneeling in front of a baby carriage protecting it while opposite him a Hizbollah fighter with a rifle kneels behind a baby carriage.

The Palestinians' message is also simple and understandable. Every question can be answered in three words: "End the occupation." Israel's message tends to be garbled, especially when delivered by gruff Israeli men with heavy accents, and involve lengthy dissertations on the history of the conflict. Recently, the pro-Israel community has developed simpler and more effective messages. Its most accurate and effective declaration, boiled down to three words: "Israel wants peace."

Chapter 11

A World of Danger

THE MOST DIRECT THREAT TO ISRAEL'S SURVIVAL COMES FROM THE ENEMIES IN its neighborhood. A more indirect danger is posed by its enemies around the world who seek to weaken the Jewish state and undermine its legitimacy. Many of these efforts emanate from Europe where a long tradition of classical anti-Semitic attitudes toward Jews has gradually been replaced by a new form of anti-Semitism focused on Israel. While an increasingly hostile environment has aroused old fears for Jews, the international status of Israel has dramatically improved and may actually be better today than ever before.

It is not surprising that Jews are concerned by what they view as a growing effort to delegitimize Israel. As Phyllis Chesler has noted in her book, *The New Anti-Semitism,* "Old-fashioned anti-Semitism was justified in the name of ethnic, Aryan, white purity, superiority, and nationalism" while the new anti-Semitism is cast "by politically correct people in the name of anticolonialism, anti-imperialism, antiracism and pacifism."[1] Jews and the Jewish state are indistinguishable when the rhetoric is examined, as the anti-Semite tries to hide behind the label of Zionism. For the Europeans grappling with their own history in the Holocaust, the frequent comparison of Zionists and Nazis presents an opportunity to assuage their guilt.

The vitriol of the new anti-Semites can be disseminated globally, nonstop, via the media and the Internet. Today, literally tens of thousands of web sites are maintained by racists, Islamists, and Jew haters. I inadvertently discovered the magnitude of the problem (and its direct impact on me) when I searched for myself when the Google search engine first came online. I was very impressed that my name came up on thousands of web sites. Then I started to look at the references. It turned out that a Holocaust denier had cited an article I had written years earlier, which had nothing to do with the Holocaust, and the denier's article appeared on every racist, neo-Nazi Holocaust denial site, and there were thousands of them. The Internet is used today by post-Zionist Israelis, far left Europeans, "human rights" advocates, and the usual bigots to attack Israel.

The Internet is an ideal vehicle for the "big lie" championed by the Nazi propaganda machine. For many young people, especially, whatever appears online is the truth; they have no idea how to verify what they read and no other sources of reliable information. Thus, if a web site reports, as many do, that the Jews who worked in the World Trade Center all called in sick the morning of 9/11 or that the Mossad carried out the attack, nothing can stop the conspiracy theories from being circulated and too often believed by the uniformed or gullible.

In the modern, politically correct world, it is not acceptable to criticize Jews; however, it has become fashionable to attack Zionism instead. Depaul University professor Norman Finkelstein, for example, argues that "Zionism is inherently racist."[2] Columbia University professor Joseph Massad goes further and suggests that Zionists are the true anti-Semites. "Zionism's anti-Semitic project [was] destroying Jewish cultures and languages in the diaspora," Massad says, "in the interest of an invented Hebrew that none of them spoke, and in the interest of evicting them from Europe."[3] Detractors can suggest they are not really attacking Jews, just "Zionists," a nonreligious, amorphous group that, in their minds, coincidentally happen to be Jews. To them, Zionists engage in all manner of outrageous, immoral, and illegal activities: They moved from their native homes to their biblical homeland, stole land to create a colonial, imperialist outpost that now tramples on human rights, ignores international law, and treats the Palestinians in a manner comparable to the way Jews were treated by Nazis.

Paradoxically, it is the Zionists who were anti-imperialist and anticolonialist. The Zionists fought to drive the British imperialists from Palestine and, rather than behave as colonialists themselves by exploiting Arab laborers, the Jewish pioneers strove to do their own work. The Zionists were hardly tools of imperialists, given the world powers' general opposition to their cause. "Everywhere in the West," British historian Paul Johnson noted in *Modern Times: The World from the Twenties to the Nineties*, "the foreign offices, defense ministries and big business were against the Zionists."[4] Anti-Zionists protest that they are not anti-Jewish, but as Martin Luther King responded to a student who attacked Zionism, "When people criticize Zionists, they mean Jews. You're talking anti-Semitism."[5]

This is not to say that it is unfair, inappropriate, or impermissible to criticize Israeli policy. Anyone interested in reading criticism of Israel need only pick up an Israeli newspaper any day of the week and they will find a vigorous debate about virtually every aspect of Israeli life. The distinction between legitimate criticism, however, and anti-Semitism is usually quite clear and can be determined by what Natan Sharansky calls the "3-D" test—committing any one "D" is usually indicative of anti-Semitism.[6] The first D is the test for demonizing: Are Israel and its leaders being demonized and are their actions blown out of proportion? Equating Israel with Nazi Germany is one example of demonization. The second D is the double standards test—as when Israel is singled out for condemnation at the United Nations for perceived human rights abuses while nations that violate human rights on a massive scale, such as Iran, Syria, and Saudi Arabia, are not even mentioned. The third D is the test of delegitimization: Questioning Israel's right to exist is always anti-Semitic. Unlike genuine critics, anti-Semites are not interested in improving Israeli society; their goal is to delegitimize the state in the short run and to destroy it in the long run. There is nothing Israel can do to satisfy these critics.

Another twist is the suggestion that Israel's actions are responsible for anti-Semitism as if anti-Semitism did not exist for centuries before the rise of the modern state of Israel. Rather than Israel being the cause of anti-Semitism, it is more likely that the distorted media coverage of Israeli policies is reflecting and reinforcing latent anti-Semitic views. As writer Leon Wieseltier observes, "The notion that all Jews are responsible for whatever any Jews do is not a Zionist notion. It is an anti-Semitic notion." Wieseltier adds that attacks on Jews in Europe have nothing whatsoever to do with Israel. To blame Jews for anti-Semitism is similar to saying blacks are responsible for racism or rape victims invite violence.[7]

Some of these attitudes can be traced to centuries-old hatred of the Jews rooted in Christian dogma, to notions of the Jews as strangers who don't conform, and to outright prejudice. The shift toward anti-Zionism, however, is also motivated by cold political calculation based on the political and economic interests of nations. The Europeans have never gotten beyond seeing the Middle East as part of its sphere of influence whose only purposes are to provide oil and trade opportunities. As more oil was pumped and the Arab producers became more wealthy, these two economic benefits became more important. Israel does not fit into the Europeans' calculus since it produces no oil for them and is so small that the value of trade is not worth upsetting the Arabs.

It is an economic reality that the world depends on oil: The Muslim states have it and Israel does not. The Europeans, as well as other nations, cannot be blamed for seeking business opportunities with the Muslim world, and especially with the profligate oil producers who can spend billions of dollars on arms, consumer goods and services that benefit individuals, corporations and national treasuries. Israel may be an advanced nation that also has a great deal to buy and sell, but it is a market of only 7 million people, compared to the 300 million consumers in the surrounding countries. EU nations are still Israel's largest trading partner, although the EU also bans imports from Israeli settlements in the territories. The Europeans are particularly keen to compete with the Americans for the lucrative multibillion-dollar Arab arms market. For example, the British agreed in 2006 to sell new Eurofighter Typhoon jets to the Saudis for a reported $20 billion. By contrast, Europe has sold few arms to Israel since France ceased being a major supplier in 1967 (one exception is submarines provided by Germany), which has made Israel reliant on the United States for most of its sophisticated weaponry.

Politically, countries have little to gain from supporting Israel. In international forums such as the United Nations, where support is needed from a large number of countries to secure favorable decisions, it makes little sense to back Israel and risk alienating 21 Arab states, or the 56 members of the Organization of the Islamic Conference. The experience of the United States has also shown that even close Arab allies rarely are prepared to support its positions at the UN. Supporting Israel politically wins them Israel's one vote and loses them all the Muslim votes. It's a simple calculation for the Europeans: Should we risk oil, trade, and political support by siding with Israel and upsetting the Arabs? Despite the history of U.S.-Israel relations, which has demonstrated that it is possible to have an alliance with Israel without jeopardizing oil supplies or broader ties with the Arab world, virtually every other country in the world allows itself to be coerced by the fear of economic and political blackmail.

The internal political dynamics of European countries also discourages support for Israel. Jews make up a tiny fraction of the population, less than 1 percent, and the parliamentary systems are such that it is not possible to create an Israeli lobby or an organization such as the American Israel Public Affairs Committee (AIPAC), though efforts are being made. In most countries, the Jewish population is shrinking while the Muslim population is growing exponentially. In France, for example, which has the largest Jewish population in Europe, the estimated 10 million Muslims now dwarf the Jewish community of 500,000. A simple political calculation can tell you which constituency politicians will be most interested in satisfying.

It is true that U.S. Middle East policy also is shaped by its economic, political, and strategic interests, with securing oil as its paramount concern. Still, I would argue the United States has an ideological interest in freedom and democracy as well. Israel is a beacon radiating these values in a region that despite our best efforts has not embraced them, which is one of the main reasons the United States has remained its steadfast friend. Conspiracy theorists and anti-Semites argue this interest is a product of the omnipotent Jewish lobby (discussed in chapter 12), but the relationship with Israel is based on fundamental values and interests that the majority of Americans support.

Though he is ridiculed for his ideological commitment to bring American-style freedom and democracy to people who have never experienced these values, the American pursuit of these goals predates the administration of George W. Bush. Many Europeans see his declarations in support of freedom and democracy as hypocritical platitudes in light of some U.S. policies (for example, supporting despotic regimes in countries such as Egypt and Saudi Arabia), but Americans do believe in these ideals and, on occasion at least, act to uphold and advance them. The Europeans, on the other hand (with the exception of Tony Blair), are completely feckless. They don't even pay lip service to democracy or shared values; they have only interests. One consequence is that "Israel is the only state in the world today, and the Jews the only people in the world today, that are the object of a standing set of threats from governmental, religious, and terrorist bodies seeking their destruction," observed former Canadian minister of justice and attorney general Irwin Cotler in 2002. "And what is most disturbing is the silence, the indifference, and sometimes even the indulgence, in the face of such genocidal anti-Semitism."[8]

The tolerance of threats to Israel is a consequence of the legitimization of the new anti-Semitism, which can be traced back at least as far as the 1975 UN General Assembly Resolution 3379 slandering Zionism by equating it with racism. This was typical of the Alice-in-Wonderland nature of the UN because it singled out Jewish self-determination for condemnation as a racist act while granting legitimacy to Palestinian and other peoples' right to a homeland. The resolution was repealed in 1991, but the precedent set by the original resolution was reaffirmed a decade later when Arab nations sought to equate Zionism with racism again at the UN World Conference Against Racism in Durban, South Africa, in 2001. The United States joined Israel in boycotting the conference when it became clear that rather than focus on the evils of racism, anti-Semitism and xenophobia that were supposed to be the subject of the event, the conference had turned into a forum for bashing Israel.

The legitimization of anti-Semitism has been accompanied by a growth in violence against Jews in Europe. Just over 400 incidents were recorded in 2005. Whether this is a serious problem or not depends on one's perspective. If you think about it on a global scale, 400 incidents are not a very large number spread over an entire year and dozens of countries with significant Jewish populations. On the other hand, the sense of discomfort among Jews is especially palpable in Western Europe, a function of their governments' policies toward Israel, violent and nonviolent incidents, incessant media attacks on Israel, the growing Muslim population and the activism of Islamists.

Jews I've spoken to in France say they see no future for the community. Is it any wonder when they heard their ambassador to England, Daniel Bernard, complain in 2001 that "those people" are leading the world into World War III and that the international security crisis had been triggered by "that shitty little country, Israel"? Or when they were told by President Jacques Chirac in the midst of a series of anti-Semitic incidents that "There is no anti-Semitism in France"?[9] While most French Jews do not fear being attacked, few make any public displays of their religion, such as wearing a Star of David necklace. Several told me that the wealthy Jews are moving to the United States and the poorer ones to Israel. In fact, many wealthy French Jews have purchased expensive apartments, especially in Jerusalem, where they live only part of the year. These homes are also meant as a haven if one day they have to flee France.

The situation has also deteriorated in Great Britain. A 2006 poll of British Muslims, for example, found that 37 percent believed Anglo Jewry is a "legitimate target as part of the struggle for justice in the Middle East." More than half of those surveyed believed British Jews exerted too much influence over foreign policy and 46 percent said British Jews are in league with Freemasons to control the media and politics. The danger is quite real. The Director-General of the British MI5 said on November 10, 2006, that young

British Muslims are becoming radicalized at an alarming rate and are "moving from passive sympathy towards active terrorism."[10]

One of the most visible manifestations of the new anti-Semitism occurred in 2005 when the Association of University Teachers (AUT) announced a boycott of Israel's Bar-Ilan and Haifa universities in response, proponents said, to requests from Palestinian academics who said the Israeli schools were contributing to the occupation. The AUT was the trade union and professional association representing academic and academic-related staff at certain universities in the United Kingdom; it was hijacked by a handful of militantly anti-Israel professors who held the vote during Passover, when many Jewish members could not attend. The vote provoked an internal and external backlash in part because of the hypocrisy of an organization ostensibly dedicated to academic freedom imposing a boycott of other academics in the only country in the Middle East where universities enjoy political independence, and where the boycott's impact would be to undermine dialogue between Israelis and Palestinians. After other members of the AUT rallied support, a special session was called and the decision was reversed. A year later, proponents of the boycott tried again but were rebuffed. When the AUT merged with the National Association of Teachers in Further and Higher Education (NATFHE), the combined membership rejected the idea of restricting open debate and academic freedom by boycotting fellow teachers, who, ironically, are among the most critical of Israeli policies toward the Palestinians.

Along similar lines, Israel's detractors in the Anglican Church shocked British Jews in February 2006 when they convinced the synod of the Church of England to announce support for divesting from companies whose products are used by Israel in the territories. The archbishop of Canterbury, Rowan Williams, who supported the decision, became the highest church official to have joined a boycott campaign against Israel. The church position was especially galling given its complete silence about the persecution and disappearance of Christians in every other country in the Middle East. Williams's predecessor, George Carey, said after the vote that he was "ashamed to be an Anglican" and called the decision "regrettable' and "one-sided" because it "ignores the trauma of ordinary Jewish people" in Israel subjected to terrorist attacks.[11] Anglicans in Israel (Christ Church Jerusalem), which has been in Jerusalem since the late eighteenth century, called the divestment decision "one-sided," "anti-Semitic," and "naive," and said it would "do nothing to promote genuine reconciliation between Jews and

Arabs in the Middle East."[12] A few months after the church decision, divestment activists were defeated when the Church of England's financial advisors voted unanimously to reject the call to sell its shares of Caterpillar. The American company has been a central target of the divestment campaign because of its sale of bulldozers that, activists say, are used to demolish Palestinian homes in the territories.

As in the United States, it now appears unlikely that either the boycott or divestment campaigns will succeed in changing policy in Britain; nevertheless, the new anti-Semites will continue to pursue these and other actions aimed at advancing the Durban agenda. Even when they lose, the publicity their efforts receive helps them brand Israel an apartheid state. In fact, the person who is becoming a hero to the new anti-Semites is former President Jimmy Carter, who published a book of anti-Israel calumnies in 2006 titled, *Palestine: Peace Not Apartheid.* Curiously enough, if you read through almost he entire book, which persistently accuses Israel of apartheid acts, you arrive at page 189, where he specifically contradicts the entire thesis by stating, "The driving purpose for the forced separation of the two people is unlike that in South Africa." It is clear from the beginning, however, that facts are of little concern to Carter who sees Israel as "the tiny vortex around which swirl the winds of hatred, intolerance, and bloodshed." It is certainly true that Israel is subject to these winds; the question is why he blames the victim. Why doesn't he see the Islamist rejection of a Jewish presence in the region as the problem, or the unwillingness of the Palestinians to accept a two-state solution? Carter is entitled to his opinions, but he has falsified history to such an extent that the book often reads like a work of fiction.[13] One long-term goal of the new anti-Semitism is to make the association between Israel and South Africa so strong that it will eventually be possible to win international support for the types of sanctions used against the apartheid regime to isolate Israel.

Europeans have at least taken notice of the rise in anti-Semitic crimes and some organizations, such as the European Commission Against Racism and Intolerance (ECRI) and the European Union Monitoring Center Against Racism and Xenophobia (EUMC) have issued declarations against anti-Semitism. The EUMC also now considers denying the Jewish people their right to self-determination, such as by claiming the existence of the state of Israel, a racist endeavor, an example of anti-Semitism. Laws against hate crimes, anti-Semitism and Holocaust denial have also been adopted in various countries. Still, manifestations of the new anti-Semitism have proliferated.

The problems are not restricted to Western Europe. Anti-Zionism is also rampant in Russia and some of the former Soviet republics. Much of the anti-Semitic propaganda used around the world by the anti-Zionists, such as the czarist forgery of the *Protocols of the Elders of Zion,* originated in Russia and the Soviet Union. On the whole, however, examples of the new anti-Semitism have been less prevalent in eastern and central Europe, perhaps because those countries are still struggling with their own histories relating to the Holocaust. Few Muslims live in those countries and attacks on Israel have a negative association with the hated communist governments of the past. Though relations with Israel have improved dramatically since the fall of communism, Russia has a long history of support for Arab countries and continues to arm Israel's enemies, as does China and North Korea, all of whom have also contributed to Iran's nuclear program.

In Latin America, leftist presidents such as Hugo Chavez in Venezuela have also staked out anti-Israel positions. Argentina has still not brought to justice the terrorists responsible for the bombings of the AMIA Jewish community center and the Israeli Embassy in Buenos Aires in the 1990s. The hostility in this part of the world does not directly threaten Israel, but the Latin American countries represent a potentially large block of votes at the UN. They played a crucial role in the adoption of the partition resolution in 1947 and may side with Israel's enemies now.

This global environment of hostility and the questioning of Israel's legitimacy certainly adds to Israelis' feeling of being under siege. As in 1975 when the United Nations adopted the resolution equating Zionism and racism, the UN and its various constituent agencies remains the principal international forum for attacking Israel. UN Secretary-General Kofi Annan admitted at the opening of the 61st General Assembly on September 20, 2006, that Israel is often unfairly judged at the United Nations. "On one side, supporters of Israel feel that it is harshly judged by standards that are not applied to its enemies," he said. "And too often this is true, particularly in some UN bodies."

Starting in the mid-1970s, an Arab-Soviet-Third World bloc formed what amounted to a pro-PLO (Palestinian Liberation Organization) lobby at the United Nations. This was particularly true in the General Assembly where these countries—nearly all dictatorships or autocracies—frequently voted together to pass resolutions attacking Israel and supporting the PLO. In 1974, for example, the General Assembly invited Yasser Arafat to address it. Arafat did so, a holster at his hip. In his speech, Arafat spoke of carrying a gun and an olive branch (he left his gun outside before entering the hall). In 1975, the assembly awarded permanent representative status to the PLO, which opened an office in midtown Manhattan. Later that year, at the instigation of the Arab states and the Soviet bloc, the assembly approved the aforementioned Resolution 3379 that slandered Zionism by branding it a form of racism.

U.S. Ambassador Daniel Moynihan called the resolution an "obscene act." Israeli Ambassador Chaim Herzog told his fellow delegates the resolution was "based on hatred, falsehood and arrogance." Hitler, he declared, would have felt at home listening to the UN debate on the measure. On December 16, 1991, the General Assembly voted 111 to 25 (with 13 abstentions and 17 delegations absent or not voting) to repeal Resolution 3379. The repeal vote was marred by the fact that 13 of the 19 Arab countries—including three engaged in negotiations with Israel, Syria, Lebanon and Jordan—voted to retain the resolution, as did Saudi Arabia. Six, including Egypt—which lobbied against repeal—were absent. No Arab country voted for repeal. The PLO denounced the vote and the U.S. role. The Arabs "voted once again to impugn the very birthright of the Jewish State," the *New York Times* noted on December 17, 1991. "That even now most Arab states cling to a demeaning and vicious doctrine mars an otherwise belated triumph for sense and conscience."

To put this "triumph" in context, less than a week before repealing the measure, the General Assembly approved four new one-sided resolutions on the Middle East, including a call for a UN-sponsored peace conference with the PLO and a condemnation of Israeli behavior toward Palestinians in the territories. On the day of the vote itself, the General Assembly voted 152 to 1, with the United States abstaining, to call on Israel to rescind a Knesset resolution declaring Jerusalem its capital, to demand Israel's withdrawal from "occupied territories," including Jerusalem, and to denounce Israeli administration of the Golan Heights.

Bloc voting also made possible the establishment of the pro-PLO Committee on the Inalienable Rights of the Palestinian People in 1975. The panel became, in effect, part of the PLO propaganda apparatus, issuing stamps, organizing meetings, preparing films and draft resolutions in support

of Palestinian rights. In 1976 the committee recommended "full implementation of the inalienable rights of the Palestinian people, including their return
to the Israeli part of Palestine." It also recommended that November 29—the
day the UN voted to partition Palestine in 1947—be declared an "International Day of Solidarity with the Palestinian People." Since then, it has
been observed at the UN with anti-Israel speeches, films, and exhibits.

Today approximately 20 UN committees are dedicated to the Palestinian
issue. In 2004–2005, the UN allocated $5.5 million to the Division for
Palestinian Rights, $255,000 for the Special Committee to Investigate Israeli
Practices Affecting the Human Rights of the Palestinian People and Other
Arabs of the Occupied Territories, $60,000 for the Committee on the
Exercise of the Inalienable Rights of the Palestinian People, and $566,000
for Information Activities on the Question of Palestine. Since the United
States finances one-fourth of the UN budget, American officials have grown
impatient with efforts to politicize the organization and have taken increasingly forceful action in response to some of the more egregious agencies. In
1977, the United States withdrew from the International Labor Organization
for two years because of its anti-Israel stance. In 1984 the United States left
UNESCO in part because of its bias against the Jewish State. From 1982
until 1989, the Arab states sought to deny Israel a seat in the General
Assembly or to put special conditions on Israel's participation. Only a determined U.S. lobbying campaign prevented them from succeeding.

The United States has consistently opposed PLO attempts to upgrade its
status in the General Assembly and UN-affiliated bodies. This was particularly true in 1989, when Arafat tried to have the PLO admitted as the "State
of Palestine" and to elevate its status in the World Health Organization, the
World Tourist Organization and the Food and Agriculture Organization
(FAO). Because of the determined opposition of Congress and the George
H. W. Bush Administration, the PLO was defeated everywhere but the FAO,
when that organization decided to provide agricultural aid through the PLO,
the United States withdrew from it.

Throughout the 1990s and into the new millennium a steady stream of
anti-Israel resolutions and actions have emanated from the UN. In 2003, for
example, the organization called an unprecedented three emergency sessions
to discuss Israel—two to condemn Israel's security fence and one to criticize
Israel for openly considering the expulsion of Arafat. That year the UN held a
two-day International Conference of Civil Society in Support of the

Palestinian People with the theme "End the Occupation!" During the event, which began with a statement of support from the UN Secretary-General, the Palestinian observer to the UN, Nasser al-Kidwa, said that "violence in self-defense in the occupied Palestinian territories is not terrorism." Even when Israel is not directly involved in an issue, UN officials find ways to interject their biases against the Jewish State. For example, in April 2004, the UN envoy to Iraq, Lakhdar Brahimi, called Israel's policies "the great poison in the region." In 2005, even after a series of positive changes at the UN, a number of public events in support of the Palestinian cause were held on November 29, including a conference to mark "an international day of sympathy with the Palestinian people" and a press briefing attended by members of the Palestinian delegation to the UN, on the subject of "Promoting the Palestinian cause through dance and cultural events." A Palestinian exhibition was displayed at UN headquarters and the General Assembly held a special session to discuss a report by the Committee on the Exercise of the Inalienable Rights of the Palestinian People on "The Question of Palestine." During the celebratory events, a map of the Middle East was exhibited that did not show the UN member state of Israel; in its place was the nonexistent nation of Palestine.

Though Israel has been the target of terrorist attacks for its entire history, the UN has consistently refused to condemn the perpetrators and has often passed resolutions criticizing Israel's efforts to defend its citizens. Finally, in March 2005, after nearly five years of incessant terrorist attacks during the Palestinian war, which ultimately claimed more than 1,000 Israeli lives, the Security Council issued an unprecedented condemnation of a suicide bombing in Tel Aviv carried out by Islamic Jihad. Unlike Israeli actions that provoke resolutions, the Security Council released only a "policy statement" urging the Palestinian Authority to "take immediate, credible steps to find those responsible for this terrorist attack" and bring them to justice. It also encouraged "further and sustained action to prevent other acts of terror." The statement required the consent of all 15 members of the Security Council. The one Arab member, Algeria, signed on only after a reference to Islamic Jihad was deleted.

Two years earlier, in 2003, Israel had sought to gain support for a resolution of its own, the first it had introduced since 1976. The resolution called for the protection of Israeli children from terrorism; it did not receive enough support from the members of the General Assembly to even come to a vote. Israel had introduced the resolution in response to the murder of Israeli children in terrorist attacks during the previous three years after a similar resolution had been adopted on November 6, 2003, calling for the protection of Palestinian children from "Israeli aggression." Israel's ambassador withdrew the proposed draft after it became clear that members of the nonaligned movement were determined to revise it in a way that would have ultimately been critical of Israel. Is it any wonder that former UN ambassador Jeanne Kirkpatrick said in 1983 that what takes place in the Security Council "more closely resembles a mugging than either a political debate or an effort at problem-solving"?

Just to get a sense of the disproportionate attention given to the Palestinians, consider that of the roughly 700 UN resolutions on the Middle East conflict, approximately one out of seven refers directly to the Palestinian refugees. Not one mentions the Jewish refugees from Arab countries. The United Nations took up the refugee issue and adopted Resolution 194 on December 11, 1948. This called upon the Arab states and Israel to resolve all outstanding issues through negotiations either directly or with the help of the Palestine Conciliation Commission established by this resolution. Further, Point 11 resolves:

> that refugees wishing to return to their homes and *live at peace* with their neighbors should be permitted to do so at the earliest practicable date, and that compensation should be paid for property of those choosing not to return and for loss of or damage to property which under principles of international law or in equity should be made good by Governments or authorities responsible. Instructs the Conciliation Commission to facilitate the repatriation, *resettlement* and economic and social rehabilitation of refugees and payment of compensation... [emphasis added].

The emphasized words demonstrate that the UN recognized that Israel could not be expected to repatriate a hostile population that might endanger its security. The solution to the problem, like all previous refugee problems, would require at least some Palestinians to be resettled in Arab lands. The resolution met most of Israel's concerns regarding the refugees, whom they regarded as a potential fifth column if allowed to return unconditionally. The Israelis considered the settlement of the refugee issue a negotiable part of an overall peace settlement. The Arabs were no more willing to compromise in 1949, however, than they had been in 1947. They unanimously rejected the UN resolution.

The UN created an agency, ultimately known as the United Nations Relief and Works Agency (UNRWA), to dispense aid to the refugees. UNRWA was designed to substitute public works for direct relief and promote economic development. The proponents of the plan envisioned that direct relief would gradually be almost completely replaced by public works, with the remaining assistance provided by the Arab governments. UNRWA had little chance of success, however, because it sought to solve a political problem using an economic approach. By the mid-1950s, it was evident neither the refugees nor the Arab states were prepared to cooperate on the large-scale development projects originally foreseen by the agency as a means of alleviating the Palestinians' situation. The Arab governments and the refugees themselves were unwilling to contribute to any plan that could be interpreted as fostering resettlement. They preferred to cling to their interpretation of Resolution 194, which they believed would eventually result in repatriation.

For nearly six decades now, the Palestinians and the Arab states have refused to take steps to resettle the refugees. Even today, with the majority of the refugees under the direct supervision of the Palestinian Authority, no effort has been made by the Palestinian leadership to take their brothers and sisters out of camps and build permanent housing for them. This is particularly tragic in the case of Gaza, where the Palestinians said they planned to build high-rise apartments for refugees on the rubble of the Jewish settlements that were evacuated and, at the authority's request, demolished. More than a year later, not one building had been constructed.

Meanwhile, UNRWA has become nothing more than an international welfare agency to support the Palestinians, with American taxpayers as the largest contributors. The agency has been accused of corruption and support for terrorism and perpetuated Palestinian dependency on the international community. Though probably no more than 500,000 Palestinians became refugees in the period 1947 to 1949, today UNRWA classifies 4.3 million Palestinians on its rolls.

Because the Security Council established the diplomatic parameters for solving the Arab-Israeli conflict, UN Resolutions 242 (1967) and 338 (1973), many people outside the UN still believe it can play a useful role in bringing peace to Middle East. A careful analysis of the Security Council's actions on the Middle East, however, shows it has been little better than the General Assembly in its treatment of Israel.

Candidates for the Security Council are proposed by regional groups. Every UN member state belongs to one of five regional groups. Geographically, Israel should be part of the Asian group, but Arab states such as Iraq and Saudi Arabia have successfully prevented Israel's inclusion. In the Middle East, this means the Arab League and its allies are usually candidates. Israel, which joined the UN in 1949, has never been elected to the Security Council whereas at least 15 Arab League members have. In fact, until recently, Israel was the only one of the 185 member countries ineligible to serve on the Security Council. A breakthrough in Israel's 50-year exclusion from UN bodies occurred in 2000, when Israel accepted an invitation to become a temporary member of the Western European and Others (WEOG) regional group. This historic step helped end at least some of the UN's discriminatory actions against Israel and opened the door to the possibility of Israeli participation in the Security Council. The WEOG is the only regional group that is not purely geographical, but rather geopolitical—namely, a group of states that share a Western-Democratic common denominator. WEOG comprises 27 members: all the West European states and Australia, Canada, New Zealand, and the United States.

Since joining WEOG, Israeli candidates have been successful in winning a variety of UN posts, starting in 2003 with the election to serve on the UN General Assembly Working Group on Disarmament, Israel's first committee posting since 1961. (After 1961, the UN split the membership into regional groups and Israel became isolated.) A further advance occurred in July 2005 when Israel's Ambassador to the UN, Dan Gillerman, was elected one of 20 vice presidents who set the agenda for the next General Assembly session. Shortly thereafter, Israel was tapped to serve as deputy chair of the UN Disarmament Commission (UNDC), a General Assembly subcommittee that serves as an advisory body on disarmament issues. In September 2005, Israel announced it was applying for the first time to become a member of the

Security Council. Each year WEOG sends two of its 29 countries to the Security Council. The next available slot will open only in 2019. Every year, at least one Arab state sits on the council.

Another major breakthrough occurred on January 24, 2005, when the UN General Assembly held a commemoration of the 60th anniversary of the liberation of the Nazi concentration camps. This marked the first time that the General Assembly convened to commemorate the Holocaust, and the first time that the General Assembly held a Special Session at Israel's initiative. The session was intended to strengthen international awareness of the Holocaust and the struggle against anti-Semitism, and the related significance of the rebirth of the state of Israel and the Jewish people. Later in 2005, a resolution was adopted establishing January 27 as Holocaust Remembrance Day at the United Nations. It also calls on member states to include the Holocaust in their educational curriculums and condemn manifestations of Holocaust denial. This was the first Israeli-initiated resolution the General Assembly has ever passed.

Despite its support at various forums, the United States doesn't always back Israel. At the General Assembly, the impact is small since assembly resolutions are mainly political statements. At the Security Council, however, resolutions can be backed by international action, such as the creation of peacekeeping forces. Many people believe the United States can always be relied on to support Israel with its veto in the UN Security Council; however, the historical record shows that the U.S. has often opposed Israel in the council. In 1990, for example, Washington voted for Security Council resolutions condemning Israel's handling of a riot on the Temple Mount and its decision to expel four leaders of Hamas. In January 1992, the United States supported a one-sided resolution condemning Israel for expelling 12 Palestinians, members of terrorist groups that were responsible for perpetrating violence against Arab and Jew alike. In 1996, it went along with a Saudi-inspired condemnation of Israel for opening a tunnel in "the vicinity" of the al-Aqsa mosque.

The Bush administration has more aggressively sought to prevent UN bodies from unfairly targeting Israel and has been less hesitant to vote against resolutions singling Israel out for criticism. In 2002 the United States announced that it would veto any Security Council resolution on the Middle East that did not condemn Palestinian terror and name Hamas, Islamic

Jihad, and the Al-Aqsa Martyrs Brigade as the groups responsible for the attacks. The United States also said that resolutions must note that any Israeli withdrawal is linked to the security situation, and that both parties must be called upon to pursue a negotiated settlement. Despite the Bush administration's stated resolve, it too has been unwilling to oppose every one-side anti-Israel resolution. In May 2004, for example, the United States abstained on a resolution condemning Israel for its actions in Gaza during a military operation aimed at stopping terrorism and weapons smuggling.

The United States did not cast its first veto of a resolution about Israel until 1972, on a Syrian-Lebanese complaint against Israel. From 1967 to 72, the United States supported or abstained on 24 resolutions, most of which were critical of Israel. From 1973 to 2006, the Security Council adopted approximately 100 resolutions on the Middle East, most were again critical of Israel. The United States vetoed a total of 40 resolutions and, hence, supported the council's criticism of Israel by its vote of support or abstaining roughly two-thirds of the time.

The Arabs can avoid the United States veto by taking issues to the General Assembly, where nonbinding resolutions pass by majority vote and where support for almost any anti-Israel resolution is assured. In December 2002, for example, the United States, breaking its pattern of abstaining, voted for the first time against a UN resolution calling on Israel to repeal the Jerusalem Law, but the resolution still passed 154-5.

The politics of the UN are understandable—the fact that bloc voting affects the issues considered and the outcome of resolutions, and that most nations believe it is in their political and economic interest to support the Arab and Muslim states' attacks on Israel. What is unacceptable, however, is the way the UN has become permeated with anti-Semitic and anti-Zionist sentiment. The following comments illustrate how ugly the atmosphere has become.

"Is it not the Jews who are exploiting the American people and trying to debase them?"—*Libyan UN Representative Ali Treiki.*[14]

"The Talmud says that if a Jew does not drink every year the blood of a non-Jewish man, he will be damned for eternity." —*Saudi Arabian delegate Marouf al-Dawalibi before the 1984 UN Human Rights Commission conference on religious tolerance.*[15]

A similar remark was made by the Syrian Ambassador at a 1991 meeting, who insisted Jews killed Christian children to use their blood to make matzos.[16]

On March 11, 1997, the Palestinian representative to the UN Human Rights Commission claimed the Israeli government had injected 300 Palestinian children with the HIV virus.[17]

In 2003, the first resolution explicitly condemning anti-Semitism was offered in the General Assembly, but its sponsor, Ireland, later withdrew it due to lack of support. Meanwhile, UN officials were among those making the most outrageous statements. Jean Ziegler, the UN special rapporteur on the Right to Food, for example, called the Gaza Strip "an immense concentration camp" and compared Israelis to Nazis. Earlier, Ziegler had called on the Caterpillar company to boycott Israel. In response to complaints, UN spokesman Farhan Haq said, "His views are his own, not those of the United Nations. The United Nations believes any comparison between conditions in Gaza and those of Nazi concentration camps is irresponsible. Such a comparison does not reflect the views of the secretary-general." Dissatisfied by the failure to take punitive action against Ziegler, 70 members of Congress wrote to Secretary-General Annan to express their concern and called on him to take steps to end anti-Semitism within the UN and to fight against anti-Semitism worldwide.

The worst example of how the UN is used by the anti-Semites rather than standing against them, is the Human Rights Council (HRC). The HRC was established in 2006 to replace the former Commission on Human Rights, which had become a travesty after allowing some of the worst human rights violators to participate in deliberations and to adopt a steady stream of one-sided condemnations of Israel. The General Assembly created a new body, ostensibly to erase the stain on the UN created by its predecessor. In the first months of operation, however, the new council proved to be worse than the original commission. Of the 47 members, 17 are members of the Organization of the Islamic Conference and repressive dictatorships such as China and Cuba are also members. While Western nations struggled to focus the council's attention on the genocide in Darfur, the majority chose instead to produce a series of reports criticizing Israel. To give one example, the council did not criticize Hizbollah for attacking Israel, kidnapping its soldiers, indiscriminately firing missiles at Israel, or using Lebanese civilians as shields, but it did condemn Israel for "violations of human rights and breaches of international humanitarian law in Lebanon."

The UN has also been directly involved in Israel's security deploying military forces assembled to stop the fighting and to create the conditions for peace. In 1956 a UN Emergency Force was sent to Sinai after the war between Israel and Egypt to prevent the outbreak of another war and to ensure that Egypt did not try again to block Israeli shipping in the Straits of Tiran. In 1967, however, Nasser ordered the force to withdraw. Without bringing the matter to the attention of the General Assembly, as his predecessor had promised, Secretary-General U Thant complied with the demand. After the withdrawal of the emergency force, Egypt did block the straits, built up its forces and ultimately provoked a war.

In 1978 Israeli forces went into Lebanon to stop PLO terrorist attacks and, after Israel was compelled by the international community to withdraw, a UN military contingent was deployed. The UN Interim Force in Lebanon (UNIFIL) was supposed to prevent any further attacks against Israel from Lebanon, but it was unable and unwilling to prevent terrorists from reinfiltrating the region and introducing new, more dangerous arms. UNIFIL's failure to prevent more than 200 terrorist attacks ultimately led Israel to reenter Lebanon in 1982 to drive out the PLO. Three years later, following the expulsion of the PLO leadership and destruction of its terrorist infrastructure, Israel withdrew the bulk of its forces, leaving behind a 1,000-man force deployed in a strip of territory extending eight miles into southern Lebanon to protect towns and villages in northern Israel. The hope was that the terrorists remaining in Lebanon would be disarmed. Instead, Iran was allowed to finance and arm Hizbollah, which initially confined itself to launching Katyusha rocket attacks on northern Israel and ambushing Israeli troops in the security zone. Gradually Hizbollah escalated its attacks on Israeli civilians. UNIFIL stood by and did nothing. As the number of casualties mounted, the Israeli public began to favor a withdrawal of its soldiers. On May 24, 2000, all IDF and South Lebanon army outposts were evacuated. The Israeli withdrawal was conducted in coordination with the UN and constituted an Israeli fulfillment of its obligations under a 1978 Security Council Resolution that had called for Israel's complete withdrawal from Lebanon. Israel thought that by completely withdrawing from Lebanon in 2000, Hizbollah would have no justification for continuing its attacks—the old land for peace formula—and that UNIFIL would now do its job and prevent any further cross-border provocations. Instead, Hizbollah interpreted Israel's unilateral withdrawal as a victory for its terrorist methods. Rather than a cease-fire, Hizbollah was emboldened and believed it could continue to pursue its broader agenda of destroying Israel.

UNIFIL did nothing to stop terrorist attacks against Israel. On October 7, 2000, for example, three Israeli soldiers were abducted by Hizbollah. The terrorists crossed through a UN-patrolled area to get to the soldiers on the Israeli side of the Israeli-Lebanese border and were videotaped by UN troops. For almost nine months, Kofi Annan denied possessing any videotape related to the kidnapping. The UN finally admitted that they possessed the tape, but it was later learned they had two additional tapes and other evidence related to the abduction. When Israel demanded to see the tapes, the UN initially refused, but eventually relented after imposing a number of conditions, including editing them so as to obscure the faces of the kidnappers. The UN said it wanted to remain neutral and did not want to provide intelligence to one party in the conflict. The three soldiers were later declared dead.

In 2006, after Hizbollah killed three Israeli soldiers, kidnapped two others, and launched a barrage of rockets at northern Israel, the IDF reentered Lebanon. After a month of fighting, the UN called for a cease-fire and the creation of a new, more robust UN force. Now the UN is facing another test of its ability to play a constructive role in the Middle East. Will the force do as instructed and prevent further terror attacks against Israel? Will it take steps to disarm Hizbollah and prevent it from rearming? So far, the results are not encouraging.

✡

Given this history of the UN, which only touches the surface of how damaging its actions have been to Israel, is it any wonder that few Israelis are willing to trust the organization to contribute to its survival?

The news is not entirely bleak, however, as Israel has diplomatic relations with more countries today than ever before, and many leaders are more openly pro-Israel, such as the Canadian, British, and Australian prime ministers. In fact, few countries outside the Middle East have any reluctance to engage in diplomatic, economic, and cultural contacts. Israel has in recent years made great breakthroughs in expanding ties with China and India, and even had its first tentative meetings with Pakistan. Israel has excellent relations with a number of the former Soviet republics and, as noted earlier, a dramatically improved relationship with Russia.

In 1973, African nations were pressured by Arab oil-producing nations to sever what had been very positive and productive relations with Israel. Once the coercive power of the Arab oil producers eroded, African countries began to reestablish relations with Israel and to seek new cooperative projects. This trend gained momentum during peace negotiations in the 1990s between Israel and its Arab neighbors. Today, 40 African countries maintain diplomatic ties with Israel, and reciprocal visits by heads of state and government ministers take place frequently.

Israel's security is also enhanced by its burgeoning relationship with NATO. Though the alliance is far from a commitment to incorporating Israel under its security umbrella, the willingness to include Israel in NATO exercises and other activities have strengthened ties with member nations.

Another important actor on the international stage is the Pope. Jews, of course, have a complicated and traumatic history with the Catholic Church, but the relationship improved dramatically after the Second Vatican Council convened by Pope John XXIII issued the Nostra Aetate declaration in 1965, that cleared Jews of responsibility for the death of Jesus, renounced its traditional claim that Jews had been rejected by God, condemned anti-Semitism, and called for "mutual understanding and respect" between Catholics and Jews. During his papacy, John Paul II turned these words into action by frequently meeting with Jewish leaders, repeatedly condemning anti-Semitism, and commemorating the Holocaust. In 1994, John Paul II established full diplomatic ties between the Vatican and Israel. He said, "For the Jewish people who live in the State of Israel and who preserve in that land such precious testimonies to their history and their faith, we must ask for the desired security and the due tranquility that are the prerogative of every nation. . . ."[18] He visited Israel in 2000, publicly apologizing for the persecution of Jews by Catholics over the centuries, including the Holocaust, and depositing a note pleading for forgiveness in a crack in the Western Wall.

While John Paul II was regarded warmly by Jews, not all of his statements and actions were sympathetic to Israel. He was frequently critical of Israeli actions and largely silent on the mistreatment of Christians by Arabs and Muslims. In February 2000 the Pope and Yasser Arafat issued a joint condemnation of any unilateral decision that would "change the unique character of Jerusalem," terming such a decision "legally and morally invalid." Arafat and the Pope, meeting in the Vatican, called for international status to be granted to Jerusalem. The Pope was also unwilling to criticize his predecessors or accept the church's institutional responsibility for anti-Semitism in the past. Still, when John Paul II died on April 2, 2005, at the age of 84, he made one final gesture to the Jews when he mentioned "the rabbi of Rome." Rabbi Elio Toaff and John Paul's long-time secretary were the only living people mentioned in the will. Toaff called the reference a "significant and profound gesture for Jews" and "an indication to the Catholic world." John Paul, he said, "wanted to indicate a road aimed at further destroying all the obstacles that have divided Jews and Christians through the centuries."[19]

When Joseph Ratzinger was elected John Paul's successor, some people expressed concern that he had been a member of the Hitler Youth. He explained, however, that he had been required to join when membership became compulsory in 1941, but that once he was out of the seminary he attended, he never renewed the association. A number of Jewish leaders also immediately noted the role Ratzinger had played in establishing Vatican relations with Israel and preparing the Vatican document on the Holocaust that discussed the church's historical "errors" in its treatment of Jews. He had also made remarks that raised concern among Jews. In 2001, for example, Ratzinger said that the church is waiting for the moment when Jews will "say yes to Christ." When asked if Jews should acknowledge Jesus as the messiah, Ratzinger said, "We believe that. The fact remains, however, that our Christian conviction is that Christ is also the messiah of Israel." In a Vatican sermon marking his installation as the new pontiff, Pope Benedict XVI extolled Jews for sharing a "spiritual heritage" with Christianity. Benedict offered greetings to "my brothers and sisters of the Jewish people, to whom we are joined by a great shared spiritual heritage, one rooted in God's irrevocable promises."

On August 19, 2005, Pope Benedict visited the synagogue on Roonstrasse in Cologne, Germany, in what was viewed as a reflection of his interest to maintain the warm relations with world Jewry fostered by his predecessor who had been the first pope to visit a synagogue. "It has been my deep desire, during my first visit to Germany since my election . . . to meet the Jewish community of Cologne and the representatives of Judaism in Germany," the pope said. He reflected on the Holocaust and anti-Semitism:

"In the darkest period of German and European history, an insane racist ideology, born of neo-paganism, gave rise to the attempt, planned and systematically carried out by the regime, to exterminate European Jewry. . . . This year marks the 60th anniversary of the liberation of the Nazi concentration camps, in which millions of Jews—men, women and children—were put to death in the gas chambers and ovens."[20] The pope spoke in a German synagogue, met with Israel's two chief rabbis, and celebrated the 40th anniversary of the Nostra Aetate document, pledging to continue the Jewish-Christian dialogue. In his first meeting with Rome's chief rabbi on January 16, 2006, the pope said, "We cannot but denounce and battle with determination against the hatred and misunderstandings, injustice and violence that continue to sow concern into the souls of men and women of good will. . . . How can we not be grieved and concerned about the renewed demonstrations of anti-Semitism that are at times reported?" He added, "The people of Israel have been released from the hands of enemies on various occasions, and in the centuries of anti-Semitism during the dramatic time of the Shoah, the hand of the Almighty sustained and guided them." And in December 2006, he joined other world leaders in deploring the deniers at the conference on the Holocaust in Iran.[21]

In addition to his positive statements about Jews, the new pope also appears to have a greater understanding of Islamism. While his predecessor devoted a lot of attention to Muslim-Christian dialogue, Benedict signaled he may go in a different direction when he quoted the medieval emperor who said Muhammad had spread his faith by the sword. The pope later apologized for the hostile reactions of Muslims who took offense and said he did not share the views of the emperor. Nevertheless, a number of commentators have suggested that Benedict is staking out a more aggressive position toward the Islamic world. I hope they are correct in believing that he recognizes the plight of Christians in the Muslim world and wants to improve their situation, that he does not think Islam will reform, and that he is prepared to confront Islam in Europe in the same way his predecessor took on communism.

Paradoxically, Israel's position may actually be improving as the Muslim population grows. While Muslims have assimilated in the United States, acculturation has not occurred in Europe where many Muslims have chosen to remain apart from the broader population and to reject the values and institutions of the nations in which they live. The head of Britain's MI5 intelligence service said in November 2006 that hundreds of young British Muslims are being radicalized, groomed and set on a path to mass murder. Similar warnings have come from other European intelligence agencies. Consequently, the Europeans are beginning to recognize the danger of a growing, hostile minority that includes Islamists committed to the destruction of their societies. They have become increasingly xenophobic, anti-Islamic, and prepared to adopt tougher terror laws. Polls also indicate a growing sense in Europe that instability in the Middle East is a product of Islamic extremism rather than Israeli policies. That feeling is far stronger in certain countries, such as Germany, than in France or the UK where Israeli policies are still viewed as nearly as responsible. For example, 27 percent of the public in the United Kingdom believe Islamic extremism is more responsible and 18 percent say Israeli policies. In France, the respective figures are 42 percent and 23 percent, but in Germany it's 50 percent and 15 percent. By comparison, 63 percent of Americans blame Islamic extremism and only 15 percent Israeli policies.

Can Israel stand up to the entire world? For much of the Cold War it was forced to do just that. Today, despite the one-sided verdicts of the UN General Assembly, on balance Israel stands tall on the world stage. Diplomatic and economic relations are expanding with countries around the globe, including countries such as India and China. Russia, once Israel's most dangerous enemy, now has normalized relations with Israel and might even be regarded as a friend. Israelis have returned to African nations with which they had a history of development assistance. Inroads have also been made with Muslim nations, such as Pakistan and the Persian Gulf states.

The spread of Islamism outside the Middle East is beginning to open the eyes of many international leaders who preferred to believe the danger was confined far from their borders. As the threat escalates, Europeans especially may find common cause with Israelis. In the short-run, however, the growing Muslim populations in democratic countries raise the possibility that this constituency will adversely influence government policies toward Israel.

While disturbing and sometimes dangerous, the new and possibly worsening anti-Semitism poses no threat to Israel's existence as long as the United States remains steadfast in its support of Israel and is prepared to prevent any international action that could undermine its security.

Chapter 12

Israel's American Protector

It is taken for granted that the United States is Israel's staunchest ally and protector and that it has little to fear from external threats as a result. History has shown, however, that Israel cannot necessarily count on the United States. With the exception of the 1973 war, the United States has not actively contributed to Israel's military campaigns and in several of them actually impeded the Israeli war effort. President Dwight Eisenhower used aid to Israel as a stick to force an Israeli withdrawal from the territory it captured in the 1956 war, and even President George W. Bush, generally regarded as the most pro-Israel president yet, has not hesitated to take punitive actions against Israel.

The United States has had a special relationship with Israel predating the establishment of the state. It also has relations with the Arab and Muslim world, and American policy often has to balance its interests in Israel's peace and security with its need for Persian Gulf oil, its desire to expand trade relations with Muslim nations, many of which are extremely wealthy, and its frequent need for political support from a large block of UN votes. So far, the balance has remained in Israel's favor, and the United States has remained steadfast in its political, military, and economic support for Israel. Israel's survival depends on the continuation of that support.

The conflict between Israel and Hizbollah in Lebanon in the summer of 2006 was a good example of the delicate balancing act executed by American officials. In July Hizbollah terrorists crossed the border into Israel and launched an unprovoked attack against a military patrol, kidnapping two soldiers. In response, Israel launched a military campaign to win the release of the soldiers and to end the threat long posed by Hizbollah's presence near the border. That threat was quickly displayed when Hizbollah began to fire thousands of rockets indiscriminately at Israeli towns throughout northern Israel and beyond, ultimately reaching Haifa, Israel's third largest city. The entire world initially condemned Hizbollah's provocation, but almost immediately after Israel began to fight back, international opinion turned against Israel. Reports that Israel's attacks had uprooted hundreds of thousands of Lebanese refugees and had killed hundreds of civilians provoked a widespread outcry and calls for an immediate cease-fire.

A cessation of the Israeli campaign would have spared civilians in Lebanon but would not have ended the threat posed by Hizbollah to Israel's population because the terrorists would have remained along the border and been allowed to obtain new supplies of rockets from its patrons in Syria and Iran. If it were not for President George W. Bush standing firm, Israel would have lost that battle in the opening days. It could not have fought against U.S. threats or pressure, which had forced Israel's withdrawal from the Sinai in 1956 and a cease-fire in previous campaigns in Lebanon during the Reagan administration.

As is so often the case in Middle East affairs, the U.S. president appeared to be fighting with his own State Department when the secretary of state, Condoleezza Rice, made her first statement calling on Israel to show restraint at the same time that the president was asserting Israel's right to defend itself. In this instance, the president took control of the State Department immediately and got Rice to operate from the same playbook. Pressure continued to build on Bush to join the chorus of opinion as civilian casualties mounted. Finally, after one particularly unfortunate attack against a building in which missile launchers were believed hidden, resulting in 28 civilian casualties, many of them children—initial reports of 56 dead were inaccurate but played into the Lebanese theme echoed by the media that Israel was indiscriminately killing large numbers of civilians—the president succumbed to the pressure and pressed Israel to stop fighting. By forcing Israel to cease its campaign before Hizbollah was decisively beaten, the president may have sowed the seeds of a future conflict—something misguided U.S. diplomacy has repeatedly done in previous wars.

The U.S. Middle East policy balancing act has been a feature of American decision making since the battle for Israel's independence. Recalling the history of U.S.-Israel relations, one begins with President

Truman's decision to support the UN partition resolution to create a Jewish and Arab state. A lot has been written about the vigorous lobbying campaign by what is sometimes referred to as the "Jewish lobby" and the pressure consequently exerted by the administration on UN delegations to vote for the creation of Israel. What one rarely hears about, however, is that an equally vigorous lobbying campaign against the resolution was mounted by the Arabs and their supporters at the UN. More significantly, opposition from within Truman's own administration nearly torpedoed the partition resolution, threatening to undermine the president's policy and to render the birth of the Jewish state stillborn. At the time of partition, two of the most influential members of Truman's cabinet were staunchly opposed to the creation of a Jewish state, Secretary of State George Marshall and Secretary of Defense James Forrestal. Echoing an argument that is repeated to this day, Forrestal warned the president that support for the Jewish state would jeopardize America's relations with the Arab states in general and, more specifically, our supply of oil. The Arabists, State Department officials who held the view that U.S. policy should be primarily determined by how it affects relations with the Arabs, tried to undermine the partition resolution by proposing to replace it with a plan that would have at least stalled the creation of a Jewish state. When they failed to prevent the Zionists from declaring their independence on May 14, 1948, the Arabists did their best to strangle the newborn state by convincing Truman to impose an arms embargo on the Middle East that left the Jews at a disadvantage against the five Arab states that then invaded. Each Arab state had larger, better armed forces to begin with and had no difficulty finding alternative weapons suppliers. The best fighting force, the Jordanian Arab Legion, was actually armed and trained by the British and led by a British officer.

Israel ultimately emerged victorious in its war of independence. Israelis might argue that they could have created a state without the United States given the momentum they had created for statehood. After all, they had established most of the institutions for governance and were determined after the Holocaust to ensure a haven existed in the Jewish homeland. At a minimum, without U.S. support it would have taken much longer than it did and would have suffered from a lack of international legitimacy. Of course, even with international support, the Jews had to fight and won without the help of any other nation. Had the Arabist view prevailed, it is likely the UN would have voted to create a unitary Arab state and the United States could have forced the Jews to accept this outcome. Yet many people continue to believe that U.S. support for Israel is attributable to the omnipotence of the Jewish or Israeli lobby and that this relationship is to blame for a whole host of ills as well as most failures of broader Middle East policy.

The view of a nefarious lobby is typified by a paper published in 2006, "The Israeli Lobby and U.S. Foreign Policy," written by Stephen Walt, then academic dean of Harvard's John F. Kennedy School of Government, and John Mearsheimer, a University of Chicago political scientist. It took 16 pages on the Jewish Virtual Library web site to rebut the nonsense in their 41-page paper, which is now widely circulated and treated as worthy of debate in the way that Holocaust denial is sometimes taken as an opinion meriting a response. Rather than repeat their canards here, let's look at the truth about the Israeli lobby and its anti-Israel counterpart (which Walt and Mearsheimer ignored).

✿

What I refer to as the Israeli lobby consists of Americans who believe that Israel should be an independent Jewish state and that it is in the interests of the United States to have a strong U.S.-Israel relationship. Jews and non-Jews (hence the rejection of the term "Jewish lobby") share this belief, otherwise it would be impossible for the lobby to have any influence. Because the U.S. has a Jewish population of only six million Jews, the Israeli lobby is dependent on the support of non-Jewish groups and actively works to form coalitions with broad segments of American society. The lobby has successfully built coalitions consisting of unions, entertainers, clergymen, scholars, and black leaders. The coalitions allow the lobby to demonstrate a broad public consensus for a pro-Israel policy. This consensus is reflected in public opinion polls that show Americans support Israel over the Arabs or Palestinians by three and four to one (see chapter 10). The gradual evolution of the relationship from friendship to alliance could not have been achieved without the support of the American public. Americans see much of themselves in the Zionist struggle. Like the early American pioneers, the Jews who originally settled the land had a commitment to manual labor to build the nation. Like newcomers to America, immigrants to Israel have tried to make better lives for themselves and their children. Americans' affinity for Israelis also stems from our shared Judeo-Christian heritage.

Public sympathy toward Israel can be influenced by presidential attitudes and events, as occurred during the first Lebanon war when support dipped to its all-time low after Ronald Reagan's criticism of Israeli actions. On average, less than half of Americans over the last 40 years have said they sympathize with Israel, so the public has never loved the Israelis. Those same polls show virtually no support, however, for the Arabs, so the affinity toward Israel has less to do with affection for Israel than dislike of the Arabs. It was not until the late 1980s and early 1990s that Americans began to distinguish between Arab countries and, in a few instances, to feel more positively about Arab countries than Israel. Even so, the rise of Islamic fundamentalism and dramatic terrorist incidents attributed to Arabs have perpetuated negative stereotypes that have helped ensure Israelis are viewed in a relatively favorable light.

A broad range of mostly Jewish organizations actively promote U.S.-Israel relations, though most are nonprofits (such as B'nai B'rith and Hadassah) that are not permitted to devote much of their time or resources to lobbying. Nevertheless, they do disseminate information and encourage their members to become involved in the political process. The main coordinating body is the Conference of Presidents of Major American Jewish 'organizations, which is composed of leaders of 51 different organizations and is responsible for formulating and articulating the "Jewish position" on most foreign policy matters. It is hampered, however, by a policy of consensus, which, given the diversity of its members, means that it often cannot take a position, or at least an effectively strong one, on the most controversial issues. Nevertheless, the conference allows the lobby to speak with one voice in a way its opponents cannot.

The principal vehicle for relating the pro-Israel viewpoint is a registered lobby, the American-Israel Public Affairs Committee (AIPAC). Originally called the American Zionist Committee for Public Affairs, the lobby was founded in 1951 by I. L. (Sy) Kenen to appeal directly to Congress for legislation to provide aid to Israel to circumvent State Department opposition. In the late 1960s, the organization was essentially a one-man operation run by Kenen. In the late 1970s, AIPAC still had only a handful of staff based in Washington. Today it is considered the most powerful foreign policy lobby in Washington with approximately 200 employees, ten regional offices and a budget of nearly $50 million. AIPAC lobbies the Executive as well as the Legislative branch. Because of its name, AIPAC is sometimes mistakenly thought to be a political action committee (PAC), but the organization does not rate, endorse, or finance candidates.

While AIPAC has a handful of lobbyists who meet with officials to make their case, it has the luxury of many allies in Congress who can do this for them. Its principal weapon is the network of key contacts around the country who can be mobilized to make calls, arrange meetings and send letters to their representatives. These are not average citizens whose communications are pawned off on interns; they are people who have personal relationships based on friendship, shared political ideology, and/or financial support. The name of the game in lobbying is obtaining access, and AIPAC's members have the ability to get their feet in doors closed to most other citizens.

The lobby strives to remain nonpartisan and thereby keeps friends in both parties. By framing the issues in terms of the national interest, AIPAC can attract broader support than would be possible if it was perceived to represent only the interests of Israel. This does not mean AIPAC does not have a close relationship with Israeli officials; it does, albeit unofficially. (To do so officially would require the organization to register as a foreign agent, something its opponents claim that it is.) On occasion, AIPAC has come into conflict with the Israeli government, but it tends to reflect Israeli government policy fairly closely. In fact, its policy can shift 180 degrees when the government in Israel changes, because AIPAC reflects the general Jewish view that major policies affecting war and peace should be determined by the democratically elected government in Israel.

AIPAC has also attracted its share of negative attention, most recently when two employees were accused of accepting classified information on U.S. policy regarding Iran from Larry Franklin, a Pentagon analyst, and of passing it to an Israeli diplomat. The two men, Steve Rosen and Keith Weissman, were fired by AIPAC. Franklin subsequently pled guilty to charges related to disclosing classified information and agreed to help prosecutors in the case against Rosen and Weissman. Franklin was sentenced to 12 years and 7 months in prison and a $10,000 fine. Rosen and Weissman were indicted on charges of violating the Espionage Act of 1917, a law intended to stop government officials from disclosing state secrets, which has only been applied in the past to spies, not to citizens who have received information. The accused have said they are not guilty and argued that they were doing what most lobbyists in Washington do every day; that is, exchanging information. Media groups have also expressed concern because journalists would also presumably be guilty of a crime if they accepted classified materials, something that is now almost routine. Most observers believe the government has a difficult case to prove and that it will likely be appealed ultimately to the Supreme Court if the two men are convicted. Regardless of the cases outcomes, the negative impact on AIPAC to date has been minimal because the organization itself is not accused of any misdeeds.

The more serious threat to AIPAC is caused by divisions within the pro-Israel community. Not all Jews share the view that Israelis are best qualified to make decisions about their future. In recent years, a growing number of Jews have adopted the view that Israel needs to be saved from itself and have staked out positions that often conflict with AIPAC. Groups such as the Israel Policy Forum and Americans for Peace Now have become increasingly assertive in rejecting the community consensus and arguing for greater U.S. intervention in the Arab-Israeli conflict. In particular, left-of-center groups have called for the United States to use foreign aid and other levers to pressure Israel to dismantle settlements and withdraw from territory. These groups have had very limited impact on policy to date, though in 2006 they did manage to water down some of AIPAC's legislative efforts to limit U.S. financial support for the Palestinian Authority after Hamas took control of the government. These groups have weakened the lobby by creating a greater sense of disunity, raising doubts about Israeli actions, and giving politicians who may question particular Israeli policies cover for opposing them. Many of the supporters of these groups believe that AIPAC has become too conservative and too closely associated with the Republican Party. They fail to understand that it is politically necessary to work more closely with the party in power, which for most of the last quarter century has been the Republicans. Reports began to surface in late 2005 that a move was afoot to create a new lobby to rival AIPAC, but this has not yet materialized.

While some fractures are visible in the Jewish community, support for Israel is rooted in Judeo-Christian values and is particularly strong among religious Christians. A Pew survey in August 2006, for example, found that "large majorities of those who view the Bible as the literal word of God say that Israel was given by God to the Jews and that Israel is the fulfillment of prophecy. . . . These figures are much lower among those who do not believe the Bible is the actual word of God." Not surprisingly, these results are reflected in a comparison of the Bible Belt and the Northeast. In the South, 56 percent said the land of Israel was given to the Jews by God and 45 percent said the state of Israel fulfilled biblical prophecy. The comparable figures for the Northeast were 24 percent and 22 percent, respectively. White evangelical Protestants had the strongest level of belief that the land of Israel was given to the Jews by God (69 percent) and 59 percent said Israel fulfilled biblical prophecy. Black Protestants held similar views, but less than a third of Roman Catholics and other Protestant churches—Episcopalians, Presbyterians, and Lutherans share this view.

Under George W. Bush and the GOP majority in Congress, the evangelicals have found a sympathetic ear that has magnified their impact. To take advantage of their clout, Christians who support Israel organized themselves into a lobby in 2006. These "Christian Zionists" believe the return of the Jewish people to its biblical homeland in Israel is in line with biblical prophecy and is necessary for Jesus to return to earth as its king. Many Jews, however, are uncomfortable with people who support them only because they hope they will convert and that Israel will ultimately be destroyed to bring the messiah. One of the earliest expressions of support for the return of the Jews to their homeland came from John Adams, who told American Jewish newspaper editor, politician, diplomat, and playwright Mordecai Manuel Noah after reading his travel book, "Farther I could find it in my heart to wish that you had been at the head of a hundred thousand Israelites . . . & marching with them into Judea & making a conquest of that country & restoring your nation to the dominion of it. For I really wish the Jews again in Judea an independent nation." The last sentence is often quoted as an example of the earliest U.S. expression of support for the Zionist enterprise; less often cited is the rest of Adams' remark, which clarified the reason for his sympathy. "I believe [that] . . . once restored to an independent government & no longer persecuted they [the Jews] would soon wear away some of the asperities and peculiarities of their character & possibly in time become liberal Unitarian Christians for your Jehovah is our Jehovah & your God of Abraham Isaac and Jacob is our God."[1]

Christian Zionists interpret both the Torah and the New Testament as prophetic texts that describe how the world will one day end with the return of Jesus from heaven to rule on earth. Israel and its people are central to their vision.

Many Jews think that Christians believe in replacement theology (the notion that the Jews are no longer the "chosen people" and that the church has replaced Israel in God's plan). That view has been largely superseded by the dispensationalist view that Christianity did not come into existence to replace Judaism but to restore it. This change does not offer comfort to most

Jews. In the meantime, most Christian Zionists deny this is part of their theology and say they do not believe they can speed up the Second Coming of Christ. Pastor John Hagee, long a supporter of Israel, who is based at the Cornerstone Church in San Antonio, Texas, heads Christians United for Israel (CUFI) and has denounced replacement theology. "We believe in the promise of Genesis 12:3 regarding the Jewish people and the nation of Israel," he said. "We believe that this is an eternal covenant between God and the seed of Abraham to which God is faithful."[2] Evangelical leader Pat Robertson echoed this statement while on his tour of Israel during Israel's 2006 campaign against Hizbollah: "The Jews are God's chosen people. Israel is a special nation that has a special place in God's heart. He will defend this nation. So Evangelical Christians stand with Israel."[3] Hagee claims that he and other Christian Zionists support Israel because they owe a debt of gratitude to the Jewish people, and not because they want Jews to convert to Christianity. Even if the Christians are supporting Israel only to advance their own messianic agenda, many Jews take the position that they need friends wherever they can find them and can't be too concerned about post-apocalyptic scenarios. Meanwhile, Christian friends of Israel such as Hagee have raised millions of dollars for Israel.

It is not only theology that makes Jews and Christian Zionists odd bedfellows. The majority of American Jews are politically and socially liberal. Christian Zionists are on the whole politically conservative Republicans who, for example, oppose liberal Jewish positions on abortion, gay marriage, and prayer in public schools. Christian Zionists are also more hawkish on issues relating to Israel than many Jews. They generally oppose territorial concessions to the Palestinians and believe Israel should never give up any of the land promised to the Jews by God. After their prime minister Ariel Sharon implemented the Gaza Strip disengagement plan and fell ill a few months later, Pat Robertson claimed that his illness was divine retribution for giving up part of biblical Israel.

Christians first flexed their political muscles in the late 1970s when Jerry Falwell established the Moral Majority, consisting of conservative Christian political action committees that succeeded in mobilizing like-minded individuals to register and vote for conservative candidates. With nearly six million members, it became a powerful voting block during the 1980s that helped elect Ronald Reagan to the presidency. One of the Moral Majority's four founding principles was "support for Israel and Jewish people everywhere." In 1980, Falwell, who ran a television ministry that reached millions of viewers, said of Israel: "I firmly believe God has blessed America because America has blessed the Jew. If this nation wants her fields to remain white with grain, her scientific achievements to remain notable, and her freedom to remain intact, America must continue to stand with Israel."

Politicians associated with the Moral Majority said all the right things about Israel, but the major test of their loyalty came when President Ronald Reagan decided to sell sophisticated AWACS radar planes to Saudi Arabia in 1981. AIPAC mounted a vigorous campaign to block the sale and had a majority of senators, including those associated with the Moral Majority, on record against it before the president began to insist the sale was crucial for American national security. Reagan demanded the support of all Senate Republicans, including his conservative base, because this was the new administration's first major foreign policy initiative. In the end, the conservative Christian senators showed their loyalty was more to Reagan than to Israel and voted for the sale. As AIPAC's former legislative director Doug Bloomfield put it, the Moral Majority "may have given us their prayers but they never gave us their votes."

Falwell disbanded the Moral Majority in 1989, but conservative Christians have remained vocal supporters of Israel and their influence grew with the election of George W. Bush and the Republican takeover of Congress. Until Hagee formed his organization in 2006, they lacked a formal structure for political action, yet within months mobilized thousands of pro-Israel Christians to travel to Washington to lobby members of Congress. Although these additional voices reinforce the message of the pro-Israel community, it is not clear that they have exerted decisive influence on any policies. Moreover, their clout is expected to decline now that the Democratic Party, with which they have more tenuous connections, has regained the majority in Congress. If a Democrat wins the White House in 2008, the Christian influence may be marginalized.

One way that lobbyists attempt to educate politicians is by taking them to Israel on study missions. Once officials have direct exposure to the country, its leaders, its geography, and security dilemmas, they typically return more sympathetic to Israel. Politicians also sometimes travel to Israel specifically to demonstrate their interest in Israel. For example, George W. Bush made his one and only trip to Israel before deciding to run for president in what was widely viewed as an effort to win pro-Israel voters' support. He was particularly influenced by a helicopter tour given to him by a man he would later work with as a fellow head of state—Ariel Sharon. In 2005 alone, more than 100 members of Congress visited Israel, some multiple times.

Jews also occupy more positions of influence today than ever before. For example, in the 110th Congress, Jewish members comprise 13 percent of the Senate and nearly 7 percent of the House. Bill Clinton nominated two Supreme Court Justices, both Jewish. In his first term, he had two Jewish Cabinet members and dozens of Jews held other key administration posts. During Clinton's tenure a Jew (Dennis Ross) was America's principal Mideast negotiator and the U.S. ambassador to Israel was, for the first time, Jewish. Clinton's national security adviser, Sandy Berger, was also Jewish.

The Bush administration has had fewer Jews in the most senior positions, yet, ironically, many of Bush's harshest critics, especially those opposed to the Iraq war such as Walt and Mearsheimer, have blamed the Jews for what they believe are the failings of U.S. Middle East policy. In fact, the most high level Jewish members of the administration, former press secretary Ari Fleischer, Homeland Security czar Michael Chertoff, chief of staff Josh Bolten, and White House political director Ken Mehlman, have little or nothing to do with Middle East policy. The real villains in the minds of critics were neoconservatives in the Pentagon, many of whom happened to be Jewish, including the former Undersecretary of Defense for Policy Douglas Feith and especially former Deputy Secretary of Defense Paul Wolfowitz. Even though they were influential advisors, there is no evidence that their views conflicted with those of their boss, Donald Rumsfeld, or that they were more influential than the views taken by other non-Jewish senior advisers such as Vice President Dick Cheney, Colin Powell and Condoleezza Rice.

Israel's detractors, such as Walt and Mearsheimer, conveniently neglect to mention in their diatribes against the Israeli lobby that Israel is often opposed by a variety of interest groups unrelated to the Middle East (for example, conservative groups that have nothing against Israel but oppose foreign aid on principle) as well as those individuals and organizations with economic or political interests in the region.

The Arab lobby in the United States is at least as old, perhaps older than the Israeli lobby. It is composed of what AIPAC's Kenen called in his memoir "the petrodiplomatic complex," consisting of the oil industry, missionaries, and diplomats.[4] According to Kenen, there was no need for a formal Arab lobby because the petrodiplomatic complex did the Arabs' work for them. For example, in 1951, Saudi Arabia's King Saud asked U.S. diplomats to finance a pro-Arab lobby to counter the American Zionist Committee for Public Affairs (later the American Israel Public Affairs Committee or AIPAC). The Arab lobby became an official, active, and visible spokesman for the Arab cause in the wake of the oil embargo. "The day of the Arab-American is here," "boasted National Association of Arab-Americans (NAAA) founder Richard Shadyac, "the reason is oil."[5]

A quarter century ago, particularly following the 1967 and 1973 wars, oil did drive much of America's Middle East policy and major oil companies, particularly those affiliated with the Saudi-based Arabian American Oil Company (ARAMCO), did not hesitate to try to manipulate public opinion and foreign policy. Participation in the public relations campaign for the Arab world amounted to the price of doing business in the oil-producing nations. While oil is no less vital today, the oil companies have been far less aggressive in advocating on behalf of the Arab states than they had been when company officials would threaten the cutoff of oil supplies if the United States carried out this or that policy toward Israel. These threats may no longer be common today because they were carried out only once, when the Arab oil producers instituted an embargo in 1973. The United States has since taken measures to insulate itself from short-term oil blackmail.

Other companies outside the oil industry have also participated in the Arab lobby; the most well known being the international engineering firm Bechtel. Since the AWACS fight in 1981 the lobbies have had no major confrontations because the Israeli lobby hasn't opposed any significant arms sales or other economic investments in the region. The Arab lobby has never gained strength because it has always been largely disunited and disorganized, with small fringe organizations vying for attention. Shadyac intentionally set out to duplicate AIPAC but never succeeded, in large measure because the Arab American population is small, deeply fragmented, and mostly unsympathetic to the agenda set by the largely self-appointed leaders of the Arab lobby.

Israel gets disproportionate attention from the press and decision makers, but the discrepancy between numbers of supporters and publicity is even greater in the case of the Palestinians. There are approximately 1.2 million Arabs in the United States, and roughly 38 percent of them are Lebanese, primarily Christians. The Lebanese Americans tend to be unsympathetic to the Arab lobby's goals because many fled their country to escape the persecution of

Muslims and other Arabs, especially Palestinians, who also helped spark the Lebanese civil war. This reflects another major problem for the Arab lobby— inter-Arab disunity. This disunity is reinforced by the general discord of the Arab world that has 21 states with competing interests. The Arab lobby is thus precluded from representing all Arabs. Only about 70,000 Palestinians (6 percent of all Arab Americans) live in the United States, but their views have received disproportionate attention because of their political activism. Similarly, a great deal of attention has focused on the allegedly growing political strength of Muslims in the United States, but fewer than one-fourth of all Arab Americans are Muslims.

One reason the Arab lobby has had no legislative success is because it has insisted on adopting an anti-Israel agenda, such as seeking to reduce aid to Israel, rather than a pro-Arab one. Thus, it inevitably must fight the Israeli lobby head on and it cannot win these battles in Congress. Compared to the Israeli lobby, the Arab lobby finds it more difficult to make its case because much of the Arab world opposes U.S. interests and shares few of its values. Even America's Arab allies are more often than not at odds with American policy, while Israel never attacks U.S. interests. Israel has periodically acted contrary to them, as in Suez and Lebanon, but these anomalies are a far cry from Arab states' routine criticism of U.S. policy; their often active support for America's enemies, such as the Soviet Union, Iran, and Libya; and their direct opposition, as in the refusal to allow U.S. troops to be stationed in many of their countries.

One quantitative index of the relative support of Israel and the Arabs for U.S. policy is the consistency of voting with the United States at the UN. Israel has annually been at or near the top of those countries voting most often with the United States, while the Arab states, including friendly nations, have always been at the bottom. In 2005 Israel was America's top ally at the UN, voting with the United States more than 90 percent of the time. By comparison, the Arab states on average opposed U.S. positions on nearly 90 percent of the votes.

The other major difference between the two lobbies is the use of paid foreign agents by the Arab lobby. Pro-Arab U.S. government officials can look forward to lucrative positions as lobbyists, spokesmen, and consultants for the Arab cause. One contractor, Qorvis Communications LLC, was paid more than $10 million just to promote Saudi Arabia's image. Despite the help of former officials, the Arab lobby has never had a fraction of the access granted to the Israeli lobby. Paradoxically, this began to change, albeit marginally, after 9/11. While the attack raised awareness of the danger of Islamism, the Bush administration was so afraid of being accused of bigotry against Arabs or Muslims, it began to cultivate relationships with the Arab lobby, including some organizations that either refused to condemn Muslim terrorism and Islamism or were believed to be active supporters of radical Middle East groups such as Hamas and Hizbollah. Administration officials who once shunned them now speak to Arab lobby groups.

In addition to the political and economic interest groups, the Arab lobby also enjoys the support of many Christian groups. While evangelical Christians supporting Israel have gotten a lot of publicity, the World Council of Churches, the American Friends Service Committee (the Quakers), and other denominations have long been virulently anti-Israel. In 2005 the Presbyterians voted to divest from Israel, a decision made by some of the leadership with little input from the rank and file. Vigorous lobbying by the Jewish community and months of dialogue helped overturn that decision in 2006. Still it should not be taken for granted that all Christians are supportive of Israel.

The reason the Israeli lobby can exert influence on Congress and, to a far lesser degree, the White House, is usually attributed to its role in elections. Jewish voting behavior is a key element. American Jews recognize the importance of support for Israel because of the dire consequences that could follow from the alternative. They also fear what might happen in the United States if they do not have political power. Consequently, Jews have devoted themselves to politics with almost religious fervor. This is reflected in the fact that Jews have the highest percentage voter turnout of any ethnic group. Though the Jewish population in the United States is roughly six million (about 2.3 percent of the total U.S. population), roughly 89 percent live in 12 key Electoral College states. These states alone are worth enough electoral votes to elect the president. If you add the non-Jews shown by opinion polls to be as pro-Israel as Jews, it is clear the Israeli lobby has the support of one of the largest veto groups in the country. About half of the Arab population is concentrated in five states with large numbers of electoral votes—California, Florida, Michigan, New Jersey, and New York. Still, the Arab population is dwarfed by that of the Jews in every one of these states except Michigan.

The political activism of Jews forces candidates for political office to consider what criticizing Israel may mean for their political future. There are no benefits to candidates taking an openly anti-Israel stance and considerable costs in both loss of campaign contributions and votes from Jews and non-Jews alike. Politicians therefore have an incentive to be pro-Israel; this reinforces support for Israel in Congress. Given the sensitivity to the concerns of Jewish voters, it should not be surprising that the foreign policy of elected officials will be influenced, although not bound, by the promises they made regarding Israel during the campaign. Similarly, presidential candidates have little to gain in their campaigns from hostility to Israel, although they have a long record of shifting positions once in office. Political campaign contributions are also an important means of influence and Jews have been major benefactors. It is difficult to assess the impact of campaign giving on legislative outcomes, particularly with regard to Israel-related issues, for which support or opposition may be a consequence of nonmonetary factors.

Initially, the Jewish community feared that post-Watergate election campaign financing reforms would reduce their influence, but the changes actually stimulated greater political activism as more donors became involved and learned how to be more sophisticated in targeting their contributions. The first pro-Israel Political Action Committee (PAC) was formed in 1978, but there was little activity until 1982 when 33 pro-Israel PACs contributed $1.87 million to congressional candidates. Like other PACs, most of this money was given to incumbents and, because of the long association of Jews with the Democratic party, nearly 80 percent went to Democrats (the figure has slipped to 69 percent overall since 1990). In 2004, pro-Israel PACs gave a little more than $3 million to candidates, and individuals contributed nearly $3 million more. According to the Center for Responsive Politics, pro-Israel contributors have donated $57 million in individual, PAC, and soft money contributions to national-level candidates and national party committees between 1990 and early October 2006. Even these contributions are dwarfed by those of labor unions, lawyers, doctors, and trade associations; out of 80 "industries," the pro-Israel contributors rank only forty-first. Still, pro-Israel donors outgive pro-Arab contributors. Only three pro-Arab PACs spent a trivial sum through 1988. Since 1988, Arab and Muslim communities combined contributed only $297,000.

Like other interest groups, the Israeli lobby has targeted its opponents. Since very few members of Congress are hostile toward Israel, contributions by Jews to races for those seats tend to attract a lot of attention. In one of the early examples of targeting a candidate, an effort was made to defeat pro-Arab congressman Paul Findley of Illinois in 1982. The congressman's district suffered from a high unemployment rate and had been gerrymandered to his disadvantage, but Findley still blamed the lobby for his defeat and subsequently founded an anti-Israel organization, the Council for the National Interest.

In 2002, the lobby attracted attention for working to defeat two African American House members known for their criticism of Israel, Earl Hilliard of Alabama and Cynthia McKinney of Georgia. Though it provided no money to the candidates and was not directly involved in the campaigns, AIPAC found itself under fire from members of the Black Congressional Caucus, who were angry that two of their own were being targeted and that much of the funding for the races came from outside the congressional districts (which was also true of the support for the candidates that came from pro-Arab donors). While caucus members understood the opposition to Hilliard and McKinney's views, they were angered by the fact that the two main targets of the Israeli lobby were black, and they were frustrated by the lack of support for caucus members who were supportive of Israel. This provided an important lesson to the lobby that it needed to spread its financial support to friends in safe districts as well as to those opposing enemies. AIPAC could no longer take anyone for granted. The Arab lobby has never had this capacity to influence races based on the candidates' views on the Middle East.

Overall, the comparative impact of the two lobbies on elections was probably best summed up by Harry Truman when he said, "I won't tell you what to do or how to vote, but I will only say this. In all of my political experience I don't ever recall the Arab vote swinging a close election."

A more serious threat to the lobby's dominance of congressional debate may be changing demographics. In 1992 Marcela Kogan and I wrote an article that noted Hispanics were projected to become the nation's largest minority group and that the day when Hispanics might play key roles in debates on Israel would not be far off; therefore, it behooved the Israeli lobby to build ties with their communities. In the 15 years since that story appeared, shockingly little has been done to cultivate relations with Hispanic leaders. Some organizations, such as the American Jewish Committee and increasingly AIPAC, have recognized the problem, but these communities do not have long experience with Jews or naturally warm feelings toward Israel. The Hispanic communities require far more attention than they have received to date if a Congress of Hispanic members is expected to maintain the U.S.-Israel alliance.

By contrast, the pro-Israel lobby has spent a great deal of effort in cultivating the African American community. The Congressional Black Caucus has been very supportive, but support for Israel in the wider community (except for religious African Americans) is lower than it is for any constituency. Blacks have long expected quid pro quo on their issues and have been frustrated by their failure to get it. While the lobby thought, for example, that blacks should be impressed by Israel's rescue and absorption of black Jews from Ethiopia, the reaction of the black community was, "That's nice, but why aren't you supporting us on affirmative action?" Jews see themselves as leaders of the civil rights movement and allies on most issues other than affirmative action, but this has not translated into sympathy for Israel among the broader black community. Ironically, Jews are the most liberal group in America other than African Americans.

Despite its access to decision makers and the disproportionate role in the electoral process, the Israeli lobby is still not nearly as influential as its detractors paint it. When I did my doctoral research on Middle East policy decisions made over a nearly 40-year period from 1945 to 1984, I found that it was very circumscribed. Contrary to conventional wisdom, for example, there was no evidence that the president's position on Israel-related issues was significantly affected by the electoral cycle despite the frequent appearance of pandering to Jewish voters.

In addition, it turns out the Israeli lobby has very limited influence on security and political issues. The main area where it does exert some power is on economic matters, such as foreign aid, which are decided in the Legislative rather than the Executive branch. Even in Congress, where support for Israel is nearly unanimous, the lobby's influence is circumscribed because of the tradition of deferring to the president on matters of foreign policy, particularly when the issues are cast in terms of the national interest. For example, legislation placing restrictions on the activities of the PLO, funding for Hamas and relocating the U.S. embassy to Jerusalem reflected victories for the Israeli lobby. In each case, the lobby succeeded in pushing legislation through Congress opposed by the Executive branch with the aim of shaping U.S.

policy, but each time the legislators ultimately caved in to the White House and added waivers that neutered the legislation.

✡

U.S. Middle East policy is not made by Congress. It is formulated by the president, and he is relatively insulated from the lobby's pressure. Through Congress, the lobby can set parameters within which the president can operate, but decisions affecting peace and security are in the hands of the person in the Oval Office. And how does the president determine policy toward Israel? It is based in large measure on ideology.

The two presidents who were least sympathetic toward Israel, Dwight Eisenhower and George H. W. Bush, saw the Jewish state as just another country. Bush's secretary of state, James Baker, viewed the Arab-Israeli conflict as no different from a management-labor dispute, so he saw no need to be especially sensitive to Israel's concerns. Bush demonstrated that a president openly critical of Israel could affect the quality of the relationship. Bush also set the negative precedent of openly interfering in an Israeli election, making no secret of his contempt for Yitzhak Shamir and his desire to see Yitzhak Rabin elected prime minister. Still, under Bush, aid to Israel was maintained, strategic cooperation enhanced and a $10 billion loan guarantee package approved (albeit with punitive deductions for the construction of settlements).

Presidents Lyndon Johnson and Jimmy Carter felt more of a religious-moral attachment to Israel. Johnson, for example, spoke about how "the Bible stories are woven into my childhood memories as the gallant struggle of modern Jews to be free of persecution is also woven into our souls."[6] And Carter wrote in his memoirs that he "believed very deeply that the Jews who had survived the Holocaust deserved their own nation, and that they had a right to live in peace among their neighbors. I considered this homeland for the Jews to be compatible with the teaching of the Bible, hence ordained by God. These moral and religious beliefs made my commitment to the security of Israel unshakable."[7]

Truman and Reagan felt gut-level, emotional sympathy toward Israel, which was translated into landmark decisions that established and strengthened the relationship. Bill Clinton falls into a similar category and is now considered, along with George W. Bush, the most pro-Israel president in history. Nevertheless, Clinton followed the senior Bush's precedent of interfering in Israeli politics by trying to help the reelection effort of Shimon Peres. Clinton's pro-Israel reputation was largely won by what he did not do, that is, he did not publicly criticize Israel or take punitive measures against it. For most of his first term, Israeli policy was far more compatible with U.S. policy than in the past, which ensured a low-level of conflict. In those few cases where disagreements arose, Clinton essentially looked the other way. In terms of new initiatives, Clinton did little beyond creating the U.S.-Israel Science & Technology Commission, a small program for cooperation in high technology announced early in his presidency that took most of his first term to get off the ground. By all accounts, however, when he left office the U.S.-Israel relationship was stronger than ever before.

Even Democrats who revile his other policies acknowledge that George W. Bush has been a great friend of Israel. But like his predecessors, including Reagan, Bush has occasionally taken punitive steps against Israel. During the first year of the Palestinian war (2000-2005), the United States imposed a sales embargo on spare parts for helicopters to protest the Israeli use of U.S.-made attack helicopters for "targeted killings." The embargo was lifted after the 9/11 attacks. In 2003 an annual interagency strategic dialogue was suspended because of U.S. anger over Israeli arms sales to China. Israel was forced not only to forego a $1 billion deal to supply China with an advanced early warning system, but also had to pay $350 million to compensate the Chinese. Talks resumed in 2005 after the arms issue was resolved. In another conflict about arms—this one over Israel's agreement to upgrade Chinese unmanned aerial vehicles that the United States feared could be used against Taiwan—the Defense Department suspended cooperation with Israel on a number of programs, including the Israeli Air Force's involvement in the Joint Strike Fighter aircraft. The U.S. pressure was particularly galling, some might say hypocritical, given that 7 percent of China's arms imports come from the United States. The U.S. decision shut Israel out of China's $15 billion military import market. Israel's military exports are estimated at $2.5 to $3.5 billion yearly, about 10 percent of the world's total, but the price of access to U.S. technology is that Israel agreed to give the United States a veto over its arms sales. These incidents reveal Israel's dependence on the United States in military matters. Israel was forced to agree to get U.S. permission to sell many of its weapons systems and has lost billions of dollars in revenues because of American opposition to sales not only to China, but also to Venezuela, which wanted to upgrade its fighter jets. The reason for these restrictions is related to fears that some systems including American components might fall into the wrong hands or be used by either enemies of the U.S. or against its allies. Because Israel's military depends almost entirely on the ability to procure U.S. weapons systems (few other countries will sell them arms and Israel prefers U.S. weapons since they are usually the best) and the military aid to pay for them, Israel can't afford to upset the United States. For critics of Israel, it shows the type of leverage the U.S. can exert if it wants to and also shows friends of Israel the potential danger should a president unfriendly to Israel ever be elected.

President Bush, though, is certainly friendly. His policy toward Israel is shaped by a worldview comprised of four key elements that I have labeled Straight Shooting, Triumphalism, Fraternity, and Faith.

George W. Bush has a stereotypical Texan approach to people that we associate with the straight shooter. He is not interested in flimflam, small talk, or deception. Bush wants information to be short, to the point, and honest. In this, he resembles Harry Truman who was known for his plainspokenness and his disdain for flash or indirection. A key instance where this value affected Bush's policy was in the *Karine-A* affair. On January 3, 2002, Israel seized the *Karine-A*, a ship laden with 50 tons of arms bound for the Palestinian Authority. When Bush learned of the ship's seizure, he called Arafat and asked him to explain the shipment. Arafat acted as though he knew nothing about it. U.S. intelligence verified the Israeli account that Arafat's "money man" had paid for and arranged the arms shipment, so Bush knew that Arafat was lying to him. From that point on, the United States deemed Arafat "compromised by terror," and the administration began to push for his removal as leader of the Palestinian Authority.

Ariel Sharon clearly understood the importance of being straight with Bush. For example, he promised that Arafat would not be harmed, and he kept that promise throughout Israel's military operations in the territories. On the other hand, he also promised to remove illegal outposts from the territories, which provoked the president's anger when he failed to act on his pledge. According to the former U.S. ambassador to Israel, Daniel Kurtzer, whenever he met with Sharon, the prime minister would bring up the outposts and apologize for not fulfilling his promise.

Many people don't remember now that much of the pro-Israel community opposed the election of George W. Bush, fearing that he would adopt his father's hostility to Israel. The younger Bush, however, is more like Ronald Reagan. He is an ideologue who sees the world in black and white or, more

accurately, as good and evil. Because of his Christian beliefs, he trusts in the ultimate victory of the good. Like Reagan, who labeled the Soviet Union an "Evil
Empire," Bush described an "axis of evil" comprising North Korea, Iran, and
Saddam Hussein's Iraq, and he routinely refers to terrorists as "evildoers."
Reagan had a gut-level, emotional attachment to Israel. He viewed it as a nation
with similar Judeo-Christian values and as an opponent of communism. His
successor, George H. W. Bush, had no such feelings toward Israel. If anything,
he saw U.S. ties with Israel as complicating American strategic and economic
interests in the Arab world. George W. Bush, however, shares more of Reagan's
religious and emotional attachment to Israel and clearly sees Israel as one of the
"good guys" that is fighting the battle with America against the evildoers.

Bush's detractors deride his Manichean view of the world and also
ridicule his reputation as a beer guzzling, lightweight, fraternity brother who
partied his way through Yale. Regardless of whether one accepts this charac-
terization, it is relevant in the sense that it reflects Bush's easygoing personal
style and the way in which he relates to people. Though he no longer drinks
alcohol, the quickest way to get a sense of whether Bush is likely to get along
with another world leader is to picture that foreign official having a beer with
Bush at the frat house. Sounds silly, perhaps, but consider Bush's relationship
with Tony Blair. Bill Clinton seemed to be Blair's soul mate because they were
similar in age, experience, and world view. Bush could not be more different
from Clinton and yet he enjoys nearly as good a relationship with Blair. How
can this be explained? In part, because you can see Bush and Blair hoisting a pint
together at the frat house.

Now relate this fraternity factor to the Middle East. Can you picture
Bush having a drink with any of the Arab leaders? Forget the fact that as
Muslims they're not supposed to drink alcohol and that Bush no longer
drinks. Perhaps the only one is King Abdullah of Jordan and, not coincidentally, Bush gets along very well with the young monarch. On the other hand,
can you imagine Bush ever drinking with Yasser Arafat? Not likely. What
about Ariel Sharon? Well, it might be hard to picture him as a drinking
buddy, but despite his gruff public image, the private Sharon was well liked
even by his political opponents, and they got along well from their first
encounter in the helicopter over the West Bank.

Most U.S. presidents have felt a certain kinship with the Jewish people
because of their own Christian beliefs and values. Many cite their reading of
the Bible for their feelings toward Israel. President Bush has made no secret

of his belief in the power of prayer and his commitment to Christian values. Recognizing the centrality of religion in President Bush's life is critical to understanding his worldview and policymaking. While Bush's faith is most often referenced with regard to domestic issues such as abortion, it is especially relevant to his attitude toward Israel. As the birthplace of Christianity and the site of so many Christian shrines, the Holy Land is of particular interest to the president. The fact that Israel is a Jewish state is also important because it is not just another political entity; it is a nation based on faith. Unlike the Islamic states, which are also based on religion, Israel shares Judeo-Christian and Western values with the United States. Bush is, therefore, naturally drawn to sympathize with Israel.

In an address to the National Commemoration of the Days of Remembrance on April 19, 2001, Bush observed: "Through centuries of struggle, Jews across the world have been witnesses not only against the crimes of men, but for faith in God, and God alone. Theirs is a story of defiance in oppression and patience in tribulation, reaching back to the exodus and their exile into the diaspora. That story continued in the founding of the state of Israel. The story continues in the defense of the State of Israel."

✡

While the American president determines U.S. policy toward Israel, the relationship of the two nations is based on more than the ideology of an individual president or the activities of the Israeli lobby. The state of the alliance is usually interpreted through the lens of conflict. What makes the friendship between the countries so strong is the web of military, economic, academic, bureaucratic, and personal connections among the peoples and institutions that insulates it from political vagaries. It is the bedrock values and interests that the two nations share that gives me confidence the United States will remain Israel's staunch ally.

For example, when Benjamin Netanyahu was elected prime minister of Israel in 1996, many in the media predicted U.S.-Israel relations would deteriorate; after all, President Clinton had done everything he could, short of making a joint campaign appearance, to aid in the election of Shimon Peres. Moreover, Netanyahu's platform with regard to the peace process was at odds with American policy. Within weeks of Netanyahu's victory, however, it became clear that while differences might exist on policy matters, the overall relationship was as close as ever. If anything, in the succeeding months, the alliance grew closer.

One of the pillars of the special relationship is based on mutual strategic interests. Up until the mid-1960s, State Department and Pentagon officials argued that Israel did not need American arms because it was strong enough to defend itself (as evidenced by the Suez campaign) and had access to arms elsewhere. Officials also worried that if the United States sold arms to Israel, it would alienate the Arabs and provoke them to ask the Soviets and Chinese for weapons, thus stimulating a Middle East arms race.

U.S. policy began to shift with John Kennedy's 1962 sale of HAWK anti-aircraft missiles to Israel, which was made over the objection of the State Department and only after Egypt obtained long-range bombers from the Soviets. Lyndon Johnson subsequently provided Israel with tanks and aircraft; these sales also were balanced by transfers to Arab countries. U.S. policy was to avoid providing one state in the region with a military advantage over the other. This policy changed in 1968 with Johnson's sale of Phantom jets to Israel. That sale established the United States as Israel's principal arms supplier. It also marked the beginning of the U.S. policy to give Israel a qualitative military edge over its neighbors. Johnson's decision was based on Israel's perceived needs (and domestic political considerations) rather than its potential contribution to U.S. security interests. Up to this point, Israel was not viewed as having any role to play in the West's defense, largely because it did not have the military might to contribute to the policy of containment. This perception began to change in 1970 when the United States asked Israel for help in bolstering the regime of Jordan's King Hussein. By the early 1970s, it became clear that no Arab state could or would contribute to the West's defense in the Middle East.

The Carter administration began to implement a form of strategic cooperation (it was not referred to as such) by making Israel eligible to sell military equipment to the United States and engaging in limited joint exercises. The relationship could have stagnated at this point, especially after the blow up between Ronald Reagan and Menachem Begin over the 1981 sale of AWACS to Saudi Arabia, but Reagan was the first president to see Israel as a potential contributor to the cold war. Prior to his election, Reagan had written: "Only by full appreciation of the critical role the State of Israel plays in our strategic calculus can we build the foundation for thwarting Moscow's designs on territories and resources vital to our security and our national well-being."[8]

The Israelis wisely played up their capability to deter the Soviet Union, while the Arab states refused to join the "strategic consensus" that Reagan's secretary of state Alexander Haig tried to create to oppose Soviet expansionism in the region. The Arabs insisted the greatest threat to them was not communism but Zionism. The Israelis never considered the Soviets their principal threat either but were prepared to say otherwise to win Reagan's favor. They began to reap the benefits of this approach on November 31, 1981, when the two countries signed a memorandum of understanding to "enhance strategic cooperation to deter all threats from the Soviet Union to the region." The agreement was diluted by opposition from the Pentagon and State Department and did not provide for joint exercises or a regular means of cooperation. Worse, it was used as a stick to beat Israel with a month later when the United States suspended the agreement because of its dissatisfaction with Israel's decision to annex the Golan Heights. Still, for the first time, Israel was formally recognized as a strategic ally.

In 1987, Congress designated Israel as a major non-NATO ally. This allowed Israeli industries to compete equally with NATO countries and other close U.S. allies for contracts to produce a significant number of defense items. By the end of Reagan's term, the U.S. had prepositioned equipment in Israel, regularly held joint training exercises, begun co-development of the Arrow Anti-Tactical Ballistic Missile, and was engaged in a host of other cooperative military endeavors.

Today, these strategic ties are stronger than ever. To cite a few examples:

Israel is linked to the U.S. missile warning satellite system, which will provide Israel with real-time warning if a missile is launched against it.

Military exercises are held involving the army, navy, and special forces.

A hotline was established between the Pentagon and the Israeli Defense Ministry.

The United States continues to fund the research and development of Israeli weapons systems and military equipment including the Arrow missile.

Israel provides intelligence to the United States on various Middle Eastern terrorist groups including Hamas and Hizbollah.

The United States prepositions hundreds of millions of dollars worth of military equipment, including spare parts, trucks, ammunition, and armor in Israel.

On average, 300 U.S. Department of Defense and military personnel travel to Israel each month, more visitors per capita than any other U.S. ally. Nearly every Israeli military commander visits the United States to tour American facilities. Senior U.S. commanders from all four service branches make regular visits to Israel for exchanges with the IDF leadership.

In 2006 alone, Congress approved more than $460 million in cooperative defense projects, including $135 million for the Arrow and funds for Short Range Ballistic Missile Defense to shield against the kind of rockets used by Hizbollah. The House also unanimously passed the Promoting Antiterrorism Through International Cooperation Act, which would create a $25 million budget for joint homeland security technology ventures between the U.S. and Israel and other allies. The strategic cooperation agreements established Israel as a de facto ally of the United States, institutionalized military to military contacts, sent a message to the Arabs that America was not afraid to risk upsetting them, and shifted at least part of the focus of relations with Israel from Congress to the Executive branch.

To further enhance Israeli security, in the Nixon Administration began what would later become an unprecedented foreign assistance program. Between 1946 and 1971, the U.S. provided Israel with an average of about $60 million a year, a 25-year total of $1.5 billion. By comparison, the Arab states received nearly three times as much aid, an average of $170 million per year, for a total of $4.4 billion. Of the total, Israel received only $162 million in military aid, all in the form of loans as credit sales. Since 1974, however, Israel has received nearly $100 billion in aid. This is the area in which the Israeli lobby has had the most clout: Israel has remained the largest U.S. aid recipient, much to the chagrin of those who want to weaken the U.S.-Israel relationship and those advocates seeking greater assistance for needy countries in Africa and Asia.

In addition to mutual defense interests, the other pillar in the alliance is the values the two nations share. While they live in a region characterized by autocracies, Israelis have a commitment to democracy no less passionate than that of Americans. All citizens of Israel, regardless of race, religion, or sex, are guaranteed equality before the law and full democratic rights. Freedom of speech, assembly, and press are embodied in the country's laws and traditions. Israel's independent judiciary vigorously upholds these rights. The political system does differ from America's— Israel's is a parliamentary democracy—but it is still based on free elections with divergent parties. And though Israel does not have a formal constitution, it has adopted basic laws that establish similar legal guarantees.

The United States signed a variety of cooperative agreements with Israel dating back to the 1950s; however, Ronald Reagan dramatically expanded the number of areas for possible joint activities. Just as he institutionalized military-to-military relations through formal agreements and mutually beneficial projects, so too he established routine bureaucracy-to-bureaucracy relations. During the Reagan administration, agreements were signed or renewed between nearly every U.S. government agency, from NASA to EPA to HHS and their Israeli counterparts. Though many of these memoranda of understanding are little more than pieces of paper, they symbolize an interest in cooperation that is broader and deeper than the United States has with any other nation. The Shared Value Initiatives undertaken through these agreements also help to tangibly reinforce the values the countries share in areas like protecting the environment, providing education, and promoting health.

The relationship also extends beyond the federal government to the state and local level. A milestone in formalizing these contacts occurred in 1984 when the Texas Israel Exchange was created to promote mutually beneficial projects between the Texas Department of Agriculture and Israel's Ministry of Agriculture. Since then, at least 23 other states have signed agreements with Israel to increase cooperation in trade, tourism, research, culture, and other activities of particular interest to the individual states. It has now become routine for governors to lead delegations of business leaders, educators, and cultural affairs officials to Israel and for state agencies and institutions to initiate joint projects. The financial benefits to the states from bilateral agreements can also be substantial; 13 states exported at least $100 million to Israel in 2005, and three exported more than $500 million, with New York leading the way with a whopping $4.4 billion.

American and Israeli scholars have had long and fruitful contacts. Many U.S. colleges have student and faculty exchange programs with Israeli institutions and several have joint degree programs. In the 1970s, two unique foundations were created to fund joint research. In 1972, a relatively unknown agreement was reached that laid the groundwork for a vast array of nonstrategic relationships between Israelis and Americans. That year the United States and Israel created the Binational Science Foundation (BSF) to promote research cooperation between scientists in the two countries. The creation of BSF set a precedent for the establishment of other foundations. In 1977 the Binational Industrial Research and Development Foundation (BIRD) was established for private sector research and development, and in 1978 a third foundation, the Binational Agricultural Research and Development Fund (BARD), was created. These groups began with little fanfare and continue to operate independent of economic or political pressures. In the last two and a half decades, they have played an important role in creating networks between American and Israeli researchers in academia, government and the private sector. Collaboration also continues outside the framework of these institutions.

American Jews sometimes fear the United States could one day turn against Israel because of the bias of the media, the prevalence of anti-Israel professors on college campuses, or the changing demographics of the electorate. The truth, however, is that Americans and Israelis are closely intertwined on so many levels that the special relationship should endure. For Israel, the strength of the alliance provides security. Israelis know their ally will maintain its commitment and be limited in its ability to apply pressure to force them into actions they oppose. Still, no prime minister wants strained relations with Israel's closest friend and the world's most powerful nation, so Israel inevitably bends to the will of the president.

For all the complexity of the alliance, the American position might have been summed up most succinctly by Lyndon Johnson. When Soviet premier Aleksei Kosygin asked him why the United States supports Israel when there are 80 million Arabs and only 3 million Jews, the president replied simply, "Because it is right."

Conclusion

Israel's Bright Future

I BEGAN THIS BOOK ASKING, "WHY DOES THE TITLE HAVE A QUESTION mark?" It should now be clear that Israel faces many daunting challenges.

Although the book has examined a number of worst case, or at least very bad case, scenarios, the future may be quite different and Israel may encounter a more positive atmosphere. The Muslims believe that time is on their side, but what if it is not? What if the region develops in a very different way than the Islamists envision? The principal reason that the rest of the world cares about Iran and the Arab states is oil. What happens when oil runs out or alternative energy sources are developed and the international community has no more interest in the Middle East than it now has in Africa?

What happens in a country such as Egypt if the population continues to grow beyond the government's ability to feed, house, and employ its people? The country might become embroiled in civil strife that weakens it and makes it less threatening to Israel.

What if democracy takes hold in Iraq and spreads into other parts of the region? Instead of Arab governments following the Iranian model, perhaps they will adopt the Turkish example where religion is secondary to the interests of the state and new leaders come to power who focus on internationalism and are willing to normalize relations with Israel.

What if the international community adopts effective sanctions or one or more nations take military action that prevents Iran from acquiring nuclear weapons? What if the backlash of the international community against the radicalism of the Islamic regime combines with anger within Iran over the repressiveness of the society and leads to reforms that once again make Iran a friend of Israel and the West, as it was under the Shah?

These are admittedly rosy scenarios, but they are all plausible and make Israel's survival more likely. And why not think positively?

Around Passover each year I watch Charlton Heston in *The Ten Commandments*. Perhaps it's heretical to say, but this cheesy old film still manages to make me think more about the heritage of the Jewish people than the Passover seders. What strikes me year after year is the portrayal of how the Israelites' faith was continually tested and how so many people failed to meet the challenge. I always wonder if I would have stood with Moses and those who feared God or with Dathan and those who feared Pharoah and preferred to assimilate. And I wonder if the Jewish people are being given a similar test today that we are not even aware of.

If I were to witness the ten plagues, would my faith be stronger or would my rational, scientific mind seek logical explanations for everything? After seeing the Nile turn to blood, the hail, the boils and all the rest, and being freed from centuries of slavery, would I have thought God would let me perish at the banks of the Sea of Reeds? After the parting of the Sea, would my thirst and hunger have led me to lose hope in the desert, to look for strength from a "god" I could see, like a golden calf, rather than one who spoke through an old man with a speech impediment?

Consider some of the "miracles" we've witnessed since the beginning of the twentieth century:

A powerless people, scattered around the globe, victims of perhaps the greatest catastrophe in human history, are granted international legitimacy to create a state of their own in their ancient homeland.

A poorly trained, poorly equipped Jewish army defeats the combined might of the Arab world. Later, a better trained, better equipped army defeats not once, but three times, Arab forces with greater arsenals and manpower. And now, a nation the size of New Jersey boasts one of the most powerful armies in the world.

A nation of immigrants from more than 100 countries, including those with authoritarian governments, becomes a democracy that is so vibrant and pluralistic that it is criticized for having too many political parties in the government.

In less than 60 years, the Jewish population of Israel has grown by a factor of twelve, from half a million to more than six million.

In those six decades, a land of deserts and malarial swamps is built by blood, sweat, and tears into one of the most technologically advanced countries on the globe, a place where America's premier high-tech companies set up research and development facilities.

Universities in Israel become world class, as does its premier hospital, Hadassah.

The ancient Jewish community of Ethiopia is transported on the wings of eagles to the Promised Land.

The long-suffering Jews of the Soviet Union witness the collapse of Communism and more than one million immigrate to Israel.

The king of Jordan and the president of Egypt stand on Mt. Herzl for the funeral of an Israeli prime minister.

The crippling Arab boycott crumbles.

Israel signs peace treaties with Egypt and Jordan.

Israel has one of the highest economic growth rates in the world.

The most powerful nation on earth develops a special relationship with the Jewish State.

Yes, "Israel is an indispensable miracle," as prominent literary critic George Steiner observed. "Its coming into being, its persistence against military, geopolitical odds, its civic achievements, defy reasoned expectation."[1] Who, except perhaps Herzl, could have predicted this outcome? Maybe the problem is that DeMille spoiled the Jewish people, that we expect miracles to look like acts of God, great natural wonders accompanied by thunder and lightning. Maybe if an earthquake swallowed up the Hamas headquarters or a tornado blew away Hizbollah, we'd believe in miracles. Perhaps it was part of the divine plan to test the Chosen People by entrusting them with a small land surrounded by hostile forces, and no oil or water. That or the Jews were just unlucky to have great milk and honey in ancient times and miss out on the more valuable resources of today.

For people of faith, it is easier to accept that what has occurred to date is God's will and the future is predetermined. Jews believe in free will and, therefore, even religious people may believe that Israel's destiny is dependent on the observance of God's commandments. Take the issue, for instance, of water. Rainfall is promised by the Torah as a reward for fulfilling the commandments and drought is a punishment for sin. "If you follow My laws and faithfully observe My commandments, I will grant your rains in their season," Leviticus tell us. "But if you do not obey Me and do not observe all these commandments . . . I will make your skies like iron" (26:4, 19).

Belief in Israel's survival does not require religious faith. Israel will endure because of the strength of its people, the support of Jews in the Diaspora and the belief of non-Jewish friends that the Jewish people are entitled to a state in their homeland. Israel was rebuilt despite the opposition of imperial powers and the fears of the local inhabitants. It became independent in the shadow of the greatest catastrophe in Jewish history. Jews from around the world, with minimal support from the international community, used their creativity, determination, and courage to establish a model society still well short of perfection, but still a light unto nations. Israelis have fought and died to keep their nation free, knowing their first defeat will also be their last. Even between these wars, Israelis have known no peace as terrorists plot against them day and night. Still, they stand tall, proud, and unafraid in their homeland.

Despite all the trials and tribulations, today Israel is flourishing. The population continues to grow and thousands of newcomers arrive each month. Its economy and military are strong. It has relations with more countries than ever before. Its principal alliance, with the United States, is stronger than ever.

Enemies still seek its destruction, but Israel can and will survive. It is evidence of the triumph of Zionism that there is an Israel for detractors to attack, and it will remain a source of annoyance to the forces of darkness into the twenty-second century. The question for Israelis continues to be how to build on the success of the Zionist endeavor. What kind of state will Israel become over the next hundred years? Will the internal tensions described in chapter 8 grow or subside?

Of course, Israelis crave peace more than anything else because they do not want to live under the threat of terror or war. Israel will, therefore, continue to take risks and compromise with its neighbors. I am confident Israel will eventually achieve peace—not perfect peace, or even the degree of normalcy the United States enjoys with Canada and Mexico, but perhaps the type of cold peace it has with Egypt or, maybe, the slightly warmer relationship it has with Jordan. The final settlement with the Palestinians appears well defined; it will inevitably resemble one of the very first peace plans proposed nearly 70 years ago in which Lord Peel figured out the only conceivable way the two peoples could live together was to create two states. There is already an Arab-Israeli peace but some threats remain. With the possible exception of the nuclearization of the region, Israel can manage the other risks.

Even though the previous chapters demonstrated the difficulties of achieving a settlement with the Muslims, we can be reassured by history that peace is indeed possible.

In 1947, the British adviser on Palestine asked a representative of the Jewish Agency why the Jews agreed to let the UN decide the fate of Palestine. "Look at the UN Charter and at the list of countries belonging to it," he said. "In order to obtain a favorable decision, you will need two-thirds of the votes in those countries, and you will be able to obtain it only if the Eastern bloc and the U.S. unite and support the decision itself and the same formulation. Nothing like that ever happened. It cannot possibly happen. It will never happen."[2] A few months later, of course, it did happen.

For years, people said an Arab leader would never make peace with Israel—it would never happen; it could not possibly happen. In 1979 it did happen, when Anwar Sadat and Menachem Begin signed the Egyptian-Israeli Peace Treaty. It took 15 more years before Jordan's King Hussein had the courage and vision to sign the Jordan-Israel treaty.

Today people say no other Arab leader will make peace with Israel. I suggest that history tells us it just might happen.

You will know that peace is at hand when the Muslim world establishes a Peace Now organization that can marshal 100,000 demonstrators as Israel's Peace Now movement does. When you turn on the news and see thousands of Palestinians or Syrians or Lebanese or Iranians march through the streets with signs saying, "Make Peace Not Terror" instead of carrying pictures of Osama bin Ladin, a new era will dawn.

We do not need more peace plans or shuttle diplomacy or U.S. engagement. The greatest hope for peace lies with mothers of the Middle East. In many places around the world, it is the mothers who have provoked political change and it could happen in the Muslim world as well. Palestinian mothers must demand that their children go to school rather than to terrorist training camps. They must encourage their kids to aspire to be doctors and lawyers instead of martyrs. They must march around the Palestinian Authority head-quarters demanding an end to the violence that has robbed their children of their present and offered them no future. When the mothers begin to march, the obstacles to peace will start to melt away.

Will Israel survive? The challenges are imposing, yet I believe that the Jewish people continue to have the qualities necessary to overcome all the obstacles—fortitude and faith. Even when times look grim, I prefer to remain optimistic, because the Jews are a people of hope, not despair. I am reminded of the song lyrics of "The Hope":

> In the Jewish heart
> A Jewish spirit still sings
> And the eyes look east toward Zion
> Our hope is not lost
> Our hope of two thousand years,
> To be a free nation in our land,
> In the land of Zion and Israel.

The song is better known as "Hatikvah," the national anthem of Israel.

At the outset, I noted that many Israelis fear for the existence of the state, but they are not abandoning their home. When asked "What state would you prefer to live in?" 63 percent of Israelis said Israel and the second choice, of only 9 percent, was the United States. Only 6 percent said their children should migrate.

During the war with Hizbollah, I received a copy of a letter from a 20-year-old woman in Israel who had just finished her army service. It captured the mood of not only the young generation but also, I believe, all Israelis. She wanted to go abroad before attending university but said she can't. "I can't leave my country. It's not that I'm thinking that my staying here will make a difference, but I guess we are all crazy in this time of war. Not only is no one leaving our country, but everyone is canceling their vacations and coming back." At the end of the letter she said that the television had just reported another 11 soldiers were killed. "Wish us luck," she wrote. "We don't ask for much more. Just our lives back."

The United States can help Israelis get their lives back and ensure their survival by demonstrating to the Muslims that time is on Israel's side, by continuing to give the people of Israel its support until there is no doubt in anyone's mind that Israel is here to stay.

I end with a poem that expresses my view on what we can all do to help bring about peace and ensure Israel's survival:

> I am only one, but I am one,
> I cannot do everything,
> But I can do something.
> What I can do, I ought to do
> By the grace of god, I will do.

Notes

Chapter 1

1. Maoz Azaryahu, "It is no fairy tale: Israel at 50," *Political Geography* 18:2 (1999), pp. 131-147.
2. Shlomo Avineri, *The Making of Modern Zionism* (New York: Basic Books, 1981), p. 219.
3. Harold W. Glidden, "The Arab World," *Middle East Review*, Winter 1974–75.
4. Hussein Agha and Robert Malley, "Hamas: The Perils of Power," *New York Review* 53:4 (March 9, 2006).
5. Bassam Jabber quotation.
6. *New York Times*, January 7, 1985.

Chapter 2

1. Official British document, Foreign Office File No. 371/20822 E 7201/22/31; Elie Kedourie, *Islam in the Modem World* (London: Mansell, 1980), 69–72.
2. *Al-Mussawar*, August 4, 1972.
3. Speech to UN seminar on religious tolerance and freedom, delivered December 5, 1984, quoted in Anti-Defamation League, *News*, February 7, 1985.
4. *Al-Riyadh*, March 10, 2002.

Chapter 3

1. Speech in Lafayette Park, opposite the White House, October 28, 2000; Capitol Hill Panel Discussion, June 18, 1998.
2. Aluma Solnick, "Muslim Clerics: The Jews Are the Descendants of Apes, Pigs, And Other Animals," MEMRI, November 1, 2002.
3. U.S. Department of State, 2005 Annual Report on International Religious Freedom, Released by the Bureau for Democracy, Human Rights, and Labor, Washington, D.C., March 8, 2006.
4. Bernard Lewis, "The Pro-Islamic Jews," *Judaism* (Fall 1968): 401.
5. Youssef Ibrahim, "Arab Majority May Not Stay Forever Silent," *New York Sun*, July 17, 2006.
6. Daniel Pipes, "Palestinian Responses to an Israeli Withdrawal from Gaza," Danielpipes.org, February 21, 2004.

7. "Arab papers slam Nasrallah, dub him irresponsible," *Jerusalem Post,* August 29, 2006.
8. *Al Jazeera,* December 15, 2005; Interview with Iranian TV station Al-'Alam, December 8, 2005.
9. Youssef Ibrahim, "Arab Majority May Not Stay Forever Silent," *New York Sun,* July 17, 2006.

Chapter 4

1. Hilary Leila Krieger and Amir Mizroch, "US Jews have future, present and past," *Jerusalem Post,* November 13, 2006.
2. Nathan Guttman, "A. B. Yehoshua sparks uproar in US," *Jerusalem Post,* May 4, 2006.

Chapter 5

1. Simon Tisdall, "Ahmadinejad on Israel: global danger or political infighting?" *The Guardian,* December 20, 2005; CNN, October 27, 2005.
2. *Lebanon Daily Star,* October 23, 2002.
3. Bernard Lewis, "Does Iran have something in store?" *Wall Street Journal,* August 8, 2006.
4. Iran Press Service, December 14, 2001.
5. *Jerusalem Report,* March 11, 2002.
6. *New York Times,* April 26, 2006.
7. "Unclassified Report to Congress on the Acquisition of Technology Relating to Weapons of Mass Destruction and Advanced Conventional Munitions, 1 July Through 31 December 2003, VA: Central Intelligence Agency, November 2004.
8. "Iran warns against sending to Security Council," *Al Jazeera,* March 5, 2005.
9. *Ma'ariv,* July 27, 2004.

Chapter 6

1. Statement to the Knesset by Foreign Minister Sharett, November 30, 1953; *Washington Times,* July 30, 1990; *Mideast Mirror,* October 7, 1991; Mitchell Bard, *Myths and Facts* (Maryland: American-Israeli Cooperative Enterprise, 2006), p. 281.
2. Martin Shernan, "Water in Israel: The Dry Facts," Herzliya: Interdisciplinary Center, April 2001.
3. Joyce Starr, *Covenant Over Middle Eastern Waters* (New York: Henry Holt and Company, 1995), p. 185.

Chapter 7

1. Mitchell Bard, "Can Israel Withdraw? Yes," *Commentary* (April 1988).
2. *Jerusalem Post,* August 4, 2004.
3. *Al-Arabi,* June 24, 2001.
4. Colin Powell, *My American Journey* (New York: Random House, 1995), p. 434.
5. Interview with Colin Powell, Cable News Network, June 27, 1993.
6. Interview with Dennis Ross, Fox News Sunday, April 21, 2002.

7. *Washington Post,* November 1, 1991.
8. Associated Press, October 22, 2001.

Chapter 8

1. Maoz Azaryahu, "It is no fairy tale: Israel at 50," *Political Geography* 18:2 (1999): pp. 131–147.
2. Adam Garfinkle, *Politics and Society in Modern Israel* (New York: M. E. Sharpe, 2000), p. 296.
3. Amos Oz, "Free at last," Ynetnews.com, August 21, 2005.
4. Haviv Rettig, "Poll: Haredim most hated group in Israel," *Jerusalem Post* (October 31, 2006).
5. Ibid.
6. Uzi Arad and Gal Alon, "Patriotism and Israel's National Security—Herzliya Patriotism Survey 2006," Working Paper, Institute for Policy and Strategy, January 19, 2006.
7. Mitchell Bard, *Building Bridges: Lessons for America from Novel Israeli Approaches to Promote Coexistence* (MD, AICE, 1997).

Chapter 9

1. Helen and Douglas Davis, *Israel in the World* (London: Weidenfeld &. Nicolson, 2005), p. 12.
2. Golda Meir, *My Life* (New York: Dell Publishing Co., 1975), p. 306.
3. Quoted in *Jerusalem Report* (October 16, 2006), p. 60.

Chapter 10

1. Yossi Melman and Steven Hartov, "Munich: fact and fantasy," *The Guardian,* January 17, 2006.
2. Tom Gross, "The media war against Israel: The Jewish state is fighting not one enemy but two: Hizballah, and those who peddle its propaganda," *National Post,* August 2, 2006.

Chapter 11

1. Phyllis Chesler, *The New Anti-Semitism* (California: Jossey-Bass, 2003), p. 88.
2. Norman Finkelstein, *Image and Reality of the Holocaust* (W. W. Norton & Company, 1995), p. 188.
3. Joseph Massad, "The legacy of Jean-Paul Sartre," *Al-Ahram Weekly Online,* February 5, 2003.
4. Paul Johnson, *Modern Times: The World from the Twenties to the Nineties* (New York: Harper & Row, 1983), p. 485.
5. Seymour Martin Lipset, "The Socialism of Fools—The Left, the Jews and Israel," *Encounter,* December 1969, p. 24.
6. Natan Sharansky, "Antisemitism in 3-D," *Forward,* January 21, 2005, p. 9.
7. Leon Wieseltier, "Israel, Palestine, and the Return of the Binational Fantasy," *The New Republic,* October 24, 2003.

8. Irwin Cotler, "Human Rights and the New Anti-Jewishness," Jewish People Policy Planning Institute, November 2002.

9. Abraham Foxman, *Never Again?* (California: HarperSanFrancisco, 2003), pp. 23 and 26.

10. *Times,* November 11, 2006.

11. George Conger, "Lord Carey 'ashamed to be an Anglican,'" *Jerusalem Post,* February 8, 2006.

12. Phyllis Chesler, "The Anti-Semitic Divestment Campaign," FrontPageMagazine.com, February 14, 2006).

13. For an extended review and refutation of Carter's book, see "Carter's Calumny," http://www.jewishvirtuallibrary.org/jsource/reviews/carter.html.

14. Speech before the UN, December 8, 1983, quoted in Harris Schoenberg, *Mandate For Terror: The United Nations and the PLO* (New York: Shapolsky, 1989), p. 296.

15. Speech to UN seminar on religious tolerance and freedom, delivered December 5, 1984, quoted in Anti-Defamation League, *News,* February 7, 1985.

16. Morris Abram, "Israel Under Attack: Anti-Semitism in the United Nations," *The Earth Times,* December 16–31, 1997.

17. Ibid.

18. From the Aposatolic Letter of John Paul II, "Redemptionis Anno," April 20, 1984.

19. MSN.com, April 3, 2005.

20. Address of His Holiness Pope Benedict XVI, Cologne Synagogue, August 19, 2005, found at http://www.vatican.va/holy_father/benedict_xvi/speeches/2005/august/documents/hf_ben-xvi_spe_20050819-cologne-synagogue_en.html.

21. Address of His Holiness Benedict XVI To Dr. Riccardo Di Segni, Chief Rabbi of Rome, January 16, 2006, found at http://www.vatican.va/holy_father/benedict_xvi/speeches/2006/january/documents/hf_ben-xvi_spe_20060116_rabbino-roma_en.html.

Chapter 12

1. "John Adams Embraces A Jewish Homeland," Chapter 33, Chapters in American Jewish History, American Jewish Historical Society.

2. John Hagee Ministries, http://www.jhm.org/beliefs.asp.

3. Tovah Lazaroff, "'Evangelicals the world over are praying for Israel,'" *Jerusalem Post,* August 9, 2006.

4. I. L. Kenen, *Israel's Defense Line* (New York: Prometheus, 1981), p. 114.

5. Congressional Quarterly, *The Washington Lobby* (Washington, D.C.: Congressional Quarterly, 1974), p, 117.

6. Speech by President Lyndon Johnson on September 10, 1968.

7. Jimmy Carter, *Keeping Faith* (New York: Bantam Books, 1982), p, 274.

8. Ronald Reagan, "Recognizing the Israeli Asset," *Washington Post,* August 15, 1979.

Conclusion

1. George Steiner, *Errata: An Examined Life* (London: Weidenfeld and Nicolson, 1997), p. 54.

2. Howard Sachar, *A History of Israel* (New York: Alfred A. Knopf, 1996), p. 280.

Index